Richard Holt Hutton

Aspects of religious and scientific thought

Richard Holt Hutton

Aspects of religious and scientific thought

ISBN/EAN: 9783337131814

Printed in Europe, USA, Canada, Australia, Japan

Cover: Foto ©Lupo / pixelio.de

More available books at **www.hansebooks.com**

ASPECTS OF
RELIGIOUS AND SCIENTIFIC
THOUGHT

BY THE LATE
RICHARD HOLT HUTTON

SELECTED FROM THE *SPECTATOR*
AND EDITED BY HIS NIECE
ELIZABETH M. ROSCOE

London
MACMILLAN AND CO., Limited
NEW YORK: THE MACMILLAN COMPANY
1899

All rights reserved

AND what are things eternal?—powers depart,
Possessions vanish, and opinions change,
And passions hold a fluctuating seat:
But, by the storms of circumstance unshaken,
And subject neither to eclipse nor wane,
Duty exists;—immutably survive,
For our support, the measures and the forms,
Which an abstract intelligence supplies;
Whose kingdom is, where time and space are not.
Of other converse which mind, soul, and heart,
Do, with united urgency, require,
What more that may not perish?—Thou, dread source,
Prime, self-existing cause and end of all
That in the scale of being fill their place;
Above our human region, or below,
Set and sustained;—

    .   .   .   .   .

         Thou, Thou alone
Art everlasting, and the blessed Spirits,
Which Thou includest, as the sea her waves:
For adoration Thou endur'st; endure
For consciousness the motions of Thy will;
For apprehension those transcendent truths
Of the pure intellect, that stand as laws
(Submission constituting strength and power)
Even to Thy Being's infinite majesty!"

        WORDSWORTH.—*The Excursion.*

CONTENTS

		PAGE
1.	CREEDS AND WORSHIP	1
2.	THE VARIOUS CAUSES OF SCEPTICISM	8
3.	THE SPIRITUAL FATIGUE OF THE WORLD	17
4.	RELIGIOUS UNCERTAINTY	24
5.	THE DEBTS OF THEOLOGY TO SECULAR MOVEMENTS	31
6.	THE WARDEN OF KEBLE ON DIFFICULTIES IN RELIGION	39
7.	THE MATERIALISTS' STRONGHOLD	45
8.	PROFESSOR CLIFFORD ON THE SIN OF CREDULITY	54
9.	PROFESSOR WACE ON BELIEF	63
10.	PROFESSOR TYNDALL ON MATERIALISM	71
11.	MR. MARTINEAU ON MATERIALISM	80
12.	DR. WARD ON THE DIVINE PRE-MOVEMENT	89
13.	THE GREAT AGNOSTIC	99
14.	A PROBLEM ARISING OUT OF THE DECALOGUE	107
15.	SCIENCE AND MYSTERY	114

CONTENTS

		PAGE
16.	Instinct and Design	120
17.	Mr. Fowle on Natural Religion	128
18.	Mr. Justice Fry on Materialism	137
19.	Professor Stokes, M.P., on Personal Identity	146
20.	The Resurrection of the Body	153
21.	The Modern Easter Difficulty	159
22.	Dr. Abbott on Natural and Supernatural	166
23.	Mr. Llewelyn Davies on Christian Miracle	175
24.	Cardinal Newman on Inspiration	182
25.	Loss and Gain in Recent Theology	189
26.	Dr. Martineau on Spiritual Authority	201
27.	The Head Master of Clifton College on the Theory of Inspiration	209
28.	Professor Jowett's Question	217
29.	Mr. Gladstone and Dr. Liddon on the Bible	224
30.	The Sacramental Principle	232
31.	Prayers for the Dead	239
32.	Canon Kingsley on Reasonable Prayer	245
33.	Canon Liddon on Prayer and Miracle	252
34.	Maurice and the Unitarians	261
35.	Mr. Maurice as Heresiarch	268
36.	Dr. George MacDonald on Hell	276
37.	Bishop Magee on the Ethics of Forgiveness	283
38.	Mr. Gladstone on the Atonement	289

CONTENTS

		PAGE
39.	Principal Tulloch on Spiritual Evolution	295
40.	Mr. J. S. Mill's Religious Confession	302
41.	Mr. John Morley on Religious Conformity	313
42.	Mr. Arnold's Lay Sermon	322
43.	Matthew Arnold's New Christian Catechism	330
44.	Agnostic Dreamers	337
45.	God, and Ideas of God	345
46.	The Limits of Free Will	353
47.	The Limits of Divine Power	359
48.	Human Sympathies and Religious Capacity	365
49.	The Christian Ethics of Forbearance	371
50.	The Modern Poetry of Doubt	377
51.	Browning's Theology	387
52.	The Humility of Science	394
53.	Tennyson's Theology	402
54.	The Late Lord Tennyson on the Future Life	409

CREEDS AND WORSHIP

1870

MR. HENRY SIDGWICK, in an essay[1] which indicates the most delicate moral discrimination on the ethics of subscription and conformity, and as such deserves the closest attention from all those who take a part in debates such as those on the Act of Uniformity and on University Tests, deprecates the use of creeds in any form of practical devotion on the following impressive ground: —"If the majority of the members of any Church," he argues, "have a right to claim that the service should be framed to meet their devotional needs, and therefore in accordance with their dogmatic convictions, the minority, on the other hand, may respectfully urge that these dogmatic convictions need not be introduced in such a manner as to give the maximum of offence to those who do not hold them, and at the same time produce the minimum of devotional effect. The formal recital of creeds is neither a natural expression of the senti-

---

[1] *The Ethics of Conformity and Subscription.* By Henry Sidgwick, M.A., late Fellow of Trinity College, Cambridge. London: Williams and Norgate.

ment of worship, nor obviously effective in stimulating devotion; and the proper place for such abridged statements of doctrine, even supposing them accurately to express the convictions of the existing generation of Churchmen (which can hardly be said of the present Creeds), would appear to be a manual of instruction rather than a formula of worship." Nothing certainly could warrant the introduction of any avowal into a devotional service, intended for men of many shades of belief, which gives "the maximum of offence to those who do not hold it, and at the same time produces the minimum of devotional effect;" but Mr. Sidgwick, in thus judging of the function and effect of recited creeds, and in describing them as being merely "abridged statements of doctrine," misses entirely, as it seems to me, the mood of sentiment which originally caused their introduction into acts of worship, and the secret of the power they still exercise. In fact, the very intellectual bewilderments and scepticisms which make men so reluctant to sign creeds, and so anxious to simplify them, lend an immeasurable depth of gratitude and even joy to the confession of the solid bases of fact, in which Christians find, as they conceive, the historical groundwork of their faith. In precise proportion to the number of influences which threaten to undermine faith, and which embarrass the "dim and perilous way" to it, whether these be, as in the world of martyrs, chiefly moral and only secondarily intellectual, or as it may at least often be in our own day, chiefly intellectual, and only secondarily moral, in that proportion must be the rest of heart, and the glad sense of exercising a faculty of vision which only God's grace can bestow, while confessing tersely, but definitely, the divine facts of a universe in many of its aspects so troubled, confusing, and confused. As it was not enough in the times of idolatry to adhere to the devotional forms of Christian worship, the heart of the Christian almost compelling him to become what was characteristically called a 'confessor' of the person and power of Christ,—and this, I take it, not by any means merely as a sign of open loyalty, but also for the sake of clearly rehearsing to his own heart the positive objects of faith on which he finally rested,—so in these days of solvent philosophies and critical reconsiderations of history, it is not enough for any Christian who can retain his Christian faith at all, however much that be, to join in the implicit devotional assumptions of his Church; for he, too, feels impelled to acknowledge with a certain wonder and awe the solid rock which he has found for his feet amid the quicksands of speculative thought. In an age when almost every educated man has at some time or other in his life considered, with more or less of that dread with which we gaze over the precipice whither we feel a morbid desire to leap, the doubts which science has suggested concerning a personal will in the Creator,—who can by any possibility feel the words, 'I believe in God the Father Almighty, maker of heaven and earth,' to be, if they come from his heart, a mere "abridged statement of doctrine," and not rather a confession as strange, as startling, as full of witness to the power of God over the tangled threads of our infantine thought, as the confession of the frightened boatmen on the Sea of Galilee, "What manner of man is this, that even the winds and the seas obey him?" In an age which has seen the *Leben Jesu* of Strauss and the *Vie de*

Jesus translated into almost every European language, and in which the tremor and vibration which such books make have spread far beyond the circle of those who have faced the doubts such books so powerfully express, who by any possibility can add the confession "and in Jesus Christ, His only Son, our Lord," whether the words in which His incarnation be recited express his belief with perfect accuracy or not, without something of the grateful wonder with which Lazarus must have heard the voice which brought him from the tomb, and while still wrapped in grave-clothes came forth to answer it? In a word, the confession of the revealing Divine acts in which we believe, whatever these may be, whether they be those of the creeds as they are, or of the creeds as we should wish to see them, seems to me one of the most natural and the happiest of the acts of worship, like the joyful confession of the man born blind, "One thing I know, that, whereas I was blind, now I see." The man who has been wandering by night upon the mountains does not recall and describe with a gladder heart the first glimpse which dawn gave him of the track he had lost, than that with which one who has found or recovered his faith in the divine government of the world and its perfect manifestation in Christ recites, if he can, the words, 'God of God, Light of Light, very God of very God,' or, if he cannot, at least recalls in the simple words of the earliest creed, the history of that crucifixion, resurrection, and ascension which, from doubtful legends, have become to him the great landmarks both of human history and of the inward life. The conscious rehearsal of the great acts on which the Christian faith is based seems to me one of the most simple and natural of the acts of worship,—and especially so in an age of bewildering speculation, when we have begun to trust our own theories less and less, and to feel that as science must at every step study anew the facts of nature and return to them to verify her conclusions, so faith must at every step study anew the revealing acts of God, and return to them to verify her conclusions. The recitation of the creed is an act of intellectual adoration, in a day when the intellect is the source of some of the deepest of our troubles.

Mr. Sidgwick apparently thinks that there is something much less jarring to a half-conformist in hearing devotional *assumptions* made in which he can only partly concur, than in hearing the same assumptions positively defined by the worshippers as an express confession of their faith. I cannot say that I so regard it. And I cannot but think that Mr. Sidgwick himself so regards it only because he looks at the creed merely as "an abridged statement of doctrine," and not an act of intellectual adoration,— a recurrence to the ultimate divine facts on which our own capacity to believe is grounded. But as Dr. Newman has pointed out in his *Grammar of Assent*, that which is a mere abridged statement of doctrine from one point of view, when you are looking to the argumentative sources of conviction, may very naturally become an act of living worship from another point of view, when you are looking to the faith which has been vouchsafed to you as the spring of life and hope in a world of perplexity and doubt. Mr. Clough has somewhere a stanza expressing the thought that it "fortifies his soul" to remember that all real truths will remain, and exercise their influence on the world, even though he himself should cease to be able to discern them. So a man who gazes on the Alps for the solitary time in his life feels it fortify his soul to know that they will continue to stand there in all their silent grandeur, when he can no longer see them, and long after his own body is part of the dust of the earth. Precisely of the same kind is the effect of the recital of their creed on those who believe it. It arrays before their minds in all their grandeur and solemnity the great facts on which their faith is based, and reminds them that those facts are so, whether their attention be drawn to them or not,—are so behind the clouds of dust in which the world's worries envelope them, as much as in the transparent moments of devotion, —in short, that their faith is the consequence of the existence of these great realities, and that these are in no degree the dream of their faith. The difference between this acknowledgment,—this 'confession,'—and the mere recitation of an 'abridged statement of doctrine' as such, seems to me as vast as the difference between an epitome of the doctrine of free will and of absolute morality, and the solemn acknowledgment that there is such an alternative for the soul as sin or virtue, made by the individual conscience when the exposition is over. No doubt a man who in the presence of Necessitarians says superfluously and perhaps combatively, 'I believe in free will,' may be fairly suspected of wishing to give battle to those who do not hold it, but the man who, even though a Necessitarian should be his companion, while canvassing the nature of a moral peril to which he was about to be exposed, should exclaim, "I believe in right and wrong, I believe in free will," would never for an instant be accused of wishing to give the maximum of offence to his companion, while producing the minimum of devotional effect on his own mind. Now, what I maintain is that the creed of the English service is in no way recited as a provocative to controversial distinctions, but as a solemn act of spiritual survey over the foundations of faith. Just as a man naturally recalls deliberately the beings for whom he prays and their needs, before praying for them, so with equal naturalness he recalls the Being *to* whom he prays and His acts, as a mode of deepening the prayer addressed to Him. What is the most moving prayer in the litany except the invocation of Christ's help on the basis of a creed,—" By thine agony and bloody sweat, by thy cross and passion, by thy precious death and burial, by thy glorious resurrection and ascension, and by the coming of the Holy Ghost, good Lord deliver us"? And what can be more natural than to survey previously, with a rapid glance, the great story on which our faith is founded, that we may distinguish the groundwork of trust from the superstructure of devotion, and compare the nature and acts of Him to whom we pray with the long list of our sorrows and our hopes? Mr. Sidgwick, while making out, I think, an unanswerable case for the frank confession by all thinking laymen of the points on which they find a difficulty in accepting the creeds, or even an insuperable obstacle to concurrence in some of their articles, and also for a general willingness to reduce the number of such disputed confessions, has, I also think, quite failed to realise how substantive an element of worship the recital of a simple creed, especially in these distracted times, really is. I suspect that it "fortifies the soul" of worship fully as much as prayer itself can melt or elevate it.

II

THE VARIOUS CAUSES OF SCEPTICISM

1878

Mr. Gladstone, in his remarkable article in the *Contemporary Review* on "The Sixteenth Century Arraigned Before the Nineteenth," and Mr. Baldwin Brown, in his not less remarkable address to the Congregational Union at Liverpool on Tuesday on the explanation of the great sceptical movements of the day, strike the same note. They hold that the truest explanation of the shortcomings of scepticism in our generation is the fault of the orthodoxy of the previous generation. It was the practical paganism of the Catholic world, say both, which gave rise to the Reformation: and it was the onesidedness of the various Reformers which gave rise to the intellectual revolts of the later heresiarchs. Thus Mr. Baldwin Brown holds that it was Calvinism which caused Unitarianism. "Take the Unitarian heresy in modern times. He held that the high Calvinistic theology, coming perilously near, as it did, to the presentation of an interior discord in the Triune Nature, which was harmonised by the Atonement, almost inevitably developed a community which could see only the unity, and felt itself called to bear witness to the vital aspect of that truth to the world." And no doubt not only is there very great truth in the general doctrine that the degeneracy of a great faith almost inevitably leads to the sincere proclamation of some half-true but energetic doctrine which is the natural protest against the spurious form in which that faith has been held,—just as idolatrous tendencies in Christianity directly promoted the spread of Mahommedanism,—but those who know the history of Calvinism and Unitarianism know how much there is to be said for Mr. Baldwin Brown's special illustration of it. At the same time, I cannot believe that explicit reaction against a degenerate and implicitly heterodox faith is the sufficient explanation of all such forms of error. Else what are we to say to the widespread atheism,—or to the still more dangerous, because colder and more indifferent, secularism,—of the present day? Is that to be explained as a legitimate reaction against the hollowness of any previous form of religious faith? It can hardly be true that *all* falsehood is half-truth, and is the proper cure for some deficiency in the previous profession of the truth. It may well be indeed that while the people of Europe were slowly learning to believe in a righteous and loving God, it was impossible for them to be taught to believe in physical law; and it may also be that now when the people of Europe are being taught the meaning and uses of physical law, it is not very easy for them to retain at the highest point,—the point of truth,—their belief in a righteous and loving God. Nobody can say that in dealing with "such creatures as we are, in such a world as the present," it is easy to give us a firm grasp of any great class of truths whatever without loosening our grasp on some other class of truths, perhaps nobler and more vital, though it may be also, for that very reason, a class of truths less difficult to recover. Still, this is a very different thing from saying that every form of explicit error is due to reaction against some still more serious implicit error in the faith of our fathers. Voltaire may have been raised up as a wholesome scourge of selfish superstitions, and yet it does not follow that every one who follows Voltaire has been driven into the rank of his followers by disgust for such superstitions. So far as I can see, the theory that the spiritual and moral law of action and reaction will account for all dominant errors, is an exaggeration of the function of a valuable, though limited principle. Doubtless, asceticism and monasticism lead to reactions in which the fibre of human character is dangerously relaxed; doubtless, mysticism encourages the growth of rationalism, and rationalism in its turn some kind of regression to idealism and mysticism. Still, these complementary phases of faith are not sufficient, or nearly sufficient, to account for all we see; nor could they be so, unless man were indeed alone in the world, and the Hegelianism which explains all his convictions as partly the growth of, and partly the recoil against, previous convictions, were true. What it leaves out of account is the free, reciprocal action—not necessarily determined by any considerations of this sort, —of God on man, and if I may say so without irreverence, since this is clearly the teaching of Christ, —of man on God. Luther never forgot this most important of all the explanations of the growth or decay of the religious life. "We say to our Lord God," he said, "that if He will have His Church, He must keep it, for we cannot keep it; and if we could, we should be the proudest asses under heaven." And Luther implied, of course, that it might please God

to humble the Church, to make it feel His presence
less at one time, as well as more at another; to give
it, for His good purposes, times of aridity, convention-
ality, and artificiality, as well as times of rich and
flowing faith. And if it be true, as Christ teaches,
that man may take the initiative with God, as well
as God with man,—that times of trust are times of
grace, that knocking leads to opening,—that when
man throws himself on God, God pours a new tide
of spiritual life into man, then, surely, one of the
explanations of a want of faith in the invisible is a
previous want of appeal to the invisible,—a self-
occupation in thoughts and things which turn us
away from the invisible, a life of absorption in the
superficial phenomena of existence, a generation of
outward interests and outward service. This is an
explanation almost opposite to that of the law of
action and reaction. That law would suggest that
to an age of too much outwardness and coldness, an
age of pietism or mysticism would inevitably succeed.
Yet such is by no means the universal experience of
men. On the contrary, the age in which it was said
that "the word of the Lord was precious in those
days,—there was no open vision," immediately preceded the age in which the Jews demanded a king,
because their faith in that succession of divine judges
by which they had been distinguished from the
neighbouring peoples, had in great measure disappeared. The times distinguished by the apparent
silence of Heaven frequently lead to periods which are
relatively periods of secularism in human history, not
to periods of true and deep religious life. And the
recent access of Atheism seems to be even more due
to an apparent dryness of the spiritual life of man
(which may be quite as much due to the will of

Heaven as to the will of man) than to any reaction from former superstitions. As Luther would have said, God has not thought fit to keep His Church as He once kept it. God may have willed that, for a time, it would be better for man to try to the full, what he could, and what he could not do, without conscious trust in Himself. He may have willed,— as He certainly appears to have willed during many generations even of the life of the people who were specially trained to reveal His mind to the world,— to withhold that stream of spiritual inspiration which is perhaps the only thing corresponding, in the religious life, to what the physicists call "verification" in the world of positive phenomena. We hear on all sides the complaint of the Agnostics that it is not their fault if they do not believe in God,—that they will believe at once, if His existence can be verified to them,—that, as Professor Huxley puts it, "no drowning sailor ever clutched a hen-coop more tenaciously" than they would clutch a belief in God which could be verified. If they do not exactly cry aloud, they yet seem to cry under their breath, with the prophet, "Oh, that thou wouldest rend the heavens, that thou wouldest come down, that the mountains might flow down at thy presence!"— in other words, that if only something physical might "verify" the divine presence for them, they would be only too happy to accept it. And yet in almost the same breath they declare,—and declare most reasonably,— that nothing physical could prove it, that happen what might, they could only interpret any physical event as a new aspect of nature, that nature is so large and so elastic, that no room is left in it for anything physical to rank as supernatural. Well, it is obvious that such a state of mind as this is one which could be changed by the direct touch of the Divine Spirit, and by that only,—by an event of the soul, not an event of the body,—by the power which convinces the conscience, not by any power which only enlarges the experience of the senses.

But it does not follow that because no such event happens,—because the only verification of which the case admits, does not take place,—the Agnostic has either, on the one hand, the least right to suppose himself entitled to assume the negative view to be true; or, on the other hand, may fairly be regarded by those who do recognise as final evidence, the influence of God over their soul, as morally inferior to themselves. Neither of these conclusions is true. The Agnostic is not right, for his negative experience, however frequently repeated, cannot outweigh a single clear experience of a positive kind. But none the less, he must not, on account of this negative experience, be treated as morally inferior to one who has verified the existence of a divine will over him and in him;—for if it has been, as doubtless it has, for the advantage of mankind that hundreds of generations should have felt the need of high social and moral laws, before ever social and moral laws were established and obeyed, and that hundreds of generations more felt the need of a clear recognition of constant physical laws, before physical laws were discovered and turned to account, why should it not also be for the advantage of man that certain classes, even in the modern times of larger knowledge and higher aims, should be taught to feel acutely the need of a divine light for the true interpretation even of those physical principles of order, which they are so strenuous in asserting and enforcing in their apparent divorce from any spiritual principle? I may say roughly, a very great thinker indeed did say,—that during the middle-ages thinking men were chiefly occupied in sounding their own minds, to see how much light the careful exploring of those minds might shed on the external order of things; and that a knowledge of the insufficiency of the study of mind to explain the laws of matter, was the first step to that true study of the laws of matter which followed. And I believe that the eminent Agnostics of the present day may be said to be discharging the similar function of exaggerating indefinitely the influence of material laws in things moral and spiritual,—in order eventually to show their well-marked limits;—that they are trying (and failing) to prove that material laws are the true keys to the knowledge of mental and moral life, just as the middle-ages tried and failed to show that moral and spiritual laws were the true keys to the knowledge of material life. And it would be just as foolish to suppose the modern physicists inferior to those who do not fall into their error, only because they are not equally fascinated by their truths, as it would have been to denounce the Schoolmen as morally inferior to the first heralds of the new science, only for trying to deduce principles of astronomy out of the *a priori* and abstract conceptions of the human mind. The truth is, that in every great stage of human progress there is, and must be, an undue appreciation of the step just made. In some sense, it may be said that Providence is the real cause of that undue appreciation. It is, of course, the divine guidance which determines the main lines of direction and intensity for human thought; and if the Creator withdraws Himself at times from the vision of men, or of some men, it is no doubt for the benefit of all men that He does so. To speak of those who do not themselves see God as "living without God in the world," is itself atheism. You might as well suppose that before the atmosphere was recognised as having weight and substance, men who did not know the difference between it and a vacuum lived without the air they breathed. God is not less behind the consciousness of men who have no glimpse of Him through their consciousness, than He is within the heart of those who worship Him; and the only real rejection of God is the resistance to His Word, whether it be felt as His Word, or only as a mysterious claim on the human will which it is impossible adequately to define. I hold that, in a sense, God is Himself, in all probability, no unfrequent cause of the blindness of men to His presence. He retires behind the veil of sense when He wishes us to explore the boundaries of sense, and to become fully aware of a life beyond. The physicists in every school are doing this great work for us now. They are explaining, defining, mapping all the currents of physical influence, and from time to time crying out, like Professor Huxley, for "the hen-coop" of which, like shipwrecked sailors, they see no sign; like Professor Tyndall, for the elevating idealism which is conspicuous by its absence in all their investigations; like Professor Clifford, for something to replace the theism of Kingsley and Martineau. To suppose that the men who are doing this great work,—who are mapping for us the quicksands and sunken rocks of physical scepticism,—are necessarily deserted by God, because they do not see Him, is to be more truly atheists than any physicist. There is a scepticism which is of God's making, in order that we may see how many of the highest springs of human life are founded in trust,—how everything else fails, even in the highest minds, to produce order, peace, and calm. The physicists of to-day are suffering for us, as well as for themselves. It is their failure to find light, which will show where the light is not, and also where it is. As Mr. Mallock well says, in the best paper he has yet written—that in the *Nineteenth Century*, on "Faith and Verification,"—the pitiful cries of modern physicists, as they raise their hands to what they deem a spiritual vacuum, are about the best auguries we could have that it is not in physical science that man can ever find his salvation.

III

THE SPIRITUAL FATIGUE OF THE WORLD

1889

Dr. Liddon, in the new volume which he has just published under the title of *Christmas-Tide Sermons*, begins with two striking sermons on St. Thomas, in which he suggests that one of the modern maladies, which palliates though it does not justify a good deal of its unbelief, is "a morbidly active imagination which cannot acquiesce in the idea of fixed and unalterable truth." Such a malady of imagination there no doubt is, and it shows itself in morbid activity; but this morbid activity is more often, I believe, the inability to rest which is due to over-fatigue, than the inability to rest which is due to abundance of life,—the restlessness of fever, not the restlessness of overflowing vitality. Look at such a book as Amiel's *Journal*, of which Mrs. Humphry Ward has just issued a new edition, with a portrait in which Amiel looks out upon the world with tired eyes that seem to be discerning in every new glimpse they take of life, some fresh difficulty which his strenuous but wearied soul cannot surmount. "Que vivre est difficile, O mon cœur fatigué!" are the words with which his long scrutiny of himself concludes; and perhaps the most characteristic thing in a journal full of characteristic things is this,—"Am I not more attached to the *ennuis* I know, than in love with pleasures unknown to me?" "Attached to the *ennuis* I know"!—is it not the condition of half the souls which are yearning for faith and unable to attain it? Shelley declared nearly seventy years ago :—

> "The world is weary of the past,
> Oh, might it die or rest at last!"

But since Shelley made that declaration, the world has grown more weary of the present than it was then of the past, and now, too, seems to be so weary of the future that it yearns after some modern form of the Nirvana doctrine of the Buddhists. When Mrs. Humphry Ward makes her dying hero, Robert Elsmere, declare that he can neither ascribe nor deny personality or intelligence to God, is it not obvious that the predominant feeling in that tired mind which is dying of its spiritual struggles is something like Amiel's "Que vivre est difficile, O mon cœur fatigué!"—the difference being, however, that Amiel was really dying when he so wrote, and that physical exhaustion may have prompted the exclamation; while there is no reason at all to suppose that Mrs. Humphry Ward intended her imaginary hero's deliberate judgment to be symptomatic of the physical exhaustion of his condition. Robert Elsmere's fatigue is purely intellectual and moral, not physical. Yet he can neither affirm nor deny the eternal spring of life in God, for it is at least clear that if God may be denied personality and intelligence, He must also be denied what forms part of the very essence of life to all human experience.

Dr. Liddon might even have suggested, what is not, I think, at all improbable, that when St. Thomas anticipated, as he remarks, "something of the positive spirit of the modern world," and was so anxious "to escape illusions and to arrive at truth by experiment," that he would trust only his own senses, it was just because he was more subject than the other Apostles to this dejection and weariness of the soul. Does not the suggestion, when Christ prepares to return to Jerusalem to restore Lazarus to life, "Let us also go that we may die with him," read like the cry of an affectionate but weary soul that could see no end to all the tragic elements which were gathering so thick about our Lord, except death, and had not a glimpse of the new life and refreshment that was about to spring from that great collapse of their recent hopes? Indeed, the question which forms the subject of Dr. Liddon's second sermon on St. Thomas, "Lord, we know not whither thou goest, and how can we know the way?" has all the air of a mind that had almost exhausted itself already in the effort to follow the vivid but mystic teaching of his master in tracks to him new and strange; and if so, there is less reason to wonder that when he was told that Christ had appeared to the ten Apostles in Jerusalem, he found the statement a new demand upon his spiritual nature to which he was hardly equal, so that he devolved, as it were, upon his senses the responsibility of faith. "Except I shall see in his hands the print of the nails, and put my finger into the print of the nails and thrust my hand into his side, I will not believe."

There is the same tone of fatigued spiritual feeling about a great deal of the scepticism of to-day. As Dr. Liddon says, men are impressed by the apparent difficulties of Christianity, and ask to put their hands into the print of the nails if they are to receive it; but in all probability they would not find it any the easier to believe if they could do so; they would immediately explain it away as subjective illusion. Most likely they have not vivid life enough in themselves to enter into so great a manifestation of the divine life:—

> "For we, brought forth and reared in hours
> Of change, alarm, surprise,
> What shelter to grow ripe is ours,
> What leisure to grow wise?"

Is it not this want of vivid life in themselves which makes men like Amiel at once unable to believe and to disbelieve, unable to reject so great and natural a consolation for the soul as faith, and yet unable to accept it? Dr. Liddon finds fault with the Poet-Laureate for saying:—

> "There lives more faith in honest doubt,
> Believe me, than in half the creeds."

But there I think that he does not quite give the significance which Tennyson meant to be given to the epithet "honest" doubt. There is a healthy doubt which may properly be called "honest," and which is in many men and women the beginning of true faith; but it is not the doubt of mere hesitation and *ennui*. It is not even the rather sickly faith which the Poet-Laureate describes in some lines which perhaps better deserved Dr. Liddon's stricture than the line praising "honest doubt":—

> "I falter where I firmly trod,
> And falling with my weight of cares
> Upon the great world's altar-stairs
> That slope thro' darkness up to God,

> I stretch lame hands of faith, and grope,
>   And gather dust and chaff, and call
>   To what I feel is Lord of all,
> And faintly trust the larger hope."

This "faint" trusting of the larger hope, this double mind of which the one self shrinks and suffers in the shadow, while the other only totters feebly towards the light, betrays, I think, a good deal more of the morbid tendency of the day, than doubt which faces calmly and boldly the testing of its true significance. I feel quite sure that a vast deal of the spiritual lassitude of the day is due much less to the magnitude of the obstacles to hearty faith than to the fatigue of spirit with which those obstacles are regarded. The modern world is far too full of small cares and interests, and the modern conception of life and its duties is far too favourable to the frittering away of life on a multitude of petty distractions. As Dr. Liddon says in the sermon I have referred to, a great deal of the scepticism of the day is due to the insufficiency of people's knowledge of Christianity, to their very superficial acquaintance with it, the complete absence of any preparation for sounding its depths, and surveying its wide horizon, and apprehending the inner harmonies of its spiritual teaching. And, in fact, this is often impossible with the meagre amount of life which remains to be thrown into the search for spiritual truth after all the other excitements of life have been provided for. There is now no adequate economy of human strength for the higher objects of life, too much a great deal being lavished on its petty interests. People are attached to their religion much as Amiel said that he was attached to his *ennuis*. They have not the strength requisite either to give it up or to give themselves up to its demands, and so they hover in a miserable state of nervous tension on the boundary that divides faith from doubt, their worldly energy being diminished by the anxious glances they cast over their shoulder at the faith which they half-believe, and their spiritual energy being "sicklied o'er by the pale cast" of sceptical hesitations. Christianity cannot be understood in any degree without being approached with a certain passion both of hope and fear. The whole history which led up to it, the whole history which has flowed forth from it, has been a history of spiritual passion, and there is no meaning in Christianity at all if it be not true that divine passion is as deep-rooted in the eternal spirit as infinite reason itself. If men come to Christ with exhausted natures they will never know what there is in Him. And they do come too often to the study of His teaching with the mere fag-end of their powers, with heart and mind both battered and fevered by the contending interests and pleasures of a life that is much too full of small excitements. No doubt Christianity offers a new life of its own, and an inexhaustible spring of that life; but it offers it only to those who can give a life for a life, who can give up the whole mind and heart that a new mind and a new heart may be substituted in their place. There must be the power to exult even in suffering for a great end, in those who would really understand the passion of Christian teaching; and the power to exult in suffering for a great end takes an intensity of nature which is very easily extinguished by a life of minute distractions and of widely distributed affections. A generation, of which the most impressive characteristic is its spiritual fatigue, will never be truly Christian till it can husband its energy better, and consent to forego many petty interests that it may not forego the religion of the Cross.

IV

RELIGIOUS UNCERTAINTY

1880

THE Rev. Edward White has just published a striking little book on *The Tone and Teaching of the New Testament on Certainty in Religion*,[1] which was preached as the Merchants' Lecture for the last October in the Weigh-House Chapel, where the late Dr. Binney was so long the minister. It would be difficult to find a more suitable subject for consideration at Christmas-time than the comparative certainty and uncertainty of the Christians of the first age and the Christians of this. Assuredly if, when the word "Christmas" is mentioned in any society, the certain convictions could be enumerated to which the mention of the word gives rise, how very small a proportion of them would be religious convictions, or perhaps even irreligious convictions, at all. Some would feel certain that they were going to suffer from seasonable conventions; others would feel certain that they were going to make themselves ill; a few young people would feel certain that they were going to be happy; many would feel certain that they were going to be rather more than usually

[1] Elliot Stock.

unreal; and how very rare would be any flash of deep and eager conviction that there is anything at all in the invisible world corresponding to the external festival to be celebrated. Mr. White's striking little book brings out very powerfully how strong a contrast to this state of mind is afforded by the mind of the writers of the New Testament. Take one passage, in which he begins his sketch of that mind:—

"Let attention be drawn to the remarkable phenomenon that these books—from the Gospel of Matthew onward to Apocalypse—though differing in style, object, and feeling, are marked by one characteristic, which pervades them in every page,—and that is, *the solemn tone of certainty* which runs through them, without one single breakdown into speculation or balancing of probabilities. At all events, these writers thoroughly believed what they wrote. This characteristic distinguishes the New Testament books, not only from all the Roman literature of the same age, but from all other Greek books that ever were written. In those literatures you have argument on both sides, guess, divination, doubt, mockery, despair. But here every page overflows with the feeling of certainty. The Evangelists and Apostles of the Gospel absolutely exhaust all the language of certainty in giving expression to their ideas. There are no words expressive of absolute truth and trustworthiness, and intense faith founded on that trustworthiness, which these men have not employed. 'This is the victory which has overcome the world' of doubters — 'even their faith.' Such thorough belief and confidence were contagious. They drove mankind before them, 'and shut them up' in the fold of faith. The Roman world at large believed nothing much—but at least these men believed, 'nothing doubting.' The New Testament stands up like a mighty and immovable rock of certainty in the midst of the wide, unstable sea of contemporary thought — in the Jewish,

Greek, and Roman world. You feel this tone of certainty in the teaching which they report from the lips of their Master—the Christ. Christ sets Himself before us as The Truth. He has no long arguments, no processes indicating inquiry on His own part, or inference, or hesitation. But every word of His is struck with a definite sovereign image of truth upon it, like gold under the descending stamp of the mint. '*Verily, verily, I say unto you:*' this is the steadfast introduction to every lesson. In Him there is no 'feeling after God' in the dark; no derivation of wisdom from earlier teachers; no modest citation of authorities: the only quotation is from prophecy, to point out its punctual fulfilment in Himself. Christ, in the Gospels, is represented to us as the Truth of Eternal Thought, alighting on the earth in the form of Man, and speaking absolutely as One who 'knew both what was in Man' and what was in God. His intellectual countenance is 'as the sun shining in its strength.'"

In discussing the vast change between this state of mind and the state of mind of the great majority of those who make up even the genuinely Christian world of the present day, Mr. White makes many suggestions tending to show the unreasonableness of the new state of mental vacillation in which Christians so often find themselves; but his subject does not lead him to consider why it is that so many who would probably quite agree in all he says are still, more or less, in the condition of mind which he condemns. I am disposed to think that the chief reason why there is so much more vacillation on the subject of religious truth, even amongst those who hold it, than the Apostles would have understood at all, is, to speak it shortly, that so much more of the modern intellect is engaged, and seriously engaged, with the surface of life, and so much less of it, in proportion, with the roots of that life. The Apostles and Evangelists belonged to a race whose most earnest life had for centuries been engaged on the unseen world, whether for good or for evil. The Jews have never been deficient in worldliness, but yet that part of them,—good or bad,—which was not worldly was very much the reverse indeed. Their intellect, whenever it was not sunk in the commoner earthly interests, was absorbed in the vision of the perfect righteousness, and the prospect of a perfectly righteous reign upon earth, or else in fierce dogmatic controversies which clouded over that vision. This was the side on which the intellect of Judaism was raised above the more selfish of human occupations. The Jewish race, so far as it rose above the earth, exercised itself in these great matters,—threw its whole heart into them.

In the modern world it is very different. A very great part of the best thought of the best men is occupied in very large degree with interests which have all the largeness and catholicity, as one may say, of something quasi-spiritual, and yet no vestige of the true spiritual world in them, no vestige in them of the great conflict between darkness and light, between evil and good, between temptation and grace. The area of perfectly disinterested and perfectly innocent and wholesome interests which are not in the least moral or spiritual interests has grown vastly in the modern world, and the effect of this is that a much larger portion of the permanent mind of good men is usually eagerly at work in tracking out clues which have neither the taint of moral danger about them on the one side, nor the inspiration of spiritual help on the other. A great part of the minds of good men is thus invested in secular interests which are not in the bad sense worldly, and which are indeed in a very real sense unworldly, though they cannot be called moral or spiritual, nay, which, far from calling up the vision of an unseen world, only tend to give a deeper intellectual fascination to the spectacle of the seen world. The vast growth of interests and studies which, like the world of the mathematician or physicist, of the geologist or botanist, of the sculptor or artist, of the economist or statistician, of the geographer or astronomer, of the musician or superficial poet,—to say nothing of the world of the mechanician and the student of all sorts of delicate practical arts,—excite the most absorbing interest, and yet not an interest which turns at all directly on the eternal issues of good and evil, holiness and iniquity,—this vast area of new interests has undoubtedly drained away a great deal of the intensity of life devoted in earlier ages to the ultimate spiritual issues of time and eternity. To my mind it seems one great reason for the comparative vacillation of religious men on religious subjects, that so many of the best of these men are now more or less absorbed in problems of a much more finite and limited character, and yet problems quite as free from the contagion of spiritual evil as they are from the attraction of spiritual good, so that when the mind reverts to the great ultimate issues it is with a sort of start, and a sense of inadequacy to grasp them with anything like the same force with which these smaller problems are grasped, that to some extent dizzies the mind, and produces that feeling of uncertainty which, as Mr. White justly says, would have been almost inconceivable to the first preachers of Christianity. To them the choice lay between living in the world of sense without God and living in the world of spirit with God. In modern times there is, as it were, a third very real alternative, namely, living in a world intermediate between sense and spirit, a world of very narrowly limited but perfectly wholesome and pure interests, to which the mind fits and adapts itself till it is absolutely bewildered by leaning once more over the great gulf which separates good and evil, which divides heaven from hell. St. Paul told his disciples, "Walk in the spirit, and ye shall not fulfil the lust of the flesh; for the flesh lusteth against the spirit, and the spirit against the flesh, and these are contrary the one to the other." But would he have said that the most ardent study of the phenomena of electricity, for instance, or even the devotion of a lifetime to the elaboration of a new form of escapement or steam-engine, was "fulfilling the lust of the flesh"? I do not think he would. Nevertheless, he would certainly not have called it "walking in the spirit." Between the spiritual world which,—whether good or evil,—was to the Jews the chief intellectual world, and the life of the flesh, there has arisen a great world of the understanding, with principles and interests of its own, the habitual inhabiting of which appears to be quite as bad a preparation for the spiritual life as it is for the life of the flesh. Those who live chiefly in this world, —and how many of us do!—come to the true spiritual world with a sense of bewilderment which makes it very difficult to attach to the judgments we form upon it the same sense of certainty which is felt concerning the intellectual issues of that more limited world to which so large a part of our intellectual life is devoted.

It is perfectly true that no true man can really avoid altogether the gravest spiritual issues, and that when he is in contact with these issues, especially when he is dealing with the personal issue of right or wrong for his own will, he begins to realise the meaning of the unseen world in the very sense in which the Christian apostles and evangelists realised it, and then perhaps he knows what religious certainty means. But the meaning and measure of certainty in that region are very different from the meaning and measure of certainty in that world of understanding in which so large a part of the better human life is now passed. And I do not hesitate to say that, quite apart from the intrinsic difficulties of religious questions, one of the chief bewilderments of modern life in relation to religion is this,—that men have learnt most of their tests of certainty in a region which is not spiritual at all, and in which certainty hardly involves the inward judgment of the true man, but only, at most, a kind of shadow of the man. Possibly, as we go deeper in knowledge, this stage may pass away. Possibly men will one day learn to trace up the principles involved in the superficial problems which occupy us so much now into the deeper world of true spirit. But I very much doubt whether all the present unreality which arises in relation to things spiritual, from the finite weights and measures and the mechanical tests of accuracy to which so many of our thoughts are subjected in the world in which so much of our lives is spent, is one for which men are themselves wholly responsible. A certain amount of shadow appears to be necessarily cast on the true spirit of man by the rapid growth in relative importance of his practical understanding. Still, true men will do all in their power to hasten the time when the understanding itself shall become as spiritual as it is now in essence carnal.

THE DEBTS OF THEOLOGY TO SECULAR MOVEMENTS

1871

MR. LLEWELYN DAVIES has taken for the subject of a very wise and interesting article in the *Contemporary Review* the debt which Theology owes to what is commonly called the World, or rather to movements which are entirely outside the theological sphere, and often headed by men who have no belief whatever in theology. Mr. Davies shows that theology has been compelled by the movement in favour of 'Toleration' to set a much higher value on that perfect spiritual freedom which is a condition of all real allegiance to God, and so to elevate the cry for 'Toleration' into the demand for setting *the heart* at liberty; that the democratic movement has compelled theology to reconsider the foundations of religious equality, and discover that Christ requires the rich and great to live for the sake of the poor multitude, and, indeed, to use their riches and power only as ministers to those who have neither riches nor power; that the economic movement has compelled theology to recognise that there is a far higher spiritual service to be done by making men truly independent, *i.e.* masters of themselves, than by so helping them in their physical difficulties as to encourage them to lean on the generosity of others; that the conceptions of justice caused by a deeper understanding of human law have compelled theology to abandon its substitutional theory of atonement; and finally, that the scientific movement has compelled theology to abandon its conception of God as showing Himself solely or chiefly in rare and strange occurrences like miracles, and to retreat on the great declaration of St. Paul's faith in "one God and Father of all, who is above all, and through all, and in all."

This assertion of Mr. Davies's is profoundly true and very striking. It is of no small importance that theologians should know that theology is just as apt to go astray if it attempt to interpret the mind of God without reference to the teaching of events and the signs of the times, as the world is apt to go astray if it attempt to interpret the teaching of events and the signs of the times without reference to the mind of God. But the essay will be very apt to give rise to a criticism of this kind; if theology can only learn the true mind of God on subjects of this importance, *under compulsion*, as it were, from the world,—if some of its highest lessons are mere afterthoughts to which it has been compelled to come under penalty of losing all hold upon the world unless it could discover some spiritual principle which would harmonise with the "manifest destiny" of social movements,—how can it be said to be in any sense the organ of revelation? If the test of human science is to *anticipate*, it should be still more the test of divine science. A theology, a science of God, which has to be kept straight, and often to be set straight, by those who do not profess to derive their knowledge in any degree from divine sources, is apparently almost as much of an imposition as a meteorology which only finds out after a hard winter is over that there was good reason for it, and which can always descant on the causes of a hurricane it had never predicted. Is there any sort of answer to this?

I think there is, and to some extent Mr. Davies gives it when he points out that most of these conclusions now adopted by theology under pressure from the world *were* anticipated in the Christian revelation, though the state of the world was then so little prepared for the complete application of these truths to quite new attitudes of the human mind, that they had been forgotten and neglected,—written, as it were, in a sort of invisible ink, which only the heat of unanticipated movements and conflicts would one day render legible, and even conspicuous. Thus our Lord's rebuke to His disciples when they asked Him to call down fire on a Samaritan village, " Ye know not what manner of spirit ye are of ; the Son of Man is not come to destroy men's lives, but to save them," is at least a clear indication of what He would have said on persecution,—persecution by miracle being at that time the only conceivable sort of persecution to which so insignificant and defenceless a sect could have had resort. The anticipation of the great democratic principle that the rich and powerful must regard themselves as servants of the poor and weak is much more pronounced,—" He that is greatest among you, let him be as the younger, and he that is chief as he that doth serve," being the great social doctrine both of the Gospels and Epistles. The economical teaching of experience that you will generally injure the poor a great deal more by giving alms than by refusing them, is simply not in the

Christian revelation at all; but then it is *only* a lesson of experience, and not of principle, and the principle that the aim of your benevolence should be not to please, but really to serve, "not with eyeservice, as menpleasers, but as the servants of Christ," is. Again, the true law of sacrifice which makes divine suffering the great remedy for sin, not by way of formal substitution, but as a proof both of the infinite love of God, and of the vastness of the disorder which all sin introduces into human society and relations, is not only anticipated in the Christian revelation, but is there in full strength. And finally, "the higher Pantheism," which, instead of obliterating the will of man, only vivifies it by rendering it more profoundly sensible to the mysterious control of God over all the avenues by which that will is reached,— turning Nature itself into a mode of the supernatural,—is, as Mr. Davies says, the great doctrine of St. Paul.

It must be admitted, however, that in all these cases theology did not apprehend the true purport of revelation sufficiently well to interpret it rightly when the moment of trial came. Theology did persecute; theology has not, on the whole, favoured the political influence of the masses; theology was against political economy; theology invented an artificial and false "system" of atonement; theology proclaimed science impious. In fact, theology could not master her own brief. What, then, has theology done for the world in these cases which the world could not have done for itself? How shall we call a science divine which had to be sent back to school by the world to learn to read its own lesson aright? The answer is suggested, I think, by asking another,—How, if the Christian theology is divine when it teaches the existence of the light that lighteth every man that cometh into the world, could it *fail* to happen that the history of human life would do as much towards interpreting theology, as theology towards interpreting the meaning of human life? If God reveals Himself *in* man as well as *to* man, how could the secular world and its history *help* contributing a grand share to the explanation of God's true meaning? Revelation itself is always asserting that theologians are quite as sure, or rather more sure, to go wrong in their own line as other men in theirs. As Dr. Norman Macleod said the other day in that fine sermon on "War and National Judgment,"[1] which the Queen had the good sense to admire and command to be published,—there was never any favouritism shown in God's lessons either to the people who received the revelation, or to the class through whom especially they received it. "'The priests,' they cried in God's name to the so-called religious people of the time, 'said not, Where is the Lord? and they that handle the law knew me not. The pastors also transgressed against me, and the prophets prophesied by Baal, and walked after the things that do not profit,'"—surely a very distinct assertion indeed that the theologians were quite as sure to go wrong in interpreting the true meaning of God's revelation as the world in discussing the true drift of His Providence. If there be any truth in revelation, the large secular human experience is as entirely pervaded by a divine guidance, though it be unconscious or less conscious of it, as is the theological teaching, and neither can really understand or do its own work right without the full co-operation of the other. Unless the teacher tries to sympathise with the learner, and the learner tries to enter into the mind

[1] Published by Strahan.

of the teacher, neither succeeds. The difficulties of the learner should give a new drift to the lessons of the teacher, and the explanations of the teacher should give a new drift to the inquiries of the learner. Revelation was in the main a record of the mind of God in relation to a particular age, or succession of ages, and a particular people, and a particular condition of human morality and society. To divine what it would have to say in relation to a perfectly new class of moral and social conditions was to solve a problem in which there were two distinct elements, the full appreciation of the new tendencies at work in human society, and the interpretation of the spiritual bearing of the former revelation on those tendencies. It seems perfectly clear that for both these elements to concur successfully, the interpreters of revelation must enter fully into the 'signs of the times,' *i.e.* the signs of the divine agency in human history, while the people must enter into the divine character, the teaching of God as to Himself. The growing necessity for 'toleration,' the increasing power of the democratic currents in modern society, the lessons of political economy, the moral bearing of popular justice, the drift of scientific discovery, are all as much divine helps to the true interpretation of theology as theology is a divine help to the true interpretation of these secular facts.

Well—but, it will be asked, if it be admitted that theology does need these external helps to prevent her from going astray, what is there of independent teaching that she can be said to contribute to the lesson of secular movements? If, in order to understand the sacredness of spiritual freedom, theology has to learn the commonplace lesson of 'toleration,' for instance, from the world, what can theology be said to teach to the world? Why, just this, that before you can ensure even 'toleration' you must go much deeper than toleration, and get at a spiritual justification for toleration, which is only to be found in the discovery that no allegiance to Truth or God is worth anything that is not really free and uncompelled. Religious persecution itself was founded on a higher spiritual basis than *mere* worldly toleration. Religious persecution did assert that *if* you could save the higher part of man at the expense of mere bodily pain and loss, you were bound to do it. In practice, no doubt, that was the excuse for all sorts of cruelty. But *in motive* it was higher than the indifference of *mere* toleration, which would never have got any real triumph without winning a spiritual alliance,—the alliance of the conviction that the allegiance of the spirit to God must be really free, or really worthless. So, again, the mere democratic principle as a doctrine of equal *rights* would have been almost mischievous; the enthusiasm it has gained has been derived from the religious principle that all men,—the rich and powerful especially,—owe to the "dim, common populations" the ministry of their lives. Theology transfigures the haggling acquisitive motive of the man who demands his fair share of the world's happiness into the generous motive of the man who demands the right to give himself up to the service of those who are most miserable and helpless. And so in all the other instances, what theology contributes is a new, and deeper, and nobler *motive* for tendencies which the world tries to justify on vulgar grounds. Where the world calls for a mere *modus vivendi*, theology makes a demand on the heart which transforms the *modus vivendi* into a deeper principle of social harmony and disinterested duty. Falsely as theology has often interpreted the meaning of God, it has always aimed high, and blundered rather in the work of interpreting the human facts of life, than in its motive. As we have said, even the doctrine of persecution was in theory a noble *kind* of error, far nobler than the doctrine of indifference and 'toleration.' The 'corruption of the higher' was, as usual, infinitely worse than 'the corruption of the lower.' Ecclesiastical persecution became a more venomous and hateful thing than Laodicean indifference had it in its power to become. But not the less the theological contempt for bodily ease and pleasure in comparison with spiritual health was of noble origin, and a fearful practical evil only because it was a mistake to suppose that spiritual health could ever be extracted out of attempts to terrify and bribe the conscience into actions which were not good unless they were free. After all, theology has done as much to keep the world from sinking into vulgar compromises with expediency, as the world has done to keep theology from cruelly trampling on the natural and the human, in its effort after the supernatural and divine.

VI

THE WARDEN OF KEBLE ON DIFFICULTIES IN RELIGION

1886

THE Warden of Keble, in the first number of a very useful and valuable series of popular and simple papers on religious subjects, called "Oxford House Papers,"[1] intended, I imagine, for use by such communities as those which are attempting to raise the moral and spiritual level of society at the East End, insists in a few very simple, pithy, and impressive pages that difficulties about Christianity are no reason for disbelieving it. By this, as he is careful to point out, Mr. Talbot does *not* mean that "the more difficulties there are, the better;" "or that Christians do not mind how much the argument goes against them;" or that Christians "believe in spite of their reason." He is quite ready to concede that difficulties "must be considered and fairly met," and that "each difficulty counts for something, at least at first sight, in an argument against religion,"—nay, he concedes that "difficulties many enough or great enough would serve to crush religion." All he insists on is that a religion without difficulties is

[1] Published by Messrs. Rivingtons.

simply inconceivable, since religion is confessedly an interpretation of human life and duty from a higher and wider point of view than any which we can occupy, an interpretation of that duty to which, of course, we cannot even take up a submissive attitude without exerting powerfully that part of our nature which looks upwards, and more or less depressing that part of our nature which pulls us downwards, nor without feeling all the qualms which such depression involves. Mr. Talbot points out very powerfully that a revelation as to the nature of God must involve infinitely larger conceptions than suit our petty local ideas, conceptions which it must strain our minds to the very utmost to grasp, conceptions to which it is even much more difficult for us to find the clue than it is for us to find the clue to the thoughts of those human beings to whom we look up as greatly above us, though that, too, is difficult enough. Again, as revelation is to be our guide, it must throw light on the hardest and most mysterious parts of our own nature; and that, as every one knows, is very difficult to understand. Further, as the Christian revelation claims to be historical, it must involve all the difficulties connected with the evidence of historical events; and finally, as a religion of conduct which, though it shows us the right way, does not compel us to take it, it involves all those most serious difficulties which arise from the weakness and guilt and self-will of those who call themselves Christians without really following the guidance of Christ. Mr. Talbot, indeed, shows most convincingly that it is not even a reasonable objection to the truth of Christianity to say that Christianity is in many respects difficult of belief. Any religion that was true must be difficult in many respects to believe, only it must be in many more and greater respects difficult to disbelieve.

I might, indeed, safely go further than Mr. Talbot, and assert that in relation to all the higher problems of our existence, difficulties are never solved except by the acceptance of principles which involve higher and more recondite difficulties of their own, though they afford an explanation of the paradoxes with which the mind had formerly been struggling. Thus, many of the difficulties of the old astronomy were explained and reconciled by the Copernican theory; but the Copernican theory, which made the sun the centre of our system, was even less in accordance with the motion of the moon than the old geocentric theory, and the discrepancy was not really explained till the law of gravitation was itself discovered. This law reconciled the difficulties of both systems; but it introduced a difficulty of a much higher and subtler order,—namely, the conception that every particle of matter is attracted by every other particle of matter, far or near, in the whole universe, in a degree varying inversely with the square of the distance. That is a conception so utterly beyond us, that though we can put it in words, we can hardly realise it in thought; and yet it is the key to mysteries less mysterious than itself. Just so it was with the theory of light. The phenomena of light could not be explained until it was assumed that a vibrating ether of which our senses afford us no trace, perfectly elastic and universally present, permeates as completely what we call a vacuum as it permeates the fluid and solid materials of the universe. Indeed, it has been truly said that we must suppose this ether to be, in its laws of vibration, much more like a solid than a liquid, since the wave vibrates through it with much more of the kind of rapidity with which waves of sound pass through solid bodies, than of that with which they pass through liquid or fluid bodies. And this marvellous vibrating medium of which we cannot find any trace through our senses, but only through our reason, is assumed to penetrate all the most distant portions of the universe, even those so distant that we cannot reach them by the telescope itself. What difficulties and humiliations to the senses are not then involved in this assumption which the reason demands for the satisfaction of her claim to explain the phenomena of light! Take, again, the explanation of the difference between chemical combinations and ordinary mixtures. In order to explain this, physicists have been obliged to assume the theory of atoms themselves indivisible, but yet so strongly attracted by specific affinities to other atoms, that, when opportunity offers, they combine together in specific proportions which are never varied. And yet this astonishing conception of potent elective affinities controlling hypothetic elements of matter of which the senses give no kind of evidence, has become the recognised explanation of all the laws of chemistry. Nay, the same doctrine, namely, that we usually find the explanation of difficulties of a lower kind by the aid of hypotheses involving difficulties of a higher kind, is even taught us in pure mathematics. Every mathematician knows that what have been called impossible quantities,—quantities "less than nothing," as though any quantity could be less than nothing,—and quantities that are strictly inconceivable, like the square roots of negative quantities, though there is no quantity conceivable which, when multiplied by itself, will yield a negative quantity,—are not only not rejected by mathematicians, but are used with such effect that they have started new developments of mathematical science. Nay, the history of mathematics is full of cases in which the confident use of functions and methods that seemed at first to be quite incapable of rational interpretation has led to the discovery of new functions and methods, in which the apparent absurdity has become the starting-point of a new calculus.

What is true of the rational progress of man is, of course, equally true of his moral progress. The maxims that there is no change without an efficient cause, and that the same causes always produce the same effects, have become the very roots of physical science. But the moment we come to ask what a cause really means, and to note the phenomena of our own nature, we find that we cannot explain our own acts of causation,—nor the emotions accompanying actions which we attribute to ourselves as their true cause,—without an entirely new departure, without assuming a cause which is not the effect of any other cause, without rising above the sphere in which so-called "efficient" causes had been traced, and assuming the reality of an uncaused cause, a volition. That assumption is, to the eye of mere science, simply inconceivable; we can no more explain in its language that which causes but was not itself caused, than we can explain in mathematics the square root of a negative quantity. Yet we cannot for a moment explain the phenomena of right and wrong without it. We are compelled to recognise it as the only solution of what we observe within us; and when we have so recognised it, we discover that our only real conception of cause itself, at least as distinguished from uniform antecedent and from energy, is will, and we find that, without will, energy is the mystery of mysteries. But the links of the mysterious chain by which we are forced to explain that which is difficult to our lower nature by some invisible and, to that part of our nature, absolutely inconceivable hypothesis, which yet recommends itself to our higher nature, does not stop here. We have no sooner well grasped the exercise of moral responsibility and referred it to free-will, than we become aware that the meaning of 'sin' which we have thus explained is only half explained by it;—that there is some all-pervading moral ether which permeates the society of moral beings, and transmits through it innumerable waves of evil and good influence, quite independently of our wills, though not so as absolutely to overpower and enslave them; and that without the conception of a "solidarity" of our race, through which alone the transmission, on the one hand, of a taint from man to man, and, on the other hand, of a spiritual grace from some source above man, a spirit of sacrifice originating in a mystery of love far beyond us, is rendered explicable, it is quite as impossible to explain the moral phenomena of human society as it is to explain morality itself without the principle of free-will.

Well, surely this short and most imperfect summary of the manner in which, from beginning to end of the history of human thought, men have always found the explanation of one class of difficulties in assumptions which involve another and a higher class of difficulties, sustains in the most ample way Mr. Talbot's assertion that a religion without difficulties would not be a religion at all,—would, indeed, be something absolutely beneath us, instead of something infinitely above us.

VII

THE MATERIALISTS' STRONGHOLD

1874

The *Guardian* of Wednesday week contained a letter from Professor Challis, the mathematician, in which he contrasted the materialistic tendencies of the great experimentalist philosophers with the deeper philosophy of true theorists, whom he seemed to identify with mathematicians like Newton or Whewell. And the *Guardian* of this week follows up the hint in a thoughtful article, in which it accepts the mathematical test as a fair gauge of truly theoretical as distinguished from empirical science, and points out that many of the most distinguished of living mathematicians, Professor Jellett, Professor Haughton, Professor Clerk-Maxwell—to whom Professor Tyndall himself, in his Lucretian apology, paid such a tribute of profound respect—Professor Stokes, and others not less distinguished in the scientific world, not to count Professor Challis, entirely reject Professor Tyndall's materialistic tendencies. Now, it is conceivable enough that a mathematician, who finds the lowest departments of the natural world governed by principles of order which it takes the highest science in any degree to fathom, should be struck with that fact, and be led by it to believe, what seems to me in the highest degree reasonable, that whatever matter may be, it is at bottom the fruit, rather than the germ, of mind. Self-existent atoms impressed with intellectually coherent laws of growth and change, but not so impressed by any mind capable of foreseeing that growth and change, are at least as mysterious conceptions as any which theology could produce, without accounting in the same way for the phenomena of moral and spiritual life. But I confess I do not like the notion of allowing our minds to be greatly influenced by the views of any particular school of science, and I suspect, not without some ground, that if the process of counting begins, a good many materialists might be counted amongst the most original and distinguished mathematicians of our day. Unless common report very much belies him, Laplace, second, no doubt, in mathematical genius to Newton, but still a mathematician of the first order, was no Theist, and certainly it seems to me pretty clear that the possession of mathematical genius and the study of mathematical principles is no adequate guarantee for the solidity or comprehensiveness of the moral and speculative judgment. Moreover, I think it unjust and erroneous to confine the name of 'theorist,' in the higher sense, to the mathematicians. Of course, only mathematicians can reduce the laws of the universe to quantitative forms, but that is not, even in Professor Challis's own sense, the criterion of a true theorist. He illustrates the name 'theorist' by contrasting what Newton did, when he considered a cause explaining the minutest motions of the planetary system, with what Kepler did in simply classifying rightly the facts concerning those motions. Well, that is a fair illustration of the distinction between an effort of empirical philosophy and the work of a true theorist. But have no true explanations of the most complex phenomena been discovered which could not be reduced to mathematical statement? What would Professor Challis say to Goethe's discovery of the radical identity of stalk, leaf, and blossom in the plant; or to Kirchhoff's, of the meaning of the dark lines in the spectrum, and their use in determining the materials of stars and sun? Were not these theories, —exercises, and high exercises, of the speculative intellect? Above all, what is Mr. Darwin's and Mr. Wallace's theory of the effect of 'natural selection' in modifying species? Can any better illustration of the discovery of a true cause for a mass of intricate and unexplained phenomena be conceived than this? If Mr. Darwin is not a theorist, and a theorist in the highest sense of the word, where is one to be found? No doubt Mr. Darwin cannot be charged with materialism. His writings, though they seem to throw doubt on the conception which makes the minutest phenomena of Nature the expression of a Divine purpose, and harp a good deal on the failures of the organic world, seem to me full of belief in an ultimate intellectual origin for the scheme of things. But what I am concerned with now is the attempt to appeal from theorists of one branch to theorists of another branch of science, in relation to the great questions involved in materialism, an appeal which seems to me hardly fair. Surely the theorists who concern themselves with the mode in which life is screwed up, as it were, to a higher phase of intelligence and beauty, are not to be shut out of the discussion, in favour of mere manipulators of lines and symbols, measurers of space, and force, and mass! If, as I am inclined to believe, the materialistic impulse which scientific thought has lately taken, is in no small degree due to a false interpretation of Mr. Darwin's great discoveries and generalisations, it would be the most unfair of artifices to appeal from a school of science which understands and has weighed Mr. Darwin's reasonings, to a school of science which knows nothing about them, only because the latter can wield the calculus and weigh the sun.

No doubt the stronghold of the modern materialism lies in the new display of the previously hidden motive forces of physical evolution, and the disappointment of ordinary thinkers at finding them, as they think, rather negative than positive, rather unfavourable to low forms of life, than actively favourable to the higher. Mr. Darwin thinks he has shown that Nature makes an indefinite number of organic attempts, as it were, of which a vast proportion fail to persist only because the few which involve the possession of an accidental advantage thrive at their expense. Both the tentative and the negative characteristics of this organon of improvement scandalise men. They ask how an omniscient mind which knows precisely what is wanted, can set Nature *groping* her way forward as if she were blind, to find the path of least resistance. And again, they ask how, if bad only becomes good by steady starvation of the worse, it is possible to see in this process the cherishing love of a divine Creator? These difficulties seem to me to be the chief causes of the new materialistic wave which is passing over England. Now, with regard to the tentative character of organic change, it is worthy of remark that the whole force of the criticism lies not in facts, but in the hasty construction which we put upon the facts. There is nothing tentative about the celestial motions, or the effect of either gravity or chemical action on matter. In this region everything is so sure that mathematical calculation can tell you what will happen in great part, and the chemist will predict with certainty the affinities and changes of combination which will display themselves. If there had been anything really tentative about the ultimate constituents of Nature, we should have found it here; we should have had the showers of atoms accidentally diverging, as Lucretius described them, from their natural course; should have discovered the signs of hesitation in the elements, and found our human science too wavering to and fro in inevitable sympathy. But notoriously this is not the case, and Professor Tyndall at Belfast was, as materialists usually are, very strong on the iron chain of necessary connection which binds everything, from the shooting meteor, up, I suppose, to the will of man. I assume, then, that if every organic form shows a tendency to vary in all directions, useful or otherwise, at every moment, and especially if the individuals of a family always diverge more or less from the parent stock, it is not from any want of steadiness in the ultimate constitution of Nature, but from the necessary variety involved in greater complexity of structure. Strictly speaking, there is nothing really tentative in organic variations. They are, in all probability, *necessary* changes, due to the unperceived variety of circumstances in which they originated. But if this be so, the appearance of tentative and temporary forms is delusive, and what scandalises our superficial reason is not the groping of Nature at all, but the mixture at every step of worse and less useful forms with the better and more useful: whereas, people think, the circumstances leading to the poorer forms of life should have been sifted away, and only the stronger forms produced, without any of that 'setting' of apparent failure, ranging from positive monstrosity up to the very borders of strong and durable types, which so perplexes the lovers of the argument from design. But this criticism really comes to a condemnation of variety itself. There could be no variety except by sudden leaps from form to form, if all that is inferior is to be—not eliminated, but never to exist; and the motive force of competition—so great and valuable a force in the lower phases of existence—would be vastly diminished, even where it was not annihilated. The more the so-called tentativeness of Nature is considered, the more it will be seen that it means simply the minute variations due to varying circumstances and operating, though within natural organic limits, still in all directions. But why, it will be asked, in all directions? Why should variations of a degenerate character ever be admitted, if there be a Divine Mind giving its law to natural change? Of course no complete answer can be given to such a question, but considering the world as the stage on which a moral freedom is to be disciplined, it is not inexplicable why that liability to degeneration which is the greatest danger in moral growth is visible to man on every side, in natural things as well as moral, as one of the catastrophes to which, both naturally and supernaturally, he is liable. Without the constant sight of the tendency to degeneration in things natural, without being daily taught that it needs, in some sense, a physical struggle not merely for Nature to keep on advancing, but to keep from falling back, the meaning and risk of the same liability in things moral and spiritual would not be half as vivid as it is. It is, after all, by no means a matter for surprise that Nature should not merely reflect back, but even in a manner anticipate, the inertia, the indolence, the degeneracy, as well as the activity, the industry, and the refining transformations, of human trial. There is no real tentativeness in Nature, only variation, for worse, as well as for better.

But then comes the difficulty as to the method of natural selection,—that progress seems to be secured rather by starving out or killing out the worse, than by accumulating the better. The imagination is shocked by what seems the destructiveness of the process, rather than the benevolence which would be expected. It is not rewards for the better, so much as penalties for the worse, by which the results of conflict are determined. It seems to be some "devil" who is "taking the hindmost," rather than a god who is smiling on the foremost. Food becomes scarce, and a race that cannot migrate perishes. Wings give their possessors a great advantage in obtaining food, and the wingless races find themselves nowhere in the struggle, and soon become obsolete. This seems more like stamping out the unimproved than encouraging the improved species,—more like extinguishing the conservatives than rewarding the progressives. But here, again, it is metaphor which deceives us. It may be that the individual of a lower and vanishing type has a somewhat shorter and less enjoyable life than the individual of a higher and multiplying type, but the difference is small at best; it is the lower *type* which suffers, not the members of it, whose individual careers, though there are fewer and fewer such careers year by year belonging to the lower type, are probably hardly distinguishably shorter or less happy than those belonging to the other.

Indeed, natural selection is not so negative as it seems. It rests upon the tendency of hereditary qualities shared by both parents, whether they be advantages or otherwise, to accumulate in the descent, and so to hasten the relative gain or loss of advantage in every generation. The interest accumulates, and the deficiency accumulates, till the one becomes a new capital, and the other is wiped out by extinction. The upward pressure, therefore, is as true as the downward pressure. The gradual development of the brain is as much the result of natural law as the gradual extinction of creatures with brain too small for their functions. In short, as it seems to me, the evidence of a controlling mind in organic laws such as these is still clearer than it is in the region of mere heat, force, and motion.

But no doubt the tendency of such studies will always be materialistic, if we forget that we must not apply to them the guiding ideas gathered from a very different region,—that of our own moral life. There, completely new principles and laws begin. Natural selection yields in man to pity and reverence; the law of competition is qualified and partly merged in the law of sacrifice. Yet to my mind this makes the materialistic explanation only the more incredible. It is hard enough to understand how gravitating force should "develop" into chemical affinity, or chemical affinity into the organic propagation of definite characteristics and forms. But if the roots of our *whole* life were in material force and physical competition, if we were the mere products of natural selection, and had no access to any store of diviner counsels, how could the Christian ideal of life ever have developed itself from such roots as these? The materialist hypothesis, even if I exclude all reference to the moral and religious life which it would treat as a superstition, is guilty of the absurd attempt to support an ever-spreading and broadening structure on a mere atom as its base. Force could hardly account for life at all, but still less for life that rises above force, and makes it the most sacred of duties to soften the severity of its own *régime*. Force abdicating its throne,—competition appealing to the conscience against the rude selfishness of competition, —is a phenomenon which it might well exhaust the inventive faculties of a materialist to account for, even though he drew freely, as no doubt he would, on ingenious moral resources, to which, of course, every materialist has access, but has access only because he cannot confine his faculties within the stony limits of his own theory.

VIII

PROFESSOR CLIFFORD ON THE SIN OF CREDULITY

1877

PROFESSOR CLIFFORD, continuing his ethical disquisitions in the *Contemporary Review* for January, dilates with much unction and more eloquence on the sin of credulity. "If I let myself believe anything on insufficient evidence," he says, "there may be no great harm done by the mere belief; it may be true, after all, or I may never have occasion to exhibit it in outward acts. But I cannot help doing this great wrong towards Man, that I make myself credulous. The danger to society is not merely that it should believe wrong things, though that is great enough, but that it should become credulous, and lose the habit of testing things and inquiring into them; for then it must sink back into savagery. The harm which is done by credulity in a man is not confined to the fostering of a credulous character in others, and consequent support of false beliefs. . . . Men speak the truth to one another when each reveres the truth in his own mind and in the other's mind; but how shall my friend revere the truth in my mind when I myself am careless about it, when I believe things because I want to believe them, and because they are comforting and pleasant? Will he not learn to cry 'Peace!' to me when there is no peace? By such a course I shall surround myself with a thick atmosphere of falsehood and fraud, and in that I must live. It may matter little to me, in my cloud-castle of sweet illusions and darling lies, but it matters much to Man, that I have made my neighbours ready to deceive. The credulous man is father to the liar and the cheat, he lives in the bosom of this his family, and it is no marvel if he should become even as they are. So closely are duties knit together, that whoso shall keep the whole law and yet offend in one point, he is guilty of all." This is eloquent and almost evangelical in its tone, but I think Professor Clifford was hardly justifiable in illustrating his position of the wickedness of credulity, as he does, by instances such as that of the shipowner who persuades himself that his old ship is still seaworthy, without satisfying himself by evidence that it is so, and who, when the ship goes down with all its crew, gets the insurance on it paid, and contents himself with the reflection that after all he acted on his own inner conviction, though his conviction proved to be mistaken. The weak point of such illustrations is that the self-interest of the man is in this case engaged on the side of his credulity, and not against it,—a circumstance which should always put us morally on our guard against not only credulity, but incredulity, or any other attitude of mind which it would be for our own interest for us to assume. Put the case the other way. Your whole fortune is embarked in a given enterprise. Some one gives you most unwelcome but, on the surface, plausible information that the enterprise is hollow, and founded on a cheat. You know that if this be true you are ruined, and also that if it be false, but be believed to be true, you are ruined by the panic which it will excite among others; it is therefore your *interest* to be incredulous, for by extinguishing the rumour at first you retain the chance of sustaining others' confidence, while if you give any credit to it, you create the panic by which others indeed may be saved, but you must be ruined. "Incredulity," therefore, is the prompting of self-interest, and in such a case, incredulity is as wrong as Professor Clifford's credulity, and for the same reason. It is the tainted motive which makes the credulity and the incredulity alike evil; while with a better motive either might be generous and noble. If instead of being a shipowner, you were the friend of the shipowner, and intending to sail in his ship, and from your absolute confidence in your friend's assurances, had rejected at once as absolutely incredible any question of the seaworthiness of the ship,—then, instead of branding your credulity with the character of a superstitious self-deception, the worst even Professor Clifford could say of it would be that it was a generous mistake. And in like manner, if the person informed of the false character of the supposed enterprise had been, not one whose capital was already at stake, but one on the point of investing, yet still able to withdraw his investment, and if the motive of his incredulity had been, *not* his selfish fears for his own property, but his complete trust in the probity of another, I should have said the same in his case. What I complain of in Professor Clifford is that he has weighted his denunciations of credulity by introducing an altogether false issue into his illustrations. And I maintain, in opposition to him, that if we free our minds from the misleading influence of his illustrative commentary, and apply his doctrine to cases in which no such taint of false motive is discernible, we shall find that his doctrine is rejected by the consensus even of that non-religious society to whose interests Professor Clifford habitually appeals, as if they constituted the true and only standard of ethics.

Let me take a sufficiently notorious case. The biographer of Columbus makes it evident to us, on the testimony of the son of the great navigator, testimony carefully substantiated by reference to the notes and memoranda collected by his father, that the magnificent enterprise which Columbus conducted to a successful issue was really the offspring of two beliefs, for which he had hardly any evidence, and which were, in fact, illusions. "It is apparent," says Mr. Washington Irving, "that the grand argument which induced Columbus to his enterprise was . . . that the most eastern part of Asia known to the ancients could not be separated from the Azores by more than a third of the circumference of the globe; that the intervening space must, in a great measure, be filled up by the unknown residue of Asia; and that if the circumference of the world was, as he believed, less than was generally supposed, the Asiatic shores could easily be attained by a moderate voyage to the west. It is singular how much the success of this great undertaking depended upon two happy errors,—the imaginary extent of Asia to the east, and the supposed smallness of the earth." And again, when in his voyage, Columbus and his pilots, to the latter's great dismay, found the magnetic needle varying more and more from the Pole star, Columbus explained it by assuring them that the true direction of the magnetic needle was not to the Pole star, but to the invisible Pole round which it circled. Here, again, it is certain that Columbus explained away most dangerous and paralysing terrors by a very ingenious but false guess, for which he had no evidence worthy of the name. Now, what language would Professor Clifford apply to these two mistaken beliefs of Columbus? Would he use the language contained in this article, and say he was guilty of a piece of mental gymnastic which did "this great wrong to Man," that Columbus "made himself credulous"? Would Professor Clifford ask concerning him, how could his friends revere truth in the mind of Columbus, when Columbus was himself careless about it, when he "surrounded himself with a thick atmosphere of falsehood and fraud," cried "Peace!" to his mariners when there was no peace; when he "entrenched himself in his little castle of sweet illusions and darling lies"?—would Professor Clifford maintain that in these acts of credulity Columbus was making himself "the father of the liar and the cheat," so that, "living in the bosom of this his family, it would have been no wonder if he had been as they"? Would he say that it matters not the least that Columbus succeeded in his enterprise, since in acting upon it, and carrying it through, he deceived himself by illusions which might far more probably have led him astray? Would he say that Columbus was not innocent in thus deluding himself and others, but only not found out? Would he assert, as he does in relation to the subject of his own illustration, that "the question of right or wrong has to do with the origin of his belief, not the matter of it; not what it was, but how he got it; not whether it turned out to be true or false, but whether he had a right to believe such evidence as was before him." I take it, Professor Clifford has too much good sense to say any of these things. They are only applicable at all, not to acts of pure credulity,—even though false credulity,—but to acts of *interested* credulity, when a man ought to have been put on his guard against himself by knowing well the swerve or bias given to his interior beliefs by his own interests. Yet Professor Clifford's argument, if it is worth anything at all, is applicable to all acts of belief on evidence which the believer, when in the exercise of his coolest judgment, would have reason to think really inadequate.

I take the case of Columbus, because I regard that case as in a very high degree illustrative of the sort of faith which is grounded not on what Professor Clifford calls evidence, but on something deeper and better. We have seen that Columbus's principal *assigned* grounds for his belief that he would succeed in his enterprise were false grounds, but no one could doubt that the general intuition of genius which gave him the pertinacity and the sanguineness of conviction essential to success was nevertheless legitimate,—and was the true forecast of those tendrils of the reason which far oftener originate the discovery of great and living truths than what our Professor means by "evidence." Now, as it seems to me, there is even in ordinary people who have no genius, some power of forecast of the same sort, on matters, however, of a very different kind;—and that with them the true secret of forecast is the affections. Love appreciates character more rapidly and far more truly than the intellect, and though it, too, like genius, may select very erroneous grounds on which to base its confession of faith,—the intuitions of love, like the intuitions of genius, are often true when the account which it renders to itself of its intuitions is false. Now it seems to me the great aim, as well as tendency, of Professor Clifford's ethical writings to encourage, even in subjects most closely intertwined with the conscience and the affections, that spirit of severe incredulity which would not only extinguish, as he desires, all the highest faiths, but also all the deepest and noblest human ties. Nothing can be less true than that the intuitions of a child,—sometimes even of a dog,—respecting the qualities of a character concerning which there is no experience to guide us, are utterly untrustworthy, although they are, and must seem to those who trust them, to be founded in a deep credulity. How mischievous, how credulous, how superstitious, according to the dictum of Professor Clifford's paper, is the child's indignation against one who accuses his father of commercial dishonesty! He has had no sort of experience of the wide divergence between men's domestic and professional consciences. He knows hardly anything except that his father has often told him what turned out to be true, and sometimes done so when it was obviously a painful task. The leap from such a little plot of experience as this to the large generalisation that the same father would not cheat a complete stranger, is, as we all know, a tremendous leap in the dark. And yet who can doubt that many a child makes it not in the dark, but in the full light of a guiding affection; while many another would shrink from making it from equally good, but quite as mysterious, instincts, which would tell him it was wrong. The ethics of belief could scarcely have been more meagrely and more misleadingly discussed than they are by Professor Clifford. I venture to say that the best and most trustworthy of all our beliefs are founded on evidence of which we cannot give even a brief summary to ourselves, and that if we attempt this, we shall wander as far from the true grounds of our belief as Columbus himself did when he gave the two false reasons on which he chiefly rested his belief in the possibility of his enterprise.

When I compare with Professor Clifford's "ethics of belief" such predictions as our Lord's, that He was come to divide father from son, and mother from daughter, to send not peace on earth, but a sword, to bring persecution on His disciples, and yet to give them a great and lasting victory over the world, I cannot but wonder at the credulity of the man who preaches the gospel of incredulity as the great cornerstone of the new ethics. Why, if, as Professor Clifford holds, a true ethic is the doctrine which fits a human society to grow stronger, more united, more fit to battle with the hostility of nature, and with the perils of anarchy, then I should say that the first requisite of a true ethic is a commanding faith which goes far beyond the bounds of what Professor Clifford means by "evidence," on the strength of the forecast due to its conscience and its affections. It was what Professor Clifford would call Christ's credulity which gave a new bond to human society, and assured the "little flock," whom He sent forth as "sheep amongst wolves," of ultimate conquest. It was precisely the same sort of credulity on a very much minuter scale which gave to Augustine, to Savonarola, to Luther, to all the great Reformers, their confidence in the divine character of their cause, and their power to bring it to a triumphant conclusion. Without such credulity there would have been little or no reconstructive force in human society after the great revolutions had spent their force. What draws human beings together and makes them into an organic whole is the great attraction of a common faith, and if intellectual truth be essential, as it is, to progress, moral and spiritual truth,—which is the truth seized by the magic of the conscience and affections,—is still more necessary to order and unity of any sort. Professor Clifford strikes at the very basis of his own ethics when he calls all belief which is either not founded on producible evidence at all, or when challenged, produces, as Columbus produced, evidence for itself which is not worth the paper on which it is written,—credulity, and brands it as both mischievous and dishonest. The simple fact is that the best and most binding faiths we have, faiths not only at the basis of popular religion, but also at the basis of domestic strength and peace, are founded on precisely such evidence as this at which Professor Clifford levels his most bitter shafts.

IX

PROFESSOR WACE ON BELIEF

1877

I DREW attention rather more than three months ago (January 6) to a striking but very misleading essay of Professor Clifford's in the *Fortnightly Review* on the sin of Credulity, and pointed out the great blunder of supposing that the structure of human society could be held together at all on the assumption that legitimate beliefs are founded solely on adequate investigation of the evidence bearing upon them, independently of those affections and half-reasoned, but often not the less, rather the more, trustworthy prepossessions of the mind, which are at the root of our deepest, and I will venture to say also of our truest, faiths. Professor Wace of King's College, and Chaplain of Lincoln's Inn, took up the same subject a few days ago, in a very thoughtful paper read at the Victoria Institute, in which he showed that the fundamental methods of science, though they may sometimes lead to beliefs first, and then to knowledge, are not at all the most commonly-used or available avenues to those personal trusts which are, as I maintained in January, the binding cement of our human society. Trust, he says very justly, is at best as much an efficient cause of truthfulness as truthfulness is a cause of trust. In other words, instead of founding trust on careful intellectual investigation, the need for such careful intellectual investigation is often dispensed with altogether by the blind power of trust. "If it is the duty of my neighbour to speak the truth, it is equally my duty to believe that he does speak it. I have no right to suspect him of violating this obligation, and to do so is, in practice, to suggest the idea of falsehood to him, and to sow the seeds of it. A corrupt society is, above all things, marked by two characteristics, —a 'universal' habit 'of questioning' all that is said, and an equally universal habit of saying what is not true. On the contrary, in a healthy society like that of England, habits of trust and of truth equally support each other; and it has now become, for instance, a principle of education that the best way to evoke truthfulness in boys is uniformly to believe them, even when appearances are against them. In place, therefore, of Professor Clifford's assertion that 'the credulous man is father to the liar and the cheat,—he lives in the bosom of this his family, and it is no wonder he should become even as they are,' we should be much nearer the experience of practical life, if we alleged this of the suspicious men." At least as regards human testimony, then, trust is natural and almost instinctive, distrust the harsh teaching of special experience; and what we ought to feel is rather that it needs specific evidence of untrustworthiness to justify suspicion, than that it needs specific evidence of trustworthiness to justify belief. We do not, even in ordinary cases of well-grounded confidence, believe because we have calculated the probabilities, and find a great balance in favour of the testimony we are weighing, but we accept that testimony at once, so long as there are no strong warnings of its positive untrustworthiness. It is, in any wholesome state of society, unbelief on all matters involving personal testimony for which we need explicit evidence rather than belief. The instincts and affections are the true basis of trust. On all matters of personal confidence, recourse is had to an intellectual estimate of probabilities, only when there is some warning of experience given us to distrust those instincts and affections,—*i.e.* that they are in danger of being abused. The initiative lies properly with those who would sap confidence; and unless that initiative be taken, trust once established, whether by a long experience of trustworthiness, or by the far more rapid process of personal affinities and insights, remains legitimately in possession of the field.

Now, what I want to call attention to to-day is the bearing of this principle on religious confidence. The root of all religion is, of course, a personal trust in God, founded on the teaching of the conscience and those spiritual impressions of care and tenderness which appear to pour in upon us from a source beyond ourselves. The root of all Christian belief is a similar personal trust in and affection for Christ as the very incarnation of God's being and the illustration of His attributes. Again, all historical belief in the Christian story depends on a similar sort of confidence in the evangelists and letter-writers of the New Testament,—a confidence which may obviously be partly shaken without any breakdown of moral trust, by anything which goes to show that these witnesses were not intellectually qualified to discriminate between what they had witnessed or derived from others, and their own inferences from such testimony. How does all this affect the absoluteness of religious trust? Must we say that till the whole armoury of scepticism has been turned against that trust, and shown to be inadequate, our trust can be only provisional, and therefore hesitating? Professor Clifford would say that a faith is not good for anything, but even evil, unless it represents well-calculated probabilities which yield a strong balance of evidence in its favour. This is clearly erroneous, but even substituting for it the truer rationale of faith, religious belief turns out to be this,—a trust in superhuman beings and in those who had closer relations than we have with such superhuman beings, which is either, in some important respects, only preliminary and provisional, or else one which has not been successfully impaired by, but has survived, a frank and full consideration of the various objections and arguments in arrest of belief forced on us by competent criticism. Is anything like absolute confidence to be founded on either state of mind, and especially on the former? May it not be said that, since we shall never be able to anticipate the new objections which new ages and new investigations may bring against our faith, even those who have examined all they have fallen in with, must not regard their faith as anything more than provisional? Still more, may it not be said that those whose learning, time, and opportunity have not enabled them to do even as much as that, have no right to ignore the difficulties which they have not even gauged? Should not both classes limit themselves to saying, 'Our mind is possessed with a belief which further knowledge might weaken or remove, and therefore, even while clinging to it, we must never forget to remind ourselves that some day it may vanish, and be succeeded by an equally legitimate unbelief?' Perhaps the true reply to these questions will best be indicated by first putting another. Would it be right for one who feels the deepest and most intimate love and reverence for a parent or friend to try and qualify that feeling by representing to himself the possibility that, under certain circumstances, the impressions on which those feelings are grounded might be wholly changed, and his love and reverence be succeeded by complete indifference or even dislike? Of course such changes are always possible. What has happened to others may happen to us, and in the case of feelings which depend on the mutual conduct of two or more variable creatures, no one can be absolutely certain that they will never change. But is it true that the habitual realising of this possibility,—the practice of giving it a substantial weight in our minds apart from any sign that the anticipation is likely to be fulfilled, would make us better friends or better sons and daughters? What I think any wise man would say of such a proposal is this: 'These affections are the best and noblest part of human nature; they lead to the life which is best worth living; they cannot exist in an atmosphere of constant distrust and suspicion; therefore the habitual contemplation of these abstract possibilities, even if it be solely due to the desire for intellectual completeness and a full survey of all contingencies, is a folly which endangers what is best in us, for the sake of a fanciful width of view which can never come near being a full survey of the horizon of possibilities. It is a waste of the highest life,—whether joy or sorrow, as the case may be,—for the sake of a trivial diminution of the intellectual inadequacy of a survey which cannot in any case even approach exhaustiveness. Let, then, the trust produced by the growth of the affections remain unchallenged by any habit of dwelling on abstract possibilities of change simply because they are possibilities. It would be just as wise to diminish the energy with which you undertake any one of life's duties by saturating yourself with the fancy that if you were to die, as you might, in the middle of it, it would not much matter how it had been begun.' If that be good sense and good faith too, as I think it is, the applicability of the considerations it involves to the case of religious faith is obvious enough. Of course, it is true that, as there are many who, from passionately believing in God, have come to be deniers of God, we, not fully knowing ourselves, may come to be counted amongst them. Of course, it is true that, as there are very many who from passionate love for and faith in Christ have come to hold the whole Christian story a fable, we, not fully knowing the drifts and tendencies of our own nature, may some day find ourselves amongst them. But it is not wisdom, but folly, to discount this bare possibility by dwelling on it, while the love, and reverence, and trust are living affections within us, filling us with a loyalty to which such anticipations are a treason. But then such loyalty as this does not imply—indeed is as far as possible from implying—that we should obstinately refuse to take in and examine fully, so far as we are competent to do so, all the facts, or even alleged facts, which are advanced by men who have ceased to be believers, as their reasons for ceasing to believe. A man who was afraid to look into the reasons alleged by another for his casting off a friendship with a common friend, would really have ceased to be loyal in his heart to his own friendship. We cannot retain our trust in God and Christ and yet admit to ourselves that we are afraid to examine the grounds of those who have ceased to put trust in God and Christ,—unless, indeed, these grounds be beyond our capacity for judgment. Of course it is quite right to refuse to examine what we could not understand. But even so, how should the knowledge that certain statements which are quite beyond our grasp are believed by many to be relevant to their disbelief, affect our belief? So far as these statements bear upon questions of scholarship and history, I think they should always inspire a certain amount of real reserve. It is an obvious rule that those who have not examined and cannot examine the true issue of a controversy, ought not to feel the confidence which is the result of examination. They must necessarily balance authority by authority, and keep room for either conviction on matters which superior learning must decide. But within all these questions of scholarship and learning, the existence of the personal life of a divine inspirer of conscience, and of the personal spell and imposing spiritual majesty of Christ, remain as clear of either history or philosophy as the existence of our own friends is clear of either history or philosophy. Some people would tell us that the existence of other beings than ourselves *is* a question of philosophy,—that if we could disprove the existence of an external world, we should have no reason to believe in the existence of any conscious being but ourselves. But we all know that this is trash,—that certainty has no meaning at all, if we are not as certain of our friends' existence as we are of our own. Such philosophical cavils should weigh no more than the abstract doubts which may always be suggested, that life may turn out to be an illusion altogether,—a dream which we have been dreaming, and from which we shall waken up to find that all the assumptions on which we supposed we were acting were as fictitious as the actions themselves. The true attitude, I take it, towards the arguments by which we know others to have been made sceptics, is to sound and gauge them thoroughly, if we can; and if we cannot, to hold our belief in reserve on any point which we can see must be seriously affected by considerations which are beyond us;—but not to concede for a moment that the attestations of our conscience and affections to the existence of that righteousness which is the ground of all righteousness, and that love which is the fountain of all love, and their highest manifestation in human life, should be shaken by the mere knowledge that other men exist who dispute that attestation, and who do not feel these affections. That would be to paralyse the life we have, in deference to those who have it not.

X

PROFESSOR TYNDALL ON MATERIALISM

1875

PERHAPS it is my own fault that the moment Professor Tyndall leaves physical philosophy, and betakes himself to the theologic or metaphysical assumptions which underlie it, I never fail to be bewildered as to what his meaning really is. He contributes, for instance, an essay to the November number of the *Fortnightly*, subsequently to appear, we are told, as a preface to his forthcoming *Fragments of Science*, which, clear as is the style of its individual sentences, and clever as are certain of its sarcasms, appears to me to remain one of the obscurest riddles in modern literature, when, even after perusing it two or three times, I lay it down, and ask what, then, really is its drift and teaching? I will attempt to state its main positions in Professor Tyndall's own words, and then to show the exceeding difficulty of understanding what jointly they amount to. The Professor is answering the various critics of his Belfast address,—chief among them Mr. Martineau, on whom he expends the main portion of his philosophical ammunition. Now, if I understand him rightly, he has two complaints to make against the ablest of these critics. In the first place, they misunderstood him to say, without his having given any excuse for such a misunderstanding, that he can "explain" mind from matter. On the contrary, he maintains and proves somewhat elaborately that he has always said just the contrary, that even granting you could know absolutely the physical conditions of the molecules of the brain which correspond to each condition of consciousness,—to each thought, feeling, hope, perception, imagination, etc.,—you would not be a tittle nearer towards bridging the impassable chasm between a state of matter and a state of mind. "You cannot," he quotes from himself, "satisfy the human understanding in its demand for logical continuity between molecular processes and the phenomena of the human mind. This is a rock on which materialism must inevitably split, whenever it pretends to be a complete philosophy of the human mind." Well, then, here is Professor Tyndall's first position. Whatever strength there may be in materialism, here is one great and impassable flaw in it. It cannot get out of itself. It cannot bridge the gulf between matter and consciousness. If it proposes to do so, it is making a vain boast which it cannot sustain. So far, then, Professor Tyndall is not a materialist. He apparently thinks it much more promising to investigate physical phenomena separately and mental phenomena separately, than to try to explain the passage from the one to the other; but as there is a whole class of phenomena of the most important kind for which he can find no key in molecular causes, he so far admits, not speculative materialism, but the speculative failure of materialism. But this position is no sooner clearly established in the reader's mind than, to his bewilderment, he suddenly finds himself overwhelmed by a very different class of equally positive and even tartly and dogmatically stated speculative opinions, such as, for instance, the following:—"Were not man's origin implicated, we should accept without a murmur the derivation of animal and vegetable life from what we call inorganic nature. The conclusion of pure intellect points this way, and no other. But this purity is troubled by our interests in this life, and by our hopes and fears regarding the world to come. Reason is traversed by the emotions, anger rising in the weaker heads to the height of suggesting that the compendious shooting of the inquirer would be an act agreeable to God and serviceable to men. . . . Our foes are, to some extent, they of our own household, including not only the ignorant and the passionate, but a minority of minds of high calibre and culture,—lovers of freedom, moreover, who, though its objective hull be riddled by logic, still find the ethic life of their religion unimpaired. But while such considerations ought to influence the form of our argument, and ought to prevent it from ever slipping out of the region of courtesy into that of scorn or abuse, its *substance*, I think, ought to be maintained and presented in unmitigated strength." Here Professor Tyndall appears to maintain that "pure intellect" has none of the speculative fault to find with materialism, which he reproached his critics so vehemently before for forgetting that he had found with it. The only flaw, he now says, in the materialistic argument is, not its inability to bridge the gulf between molecules and consciousness, on which he had previously insisted, but only man's dislike to face the conclusions of pure intellect when they are disagreeable to himself. Here, then, it is only "courtesy," not in the least an intellectual sense of the inadequacy of materialism, which makes Professor Tyndall tender with the anti-materialists. The "objective" truth of their religion has been positively riddled by logic, and if their position be worthy of respect, it is not for any grain of speculative strength in it, but solely because it is the source of a certain 'ethic life' in themselves. That very materialistic argument on the hopeless and ineradicable flaw in which he had previously insisted, when he overwhelmed his critics with reproaches for failing to recognise that he had seen and pointed out its shortcomings, he now finds one of "unmitigated strength."

These discrepancies are puzzling enough, but when I come to consider the sphere assigned by Professor Tyndall in this relation to what he terms the "potency of matter," I am more hopelessly out of my depth than ever. "Think," he says, "of the acorn, of the earth, and of the solar light and heat,—was ever such necromancy dreamt of as the production of that massive trunk, the swaying boughs, and whispering leaves from the interaction of those three factors? In this interaction, moreover, consists what we call *life*." And then he goes on to illustrate this "potency of matter" more elaborately still:—

"Consider it for a moment. There is an experiment, first made by Wheatstone, where the music of a piano is transferred from its sound-board, through a thin wooden rod, across several silent rooms in succession, and poured out at a distance from the instrument. The strings of the piano vibrate, not singly, but ten at a time. Every string sub-divides, yielding not one note, but a dozen. All these vibrations and sub-vibrations are crowded together into a bit of deal not more than a quarter of a square inch in section. Yet no note is lost. Each vibration asserts its individual rights; and all are, at last, shaken forth into the air by a second sound-board, against which the distant end of the rod presses. Thought ends in amazement when it seeks to realise the motions of that rod as the music flows through it. I turn to my tree and observe its roots, its trunk, its branches, and its leaves. As the rod conveys the music, and yields it up to the distant air, so does the trunk convey the matter and the motion—the shocks and pulses and other vital actions—which eventually emerge in the umbrageous foliage of the tree. I went some time ago through the greenhouse of a friend. He had ferns from Ceylon, the branches of which were in some cases not much thicker than an ordinary pin—hard, smooth, and cylindrical—often leafless for a foot and more. But at the end of every one of them the unsightly twig unlocked the exuberant beauty hidden within it, and broke forth into a mass of fronds, almost large enough to fill the arms. We stand here upon a higher level of the wonderful: we are conscious of a music subtler than that of the piano, passing unheard through these tiny boughs, and issuing in what Mr. Martineau would opulently call the 'clustered magnificence' of the leaves. Does it lessen my amazement to know that every cluster, and every leaf—their form and texture—lie, like the music in the rod, in the molecular structure of these apparently insignificant stems? Not so."

Now, in that fine passage, Professor Tyndall seems to me to yield all, and more than all, that Mr. Martineau asks, when he challenges the physicist really to explain the universe as a result of 'material' causes. 'Potency,' I suppose, is power; and 'potency' to do something in the future which is not yet within the reach of actual energy is power to anticipate the future and to provide for its contingencies. Preparation for conditions which are as yet neither present nor, by such minds as ours, even imaginable, implies, of course, a mastery of laws of measure and laws of quality and laws of combination and co-ordination, which involves not only what we call mind, but infinitely more than we call mind. 'Potency of matter,' in Professor Tyndall's sense, is matter with most elaborate conditions grafted on it, which have reference to the most distant spaces and the most remote times. Are such conditions conceivable except as proceeding from a being who, in some sense immeasurably higher, rather than lower than ours, *knows* those distant spaces and distant times for which these conditions are prepared. Take the case of the electrised wire, which differs from other wire only in physical conditions perfectly invisible to any man surveying it, but which were preconceived by him who sent the current through it and by him who marks off its results. Here is a 'potency of matter' of which we know the precise meaning, and it is a meaning which involves knowledge on the part of him who produced the potency. So in the case of Professor Tyndall's sounding-rod; it contains now only potencies of sound, which, if the sounding-board at the end be forgotten, may be potencies of sound never likely to reach human ears, and it must have contained once also those potencies of leaf and verdure which Professor Tyndall so eloquently describes in the case of the twig of fern. In this case, then, one set of 'potencies' have never reached their actual efflorescence to human eyes, and have been succeeded by another set of 'potencies' which may never wield their power of delight for human ears. But is it conceivable that, in either case, the 'potencies' were there without the power which knew what was in them? If it takes mind, and very refined mind, like Professor Tyndall's, even to discover these laws of adaptation of distant conditions of space and time to each other, does it not take much more than what man calls mind to embody the laws and keep them at work? It seems to me that in this talk about the 'potency' of matter Professor Tyndall gives up entirely the materialism for which he argues. Potency is an *idea* simply, without any meaning except for one who can see both ends of a long chain of complex conditions, and can see that the beginning makes provision for the end. But this is equivalent to mind plus matter, or rather something much more instead of much less than what we call mind, plus matter, and not matter alone. If it takes what we call mind, and mind at a stretch, to adapt the conditions of locomotion, say, to the conditions of the people who desire to go about a day or two in advance,—it must be something not less, but infinitely greater than mind so stretched, which adapts the conditions of a sun in space to the myriads of lives which will, sooner or later, if scientific evolution be on the right track, be evolved from the conditions so prepared. In that word 'potency' Professor Tyndall seems to me to have assumed a mental, and excluded a purely material, cause as conclusively,—and let me also say, as unconsciously,—as his 'unsightly twig' assumed its beauty and put off its unsightliness when it burst into that "clustered magnificence" of fronds of which he speaks. 'Potency' assumes the capacity to see present and future at once, and prepare the present for the future. Matter, as such, can have none but accidental 'potency,'— the potency of changing place when force is forthcoming to change its place. But force acting under rhythmical laws of specific and complex provisions, force moulding and constraining force, till matter gives out music, and beauty, and consciousness, and suffering, and joy, —this is all language without meaning, unless you credit the force so at work with all, and much more than all the qualities, which are combined in what we call 'mind.'

And yet Professor Tyndall appears to make it his main charge against Mr. Martineau, that all this inference is a mere feat of 'feeling,' for which there is no sort of intellectual defence. After explaining that the animal world is a distillation through the vegetable world from inorganic nature, he goes on :—

"From this point of view all three worlds would constitute a unity, in which I picture life as immanent everywhere. Nor am I anxious to shut out the idea that the life here spoken of may be but a subordinate part and function of a higher life, as the living, moving blood is subordinate to the living man. I resist no such idea as long as it is not dogmatically imposed. Left for the human mind freely to operate upon, the idea has ethical vitality; but stiffened into a dogma, the inner force disappears, and the outward yoke of a usurping hierarchy takes its place."

What Professor Tyndall means by 'ethical vitality' is one of the great mysteries of this beautiful but mysterious paper. I should have said that if there was a word wholly inapplicable to the conception he is here describing it is the word 'ethical.' I suppose he means by 'ethical vitality' that the notion has a charm for us which gives us new impulse, but that it has no basis at all in our pure reason. I should have said just the reverse. There is no 'ethical' vitality in this or any other idea till you put some moral or spiritual character into it, which hitherto Professor Tyndall has not done. It is to the intellectual nature of man, and to that alone, that this notion appeals with irresistible force. Here is an infinite wealth of minute correspondence between the most distant parts of space and time, which, unless we assume mind, and much more than human mind, operating in and through what Professor Tyndall calls matter, is simply a miracle of harmonious accidents, of happy rhythm in events which no one ever intended to be linked together, of poetic coincidences and convergencies of energies, the rhyme and music in which no one ever preconceived. And this the imagination of man refuses to conceive. As far as I understand Professor Tyndall, what he calls "feeling" I call "reason," and what he calls pure reason I should call, if I did not feel so much respect for him as a physicist, pure folly. Certainly he is not happy in expounding 'materialism' to his readers, in spite of the fact that he possesses, as he does, the ear of nature, and catches so much more than most of us of her hidden secrets and inspirations.

XI

MR. MARTINEAU ON MATERIALISM

1876

PROFESSOR TYNDALL'S reply in the November number of the *Contemporary Review* to Mr. Martineau's criticisms on some of the positions of his Belfast address in 1874 has elicited a rejoinder from Mr. Martineau in the new number of the same periodical, which in the clearness of its positions and the precision of its reasoning, should, at least, protect him against any reiteration of Professor Tyndall's accusation of want of lucidity in his style, and want of accuracy in his apprehensions of the issues discussed between them. Indeed, to those who look not so much at the descriptions of physical phenomena referred to for purposes of illustration, as at the exposition of the intellectual assumptions involved in the scientific description of these phenomena, and the rational inferences drawn from them, it will appear, as I ventured to intimate in commenting on Professor Tyndall's paper in the November *Contemporary*, that the charge of vagueness of conception and looseness of exposition may be made with much more truth against his own presentation of the case than against Mr. Martineau's. Indeed, I defy any one to apprehend clearly what it is that

Professor Tyndall meant to assert when he derived all the various elaborate forms of life now existing from what he called the "potency" of matter, and what it is, on the other hand, that he was angry with his opponents for supposing that he meant to assert and earnestly protested that he refused to assert. If I am not mistaken, he will find that Mr. Martineau had a much clearer conception than he himself had of the intellectual creed shadowed forth in the Belfast address; nor need he be much abashed by the discovery, since it has been one of Mr. Martineau's chief works in life to discriminate accurately between the philosophical significance of various systems of thought, while it has been his own duty chiefly to push forward science rather than to analyse its logic, or to distinguish sharply its fundamental assumptions from the rationale of the methods it pursues and the conclusions which it gathers. At the same time, when the purport of a popular address such as that given at Belfast is distinctly philosophical, as distinguished from merely scientific, when it deals boldly with the great question of origin, and calmly relegates religion to the sphere of emotion, bidding it beware of meddling with the realm of knowledge, it is not perhaps too much to expect that the thinker who delivers it should have a clearer grasp of the belief he is endeavouring to spread than Professor Tyndall appears to have had in his Presidential Address at the British Association. It will be, I believe, the destiny of that picturesque survey of the achievements and claims of Science to make converts to a system of Materialism which it is, to say the least, doubtful whether Professor Tyndall has ever held, and tolerably clear that he never accurately understood.

Materialism may be practically defined as the philosophy which lavishes on the elementary material agencies discovered to be at work in the universe, the wonder and admiration which all religious creeds reserve for the Mind by which the believers in these creeds assume that those material agencies are moulded and expanded till they produce the results which we all see. Now, whether Professor Tyndall really intended to imply that this wonder and admiration ought to be lavished on those material atoms which contain, according to him, "the promise and potency of every form of life," or whether, as I somewhat incline to believe, he intended us to suspend our judgments absolutely as to the proper object of this wonder and admiration,—in fact, wished us to indulge the emotion without defining any object for it at all, while we studied the forms in which this feeling would be apt to express itself, if the intellect refused to come to any decision as to the proper object of the emotion,—it would be a rash thing to affirm with any sort of confidence. In criticising Professor Tyndall's thesis that human emotion, not knowledge, is the true foundation for a religious philosophy, Mr. Martineau had replied that so soon as emotion proved empty, he hoped we should stamp it out, and get rid of it. On this Professor Tyndall brought a charge against Mr. Martineau, that he was kicking away the only foundation of his own faith. Mr. Martineau, as I understand him, now rejoins that he did not in the least intend to depreciate the testimony which emotion may supply to the existence of a real object for it, but that what he meant to say was that if the emotion is felt *without* a real object for it, if it makes us indulge in illusions as to an object which does not exist,—if, in fact, it wraps us in a world of phantasm,—instead of guiding us safely amid the realities of life, then, and then only, he hoped we might stamp it out. If, on the contrary, it be only a sign of something real, though as yet imperfectly apprehended, above and beyond us, then our effort ought to be to get a solid grasp, as far as our faculties admit, of the reality which arouses these emotions, but not to indulge them in the dark without any conviction that such an object really exists.

"It is for 'emotion' with a vacuum within, and floating *in vacuo* without, charged with no thought and directed to no object, that I avow distrust; and if there be an 'over-shadowing awe' from the mere sense of a blank consciousness and an enveloping darkness, I can see in it no more than the negative condition of a religion yet to come. In human psychology, feeling, when it transcends sensation, is not without idea, but is a type of idea; and to suppose 'an inward hue and temperature,' apart from any 'object of thought,' is to feign the impossible. Colour must lie upon form, and heat must spring from a focus, and declare itself upon a surface. If by 'referring religion to the region of emotion' is meant withdrawing it from the region of truth, and letting it pass into an undulation in no medium and with no direction, I must decline the surrender. In thus refusing support from 'empty emotion,' I am said to 'kick away the only *philosophic foundation* on which it is possible to build religion.' Professor Tyndall is certainly not exacting from his builders about the solidity of his 'foundation;' and it can be only a very light and airy architecture, not to say an imaginary one, that can spring from such base; and perhaps it does not matter that it should be unable to face the winds. Nor is the inconsistency involved in this statement less surprising than its levity. Religion, it appears, has a 'philosophical foundation.'

But 'philosophy' investigates the ultimate ground of cognition and the organic unity of what the several sciences assume. And a 'philosophical foundation' is a legitimated first principle for some one of these; it is a cognitive beginning—a *datum* of ulterior *quæsita*—and nothing but a science can have it. Religion, then, must be an organism of thought. Yet it is precisely in denial of this that my censor invents his new 'foundation.' Here, he tells us, we know nothing, we can think nothing; the intellectual life is dumb and blank; we do but blindly feel. How can a structure without truth repose on philosophy in its foundation?"

To this I cannot conceive any reply, unless it be that emotion may be properly aroused by even an unknown cause, when we contemplate the magnitude of the effects produced by it,—which is true so long as the emotion is limited to one of pure surprise and desire to sound what is nevertheless not to be sounded. But then if it be so limited, it is quite certain that no religion can ever be got out of it. A religion, if it be a religion in anything but name, implies moral trust in something, but moral trust is wholly unwarrantable, if all that we see can be even more securely referred to matter as "the promise and potency of every form of life," than it can to any ulterior spiritual cause beyond matter which gave matter this "promise," and implanted in it, so far as it can be said to contain, this "potency." Mr. Martineau's argumentation in his new essay is wholly devoted to showing that in no sense can the higher forms of life be really educed out of the lower, unless you already assume as latent in the lower the fulness of power which is eventually expressed in the higher. He analyses with great force and precision the real assumptions of the atomic theory, so far only as the chemistry of the universe is supposed to be implicitly contained in its mechanics, and shows, as it seems to me unanswerably, that the only sense in which qualitative differences are explicable by the assumption of differences in the bare form and motion of otherwise homogeneous atoms is a sense in which the hypothesis does not in the least *explain* the qualities thus resulting, but only finds for us a valuable scientific test and measure of their existence and their intensity,—just as the assumption as to the length of different waves of light, while it gives us a test and measure of the different colours, and enables us to predict the results of interferences, does not in the least explain the sensation of colour, any more than the expansion of the mercury or the spirit in the tube of a thermometer, while it measures for us the intensity of heat, gives us the slightest explanation of the sensations which accompany the various gradations of that heat in our own frames. Show, if you can, that the chemical qualities of a substance might be connected with the assumed form and vibratory velocities of the atoms of which it is composed, yet this only means that you have discovered certain uniform criteria of the relation between mechanical and chemical phenomena, by the help of which you can predict the latter from the study of the former. Does that make it at all more philosophical to say that the latter are contained in the former? Is the quality which we call heat (of sensation) in any way latent in the criterion which leads us to expect it? Is the beauty of the flower latent in the seed, even in conjunction with the earth and air and moisture which lend that seed the constituents of its growth? If so, as Mr. Crosskey of Birmingham finely put it in the masterly sermon which he preached before the

British Association last August at Bristol,[1] "in the attempt to reduce 'spirit' to 'matter,' matter is itself transfigured and becomes spirit." Or to quote the passage more at length—

"The words 'promise' and 'potency,' as used by Tyndall, do not exclude intellectual action or describe an imagined physical substitute for a 'Father in heaven.' 'Potency'—for what? Power exercised according to method is equivalent to power guided by controlling thought,—and where there is controlling thought, the Lord of the Heavens and the earth is near at hand. In the last analysis matter itself disappears in any tangible sense, and force alone remains. What is force restricted to definite combinations but the expression of a determining will? When 'promise' is connected with 'potency,' there must be that forecasting of the future of which we know nothing except as a mental act. If qualities commonly described as mental are referred to the 'promise and potency' associated with 'matter,' mind is not degraded to matter, but matter is uplifted to mind. The tendency of philosophical materialism is not to scepticism, but to idealism. The resolution of matter into force, and the attribution to force of those mighty qualities, connected with ordered intellectual action, render the phenomena of the universe the manifestation of an authority possessed of every characteristic the Christian ascribes to his God. In the attempt to reduce 'spirit' to 'matter,' matter is itself transfigured and becomes spirit."

To apply the same argument in a particular case, in what sense can the "struggle for existence," which

[1] *The Religious Worth and Glory of Scientific Research.* A Discourse delivered in the Lewin's Mead Chapel, Bristol, on Sunday, 29th August 1875, on occasion of the Forty-fifth Meeting of the British Association for the Advancement of Science. By Henry William Crosskey, F.G.S. London: Whitfield.

Mr. Darwin has found to be so efficient a cause in superseding lower by higher forms of life,—in other words, in producing a "survival of the fittest,"—be said to contain the "promise and potency," of the higher forms of human pity and sympathy, except only in this, that as a matter of fact, the one can be traced back in lineal descent to the other, though it so far transcends, and indeed disguises, the features of its ancestor, that the two are more like deadly antagonists than near relations? You can trace the steps of the descent, but it is mere folly to say in this case that the antecedent in any true sense carried within it the essential life of the consequent. And so, too, what spiritualists maintain, they maintain on strictly rational grounds. Man, as a speculative being, finds it reasonable to recognise in such transformations as these the moulding power of a Mind which sees the end from the beginning, rather than the magic transformations of a force which is always adding to its own conquests without any pretence of being guided by the intellectual plan of a conqueror, and which is always improving on its former achievements without any standard by which to measure the better and the worse, or any goal at which its endeavours are aiming. To go back once more to the atomic theory, with which Mr. Martineau in this paper has chiefly dealt, it seems to me that he has really justified Sir John Herschel and Professor Clerk-Maxwell in their assertion that even assuming the atomic hypothesis to be so elaborated and established as to account for the phenomena of chemistry,—which as yet it is far from being,—the atoms so assumed must be regarded as resembling much more closely "manufactured articles," *i.e.* articles full of properties carefully induced in them, than those bare and blank units of solidity which the true materialistic hypothesis requires. In other words, the different atoms must already be distinguished by such remarkable differences of form and capacity for vibration that it is certainly not wonderful that they result in different qualitative properties if they result in qualitative properties at all. Yet the fact that difference in form and vibratory character is a note of some coming difference of quality remains just as inexplicable, and as in need of a philosophic assumption to explain it, as the fact that the law of conflict and competition ultimately results in a law of sympathy and compassion. "No connection," says Mr. Crosskey, in the admirable sermon to which I have already referred, "that may be established between the act of thinking and the peculiarities of our bodily organisation can alter the fact that to exist as beings capable of thought and moved by passion, implies relationships which the elements into which our flesh and blood may be resolved do not share." And till Professor Tyndall can show that it is not a more legitimate intellectual inference to refer the less to the greater than it is to refer the greater to the less, he will hardly be able to justify his own strange teaching that religion is concerned only with the region of emotion, and that he who tries to evolve a religious creed from the operations of *all* the higher faculties of man, instead of from mere blind feeling, is on a false scent, in which he will only mislead mankind, and prepare for himself a heavy disappointment.

XII

DR. WARD ON THE DIVINE PRE-MOVEMENT

1881

I HAVE always recognised in Dr. Ward—the author of *The Ideal of a Christian Church*, which more than a generation ago made such a stir at Oxford, and till very recently the editor of the *Dublin Review*—one of the ablest and clearest of the philosophical thinkers of the day. Little as I agree with his not merely Roman Catholic, but peculiarly Ultramontane theology, I believe that he has done more service to the cause of true philosophy in England than any thinker of the day, unless I except Dr. Martineau, who, indeed, has it in his power to do far more than he has actually done for English psychology and metaphysics. But greatly as I esteem Dr. Ward's writing, I question whether he has ever published anything weightier and more effective than a pamphlet which has just appeared,—republished from the *Dublin Review* of fourteen years ago,—on *Science, Prayer, Free-will, and Miracles*.[1] It would be impossible for me, of course, in a newspaper article, to deal with the whole of this remarkable paper; and, indeed, I only contemplate touching

[1] Burns and Oates.

what Dr. Ward says of the scientific view of the uniformity of Nature in relation to that Providential view of the Universe with which it is supposed to be more or less inconsistent. No one can deny that Dr. Ward states the *primâ facie* view of the unreasonableness of prayer with sufficient clearness and energy, in the following hypothetical argument against it :—

'Your country is visited with famine or pestilence, and you supplicate your God for relief. Your only child lies sick of a dangerous fever ; and as a matter of course you are frequent in prayer. You are diligent, indeed, in giving her all the external help you can ; but your chief trust is avowedly in God. You entreat Him that He will arrest the malady and spare her precious life. What can be more irrational than this ? Would you pray, then, for a long day in December ? Would you pray that in June the sun shall set at six o'clock ? Yet surely the laws of fever are no less absolutely fixed than those of sunset ; and were the case otherwise, no science of medicine could by possibility have been called into existence. The only difference between the two cases is, that the laws of sunset have been thoroughly mastered ; whereas our knowledge as to the laws of fever, though very considerable, is as yet but partial and incomplete. The 'abstract power of prediction,'—as Mr. Stuart Mill calls it,—this is the one assumption, in every nook and corner of science. All scientific men take for granted—when they cease to do so they will cease to *be* scientific men—that a person of superhuman and adequate intelligence, who should know accurately and fully all the various combinations and properties of matter which now exist, could predict infallibly the whole series of future phenomena. He could predict the future course of weather or of disease, with the same assurance with which men now predict the date of a coming eclipse. Pray God all day long—add fasting to your prayer, if you like, and let all your fellow-Christians add *their* prayer and fasting to yours—in order that the said eclipse shall come a week earlier: do you suppose you will be heard? Yet the precise date of an eclipse is not more peremptorily fixed by the laws of nature than is the precise issue of your daughter's fever. You do not venture to doubt speculatively this fundamental doctrine of science; in our various scientific conversations, my friend, you have always admitted it. But, like a true Englishman, you take refuge in an illogical compromise. You assume one doctrine when you study science; and another, its direct contradictory, when your child falls ill. And yet I am paying you too high a compliment: for you do not *profess* that this latter doctrine is *true;* you do not *profess* that your prayer to God is *reasonable*, or can possibly be *efficacious:* your only defence is, that your reason is mastered and overborne by the combined effect of your religious and your parental emotion. As though you could please God—if, indeed, there be a Personal God at all—by acting in a manner which your reason condemns."

Well, the answer to this difficulty is given in a passage of some humour,—and my readers may be surprised to hear that there is a good deal of humour in Dr. Ward,—in which he propounds for us the view which philosophical mice imprisoned in a piano, or some more complicated instrument of the same kind, might be likely to take of "the laws of Nature," as represented by the sounds and vibrations of these instruments.

"We begin, then, with imagining two mice, endowed, however, with quasi-human or semi-human intelligence, enclosed within a grand pianoforte, but prevented in some way or other from interfering with the free play of its machinery. From time to time they are delighted with the strains of choice music. One of the two considers these to result from some agency external to the instrument; but the other, having a more philosophical mind, rises to the conception of fixed laws and phenomenal uniformity. 'Science as yet,' he says, 'is but in its infancy; but I have already made one or two important discoveries. Every sound which reaches us is preceded by a certain vibration of these strings. The same string invariably produces the same sound; and that louder or more gentle, according as the vibration may be more or less intense. Sounds of a more composite character result when two or more of the strings vibrate together; and here, again, the sound produced, as far as I am able to discover, is precisely a compound of those sounds, which would have resulted from the various component strings vibrating separating. Then there is a further sequence which I have observed: for each vibration is preceded by a stroke by a corresponding hammer; and the string vibrates more intensely, in proportion as the hammer's stroke is more forcible. Thus far I have already prosecuted my researches. And so much at least is evident even now: viz. that the sounds proceed not from any external and arbitrary agency—from the intervention, *e.g.* of any higher will—but from the uniform operation of fixed laws. These laws may be explored by intelligent mice; and to their exploration I shall devote my life.' Even from this inadequate illustration you see the general conclusion which we wish to enforce. A sound has been produced through a certain intermediate chain of fixed laws; but this fact does not tend ever so distantly to establish the conclusion that there is no human pre-movement acting continuously at one end of that chain. Imagination, however, has no limits. We may very easily suppose, therefore, that some instrument is discovered, producing music immeasurably more heavenly and transporting than that of the pianoforte; but for that very reason immeasurably more vast in size and more complex in machinery. We will call this imaginary instrument a 'polychordon,' as we are not aware that there is any existing claimant of that name. In this polychordon, the intermediate links—between the player's pre-movement on the one hand, and the resulting sound on the other—are no longer two, but two hundred. We further suppose—imagination (as before said) being boundless—that some human being or other is unintermittently playing on this polychordon; but playing on it just what airs may strike his fancy at the moment. Well: successive generations of philosophical mice have actually traced one hundred and fifty of the two hundred phenomenal sequences, through whose fixed and invariable laws the sound is produced. The colony of mice, shut up within, are in the highest spirits at the success which has crowned the scientific labour of their leading thinkers; and the most eminent of these addresses an assembly. 'We have long known that the laws of our musical universe are immutably fixed; but we have now discovered a far larger number of those laws than our ancestors could have imagined *capable* of discovery. Let us redouble our efforts. I fully expect that our grandchildren will be able to predict as accurately, for an indefinitely preceding period, the succession of melodies with which we are to be delighted, as we now predict the hours of sunrise and sunset. One thing, at all events, is now absolutely incontrovertible. As to the notion of there being some agency *external* to the polychordon,—intervening with arbitrary and capricious will to produce the sounds we experience,—this is a long-exploded superstition; a mere dream and dotage of the past. The progress of science has put it on one side, and never again can it return to disturb our philosophical progress.'"

The reader may infer very easily what that reply really amounts to. It comes to this,—that a very considerable power of tracing out the order of phenomena, and even of predicting the future order of phenomena from the past, may be acquired by creatures who are liable, nevertheless, to be entirely misled by the knowledge they so acquire, as to the most important of all the causes at work in producing these phenomena. Just as the mice were certainly wrong in supposing that, because 150 steps in the phenomenal order had been discovered, the remaining fifty would lead to no new kind of cause —no true initiative—so scientific men may be just as wrong in supposing that because they have discovered so many of the uniform links in the order of Nature, there is no divine hand beyond, which moves the whole network of physical agencies as it will, so as to produce this or that result. The player outside the order of Nature counts none the less in determining that order, even though men who confine their minds to groping about within it, convince themselves that the chain of second causes is literally endless. Some one will at once ask whether, then, Dr. Ward means that it would be as rational (if there were any excuse for it) to pray for the lengthening of the day at Christmas or the hastening of an eclipse, as to pray for the recovery of a sick child? Does the hand outside the great instrument really select all its melodies absolutely arbitrarily, or are there some which so underlie all others, that to expect their arrest is to expect that the musical instrument itself shall cease to be? It is clear that Dr. Ward would answer the two first questions in the negative, and the last in the affirmative. He regards what he calls the cosmical laws as constituting a permanent framework for our Universe, and though, of course, no less subject to the will of

God than the others, yet as so framed that changes or modifications in them can neither be necessary nor desirable for the purpose of man's education in religious trust. What happens by cosmical law cannot be inconsistent with any such special guidance of human lots, as is needful to teach men to lean on God. Within the fixed framework of these laws there is plenty of compass for such a play of special providence on the one side, and of trust on the other, as the religious life requires. Hence, though it is, of course, to be assumed that the Divine pre-movement does determine the courses of the stars, there is no reason why the laws determining them should be pliant, since their pliancy is not needful to teach man the necessity of trust in God, and therefore there can be no sense or piety in praying that they should be altered. The whole compass of human fate depends on combinations of a much more variable and composite kind—

"By cosmical phenomena we mean such as the hours of sunrise and sunset; of moonrise and moonset; the respective apparent position of the heavenly bodies, etc. By earthly phenomena we mean such as the weather; the violence and direction of the wind; the progress of disease; and others of a similar kind. The discovery of Copernicanism placed these two phenomenal classes in far more striking contrast. It appears that cosmical phenomena are produced by an incredibly vast machinery, in which this earth plays a very subordinate part; whereas earthly phenomena are due in great measure to agencies, which act exclusively within the region of our planet. From the very first, therefore, there was a real presumption that these latter agencies were subject to a pre-movement, quite different in kind from any which influenced the former; and this presumption would be very greatly increased by the discoveries of Galileo and his successors. Now it is most remarkable, and bears thinking of again and again, that the only power of indefinite prediction which science has procured concerns cosmical phenomena, and not earthly."

Nay, more, Dr. Ward might have added, had he been writing now, that even the latest investigations into cosmical laws suggest the intervention of causes existing on a very grand scale, and analogous, in some respects, to human volition, which do not seem to be immanent in these laws as they are at present known. All the great physicists regard the gradual diffusion and equalisation of heat throughout the universe as the running-down of a mechanical process, of which they cannot present to themselves the winding-up. The sun will in a certain number of millions of years burn itself out, and all its concentrated heat will be scattered throughout solar or stellar space. But when you ask how that heat—which will then, in its diffused and equalised state, be no longer a cause of motion, but a condition of rest—can be again concentrated, so as to become once more the source of new life and motion, no answer is given, and we are told that to create such a store of energy there must be the intervention of some new cause, of which at present we cannot even guess the nature. That is merely another way of saying that however uniform cosmical phenomena may be throughout long periods of time, there is yet in existence some cause, of which we know nothing, which, if it did not initiate an absolute beginning, yet could do what is quite as inconceivable—so change the phenomena as to reverse the order of things as we see it,—could play, as it were, the cosmical time backwards, and concentrate that which is now always in course of diffusion, or diffuse that which had previously been in course of concentration. Take even the cosmical laws as they are, and you find in them the necessity for some external control, which can reverse their order and revolutionise their tendency.

But, of course, if this "divine pre-movement" of which Dr. Ward speaks exists, it must be much more observed in the sphere of mind than in that of matter. Men certainly, in the exercise of their volition, cause almost as many obvious changes in the physical order of the universe as they do in the moral order; but then, all their modifications of the physical order of the universe begin in their own purposes and intentions, and may, therefore, be said to be of moral origin. And, of course, we should expect that those divine pre-movements of the physical order of the universe which alter the character of the melody or the harmony, would also begin very often at least, in the minds of men. And so, no doubt, the Bible represents it. It makes the call of a man—the divine pre-movement of his will—the commencement in the history of religion. It makes the call of a nation by its greatest prophet, the starting-point of the most important of all national histories, at least if we think that the most important which is intended to give a moral and spiritual example to the whole. It makes the call of one man after another the starting-point of one new era after another in that history, and it makes the pre-movement of an absolutely perfect human nature by God the central point of human destiny. In all these cases, a number of secondary and human causes, which spend their force as secondary causes in the usual manner, are, as it is asserted, set in motion by the "divine pre-movement," which Dr. Ward assumes as the explanation of all providential interferences with the lot of man. Even in secular history, the same importance attaches to the first entrance of a new and unaccountable moral force on the scene,—a force which I at least should find it more difficult to ascribe to any human cause, than to a definite impulse by the hand of Providence itself. Take such an impulse as that given by Socrates to Greek thought, —which he himself expressly ascribed to the teaching of a superhuman power; take such an impulse as that given to the Arabian intellect by the career of Mahommed; take such an impulse as that given to the spiritual affections and the rebellion against ecclesiastical conventions by the conversion of Luther, —and in all these, and a thousand other cases, we should see the direct modification of the order of human events, by a divine pre-movement of the mind of man. Not more certain is it that to account for the motion of the planets, you need to assume an original force of "projection" as well as a source of centripetal attraction, than it is that to account for the destiny of man, on the national, no less than the individual scale, you need to assume a constant "pre-movement," from some source of which no man who rejects revealed religion can assign the origin. Dr. Ward has done the world of thought a real service, by the hypothesis of his "philosophical mice;" for he has cleared up by it a branch of his subject on which thought is very apt to become hazy, and even to lose its way.

XIII

THE GREAT AGNOSTIC

1895

Professor Huxley has not lived to conclude his reply to Mr. Balfour's book on "The Foundations of Belief" in the *Nineteenth Century* for March. He had proposed to himself to conclude it in the month of April; but no sooner had his first indignant denial that his Agnosticism could properly be identified with the "Naturalism" of Mr. Balfour's essay been completed, than he was struck down by the fatal illness which, though it often gave us hope of its passing away, has at length terminated that eager and opulent life. There has not often been an Englishman of more brilliant gifts, of richer energies, of higher courage, and more thoroughly English combativeness. He had in him, too, all the qualities of a leader of men, though his studies and researches led him into fields of knowledge where there were but few men to follow him with any discriminating judgment. Had he ever taken to the political field, he would have been as distinguished, perhaps, as Mr. Gladstone himself, though distinguished as a benevolent Conservative rather than as a champion of democracy. He had much of the charm of manner, of the ready humour, and almost tender loyalty to his friends, which makes a great captain. And he certainly possessed that gift for popular exposition and making plausible presumptions seem a great deal more adequate and satisfactory than they are, that gives life and confidence to those who attach themselves to a leader, and who desire to tread in his footsteps. He had a rich fund of humour, and a great resourcefulness in battle. And if there were any Church to which he could properly be said to belong, it was certainly a Church militant. But none the less, there was so much of human kindliness and geniality in him that he had many more eager friends than he had eager foes, and there were probably as many sincere English mourners when it was known that the long four months' illness had ended fatally, as there were when the last Poet-Laureate died, and not a few of the same distinguished band. Indeed, it is curious that of the group which found the very unaccustomed medium of verse necessary to express their grief for Lord Tennyson's death, Professor Huxley himself was perhaps the most distinguished and the least unsuccessful, though it had been Tennyson's great purpose in life to teach men that they might much more than "faintly trust the larger hope," while it was Professor Huxley's to persuade them that they should rather frankly utter and even foster the larger doubt. Yet strangely enough, it was Professor Huxley who eagerly proclaimed Tennyson's right to a place in that grand Abbey which had grown "stone by stone:"

> "As the stormy brood
> Of English blood
> Has waxed and spread

> And filled the world
> With sails unfurled;
> With men that may not lie;
> With thoughts that cannot die."

And yet the "thoughts that could not die" in Tennyson's great verse were certainly not the thoughts which were uppermost in Professor Huxley's mind. For he, though he denied being a champion of Naturalism in Mr. Balfour's sense, gloried in being an Agnostic. It was he, indeed, who first popularised the word, and made a sort of creedless creed of Agnosticism. He held, and held to the last, that though it is not the part of any true Agnostic to deny God's existence, it is certainly not his part to affirm it; that the dominant idea of Tennyson's poetry is as questionable as it is fascinating; and we conclude that he would have held that if Tennyson was great for having put the deepest human and even Christian faith into immortal words, he would have been still greater if he had made suspense of faith the true ideal of a lofty mind. Here is Professor Huxley's deliberate confession of faith in his own words,—words which are very divergent indeed from those which he had so warmly extolled in his friend,—

"As regards the extent to which the improvement of natural knowledge has remodelled and altered what may be termed the intellectual ethics of men,—what are among the moral convictions most fondly held by barbarous and semi-barbarous people? They are the convictions that authority is the soundest basis of belief; that merit attaches to a readiness to believe; that the doubting disposition is a bad one, and scepticism a sin; that when good authority has pronounced what is to be believed, and faith has accepted it, reason has no further duty. There are many excellent persons who yet hold by these principles, and it is not my present business, or intention, to discuss their views. All I wish to bring clearly before your minds is the unquestionable fact that the improvement of natural knowledge is effected by methods which directly give the lie to all these convictions, and assume the exact reverse of each to be true. The improver of natural knowledge absolutely refuses to acknowledge authority, as such. For him, scepticism is the highest of duties; blind faith the one unpardonable sin. And it cannot be otherwise, for every great advance in natural knowledge has involved the absolute rejection of authority, the cherishing of the keenest scepticism, the annihilation of the spirit of blind faith; and the most ardent votary of science holds his firmest convictions, not because the men he most venerates hold them; not because their verity is testified by portents and wonders; but because his experience teaches him that whenever he chooses to bring these convictions into contact with their primary source, Nature,—whenever he thinks fit to test them by appealing to experiment and to observation, Nature will confirm them. The man of science has learned to believe in justification, not by faith, but by verification."

Professor Huxley, as he often and eagerly proclaimed, was no materialist or Atheist. He thought a mental origin of the universe a great possibility, but nothing more. The most celebrated passage in his most celebrated essay described human life as something like a great game of chess between men and a hidden player who always plays on the same rules, but who, as Huxley himself admitted, leaves men to find out by the use of their own wits what those rules are,—a kind of game at which no man, I suppose, would be willing to play without some sort of guidance and help from his unseen antagonist.

The passage to which I refer is a very powerful and characteristic one; and it seems to me so memorable that, profoundly as I differ from its drift, I should like, now that we are mourning this great student's death, to recall it to the memory of its first readers, and bring it to the notice of a generation which may never have read it.

"Suppose it were perfectly certain that the life and fortune of every one of us would, one day or other, depend upon his winning or losing a game at chess. Don't you think that we should all consider it to be a primary duty to learn at least the names and the moves of the pieces; to have a notion of a gambit, and a keen eye for all the means of giving and getting out of check? Do you not think that we should look with a disapprobation amounting to scorn upon the father who allowed his son, or the state which allowed its members, to grow up without knowing a pawn from a knight? Yet it is a very plain and elementary truth, that the life, the fortune, and the happiness of every one of us, and, more or less, of those who are connected with us, do depend upon our knowing something of the rules of a game infinitely more difficult and complicated than chess. It is a game which has been played for untold ages, every man and woman of us being one of the two players in a game of his or her own. The chess-board is the world, the pieces are the phenomena of the universe, the rules of the game are what we call the laws of Nature. The player on the other side is hidden from us. We know that his play is always fair, just, and patient. But also we know, to our cost, that he never overlooks a mistake, or makes the smallest allowance for ignorance. To the man who plays well, the highest stakes are paid, with that sort of overflowing generosity with which the strong shows delight in strength. And one who plays ill is checkmated,— without haste, but without remorse. My metaphor will remind some of you of the famous picture in which Retzsch has depicted Satan playing at chess with man for his soul. Substitute for the mocking fiend in that picture, a calm, strong angel who is playing for love, as we say, and would rather lose than win,—and I should accept it as an image of human life. Well, what I mean by Education is learning the rules of this mighty game."

There you see Professor Huxley in his full force. But whence was that force derived? At least as much from the want of logic with which his emotions coloured his conceptions, as from the courageous scepticism in which that passage abounds. Professor Huxley professed to know that the hidden antagonist who does not even hesitate to checkmate his human opponent for not knowing the rules of a game which he has generally had no opportunity of learning, is "always fair, just, and patient." How could Professor Huxley be an "Agnostic" if he knew as much as that? Is it true Agnosticism to assume anything of the kind? What can be less like Agnosticism than to depict the unseen antagonist as "an angel who plays for love, as we say, and would rather lose than win." A clearer case of that faith which justifies *without* "verification," I cannot imagine. The whole idealism of the picture would have vanished if Professor Huxley had held to his Agnosticism, and had told us that we do not know whether the hidden player is a fair player or even a player at all, or only an automaton without a mind and without a purpose,—perhaps fair, just, and patient, but quite as probably incapable of so much as a thought or feeling of its own,—a thing to which fairness, justice, and patience are qualities as inapplicable as they would be to the stone wall against which a man breaks his head, or the prussic acid by which he stops the action of his heart. Nothing seems to me clearer than that Professor Huxley borrowed from a religion which he thought wholly unproved, his description of the unseen player in this great game of life. And it was because he did so, in his heart, though not consciously, that he could welcome Tennyson's body to Westminster Abbey in those touching lines wherein he expressed his own secret sympathy with the leading thoughts of a poet against whose belief his criticisms had so often levelled the accusation that it was unproved and unprovable.

It was the same when, about twenty years earlier, Professor Huxley served on the London School Board, and acquiesced in the reading of the Bible as the best book for the moral education of the children. It is true, of course, that he was one of the most eager of the adversaries of any definite theological commentary on it. But how could the Bible itself be a proper influence for children if its greatest lesson, "Thou shalt love the Lord thy God with all thy heart, and with all thy soul, and with all thy strength, and with all thy mind," were a leap in the dark which a true Agnostic could not so much as excuse? In my belief, Professor Huxley had a half-unconscious craving, to which he thought it wrong to give way, for that passionate faith which he said that he desired to undermine in all cases in which there was, in his opinion, no possibility of what he termed verification. Indeed, his heart often rose up in insurrection against his scientific genius, and compelled him to feel what was entirely inconsistent with the logic of his thoughts. For he was a very lovable man, and no man is lovable who cannot deeply love. That he was a man of true scientific genius I do not doubt. All who knew his career as a biologist agree that he added greatly not only to the exposition, but to the development, of Darwin's doctrine. But from that point of view, I cannot speak of him with the smallest authority. To me he is the great Agnostic who has tried, and, as I hold, tried in vain, to regard physical science as the one sure guide of life, and has yet betrayed in some of the most critical utterances and actions of his career, that his Agnostic creed did not cover the whole of the legitimate evidence, and that he coveted for the children of his country a kind of teaching which he nevertheless proudly rejected for himself.

XIV

A PROBLEM ARISING OUT OF THE DECALOGUE

1884

In the extremely thoughtful and able address which Canon MacColl delivered at the International Conference on Education, concerning the theological teaching of the Universities,—an excellent report of which is to be found in the *Guardian* of last week,—he dropped a hint which deserves, I think, to be developed and followed out more elaborately, since it appears to me to contain impressive evidence of the reality of a Divine Revelation. While insisting on theology as the true centre of the sciences—the science which contains the key to the purpose and order and relations of all the subordinate sciences—he remarked :—" What a different meaning physical science has for those who suppose it to be the puzzling-out of riddles of which no living person has the key—nay, to which, for aught we know, there may be no key—and for those who suppose physical science to be the knowledge of natural laws which had been providentially withheld from us till the far more important knowledge of moral laws had been thoroughly impressed upon us. If the revelations of physical science had preceded those of moral law,

what a Pandemonium the world would have been.
Surely the remarkable fact that a law like the Decalogue far preceded a sound knowledge of the laws
and forces of nature, shows that there was a Power
above to impress itself upon the world, before the
powers which are below our own highest level had
had any serious attention paid to them." Now, let
me follow out a little that line of thought. Mr.
Herbert Spencer, we know, maintains that the ghost
theory, originally suggested by dreams of the dead,
is the origin of all belief in God. If so, how extraordinary it is, that in the most coherent and strictly
developed of all ancient religions there is hardly a
vestige of this ghost theory,—indeed, hardly a clear
indication, till very late in history, of any belief in
the existence of departed spirits as powers at all,—
Saul's vision of Samuel in the witch of Endor's house
is the only one I can at present recollect,—while
nevertheless the enunciation of an authoritative moral
law, far in advance of the intellectual stage of culture
which would appear to correspond to it, takes place
in the very nursery of the race, and in the very
centre of its first great scene of trial! Is it conceivable to any one that the ghost of a great ancestor
could have originated the Decalogue? Whence did
these severe restraining precepts come, if they did
not come from a real power above man? To one
who assumes the view of the purely physical origin
of man, how should so early an outbreak of what
would, on that hypothesis, be the pure superstition
of a spiritual and rigidly restraining power, be accounted for? It has often been maintained that the
conflict for existence necessarily developed a competition amongst the various tribes of early history,
a competition to determine which of them should act

with the most solidarity, and that this competition gave a great physical advantage to the one which earliest developed a strict social morality. That would explain how the aptitude for discipline, self-restraint, fortitude, and courage displayed by the Romans secured them so long a reign, but would not explain at all the very early inculcation of the conscious principle involved in such qualities, found among the Jews, unaccompanied, as I must certainly say in the case of the Jews it was unaccompanied, by any strong practical disposition to embody those qualities in actual life. Besides, as a matter of fact, the moral law of the Decalogue is altogether based on a spiritual law of which the condemnation of idolatry is the key-note. So far is it from true that the moral conditions which secure the cohesion of a race come out most prominently in the Jewish Decalogue, that that which there comes out most prominently is the worship of a Supreme Will,—the very centre and essence of the whole moral law,—the kind of law which that Will imposes being, in one sense at least, secondary to the worship of that Will. In other words, it is because the moral law is God's law, and because it unites those who obey it to the Divine nature, that it is so strenuously enjoined. It is not true that the Jews developed anything like the same capacity for carrying out the conditions of moral co-operation which their lawgiver had certainly displayed for apprehending those conditions. The Decalogue implies the inculcation of a conscious principle long before the development of any adequate capacity for embodying that principle in life; and not only that, but for developing it expressly as the will of an invisible power which, according to the materialistic theory, did not exist, and does not exist, except in the imagination of a superstitious people. Can anything be conceived more unnatural than that a pure falsehood should be conceived as the guarantee of a set of moral truths, and these, too, moral truths which, so far from being the reflections of moral experience, were far in advance of that experience— the presages, as it were, of creative genius? Surely the moral genius which could lay down such truths could never have superfluously imagined a fictitious Supreme Will by which to sanction them. And surely the superstition which would have laid a mighty falsehood as the pillar and ground of the moral and social law, would never have anticipated the true moral and social law, but would have wandered as widely from the mark in declaring that law as it had in insisting so solemnly on a false sanction for it? If the supposed lawgiver were a phantom, is it not certain that much of the law would have had on it the impress of a phantom origin?

Again, as Canon MacColl says, if the true origin of man be found in physical and material forces, how is it that the discovery and proclamation of the moral law seems to have run ahead so much of the discovery and proclamation of physical laws? If the physical constitution is the root of man, why did not the growth of the curiosity of the senses precede the growth of the curiosity of the conscience? Indeed, why should there have been any conscience, or any curiosity of the conscience at all, if man is the growth of material conditions, and if the mastery of those conditions be really the key to his earthly salvation? If the moral nature be a mere secondary thing, and the first and chief thing about man be his physical organisation, how is it that the problem of civilisation was not primarily a problem of the adaptation of physical means to physical ends—a problem primarily of the sciences and the arts, instead of a problem of the conscience and the will? What one would expect from the development of an intellect founded on the senses, would have been the steady growth of the effort to deal with the difficulties of human existence from the intellectual side,—to manœuvre the passions rather than to control or subdue them; to utilise the resources of external nature, and to strain to the utmost the elasticity of man's tastes and capacities, in order to increase the range of the conditions within which he could enjoy existence. Something of this type of character we see shadowed forth in early Greece, where the crafty, the resourceful, the pliant man seemed to be at one time likely to take precedence of the true, the good, and the great man, until other and nobler ideals won upon the susceptible Greek imagination. If the intellect had been really developed merely out of the physical constitution, we should have seen such a type of character as this, gaining on all others. Shame at poverty of resource would have taken the place of that nobler shame which men feel at easy and adroit concession to the importunity of circumstance. The man of elastic intelligence, of many shifts and wiles, would have been valued ten times as much as the man of dignity, fortitude, constancy—in one word, *character*; for character only means that there *is* a standard of inward life to which men must adhere even at the cost of the outward life itself. That implied assumption, however, is everything. It is equivalent to the assumption of a moral law for man, which anticipates, and overrides, and moulds his dealings with physical law. We can, perhaps, in part imagine what a great curiosity and a pliant intellect, exerted chiefly to interrogate the outward conditions of our life, and to adapt, as the phrase is, our wants to our "environment," and our environment to our wants, would have made of man,—a sort of potent mental chameleon, now shrinking to external conditions, now bending external conditions to his needs, without a dream or thought of any absolute internal standard to which it is needful to conform himself. Instead of that, we find that at one of the earliest of the epochs of human history an inflexible standard of character was laid down, and laid down as the command of the invisible God, a standard which was not to be trifled with and moulded and bent to suit the exigencies of the hour. The inquisitive mind itself was to pursue its ingenious questionings under the restraints of this law; what was called civilisation was declared sound only so far as it observed this law; it was this law which kept discovery from transforming not only the realm of knowledge, but the very ends and aims for which the realm of knowledge was to be used, just as opportunity might dictate. It was this which made man man, and prevented him from passing through an earthly metempsychosis of adaptation to the universe, which would have eliminated all the unity from human history, and all the definiteness from human progress. Without a fixed background of conscience, the shuttle of events, manipulated by an ever active and elastic intelligence, would have made the man of one age a totally different creature from the man of another. And this background of conscience was not only given us, but it was given by an asserted revelation before the development of scientific intelligence had reached any high level. The moral law was scored deep in human nature before science had fairly begun its lively career. We were told in many respects what we *ought* to be, long before we found out what we were. Now, could that be conceivable, if (1) there were no character in existence higher than our own to impose its law upon us, and if (2) there were nothing, and never had been anything in existence, except an endless chain of cause and effect under the shadow of which an "ought" becomes impossible since nothing could ever be otherwise than as it is? It seems to me perfectly certain that the early incorporation of such a law as the Decalogue in human history is an incontrovertible proof, first, that physical law is not the root of human character, but moral law; and next, that the moral law was revealed to us, and in us, long before the intellect had begun to stride forward with anything like its full power; in other words, that, instead of being the mere fruit borne by that power, it was the ultimate guide and ruler and director of that advancing intelligence which now claims to be its master. That seems to me, I confess, utterly inconsistent with a merely physical and material constitution of things.

XV

SCIENCE AND MYSTERY

1896

PROFESSOR BURDON SANDERSON, in the lecture which he delivered at the Royal Institution yesterday week on Ludwig and the doctrine which he called Neo-Vitalism or New Vitalism (to distinguish it from the old assumption of a vital force which was called in to explain anything which the older physiological science failed to reduce to consistency with the older physical and chemical explanations), drew a very useful distinction between falling back on vital force as a formal but very useless master-key,—really no master-key at all,—to all difficulties which could not be otherwise resolved, and the proper admission that, after comparing accurately and specifically the processes which can be reduced to consequences of the older physical and chemical laws of force and combination, and those which cannot be so explained, but leave a certain residuum of phenomena inexplicable on the old physical and chemical principles, that residuum represents an absolutely new region of science. That is a very just distinction; but I think the Professor would have made it clearer, and have interested his audience more, if he had frankly acknowledged that science, properly conceived, really makes no attempt to explain away the manifold mysteries of the world at all, but only endeavours to sort the various wonders of the universe into those which are of the same kind, and whose methods or processes may be described on the same principles, by calling some of them physical, as being reducible to the principles which govern mechanical and dynamical laws; others of them chemical, as being reducible to the laws of elective affinity; and others, again, vital, which appear to be complicated by that distinct kind of influence which organic cells, when once they have come into existence, exert on the forms of matter submitted to them. All these various regions of phenomena are equally inexplicable in themselves, but it is obvious that the processes by which they are distinguished are all of one kind in one region and all of another kind in another region, and the immense value of science is not that it explains away the mystery of any one of them, but that when it can distinguish with which region it is dealing, and what the data are, it can predict with fair accuracy exactly what is likely to take place as a consequence of the general laws which prevail in that region.

For instance, what can be more accurate than the predictions of physical astronomy? But what can be more mysterious than its fundamental assumption that every particle of matter attracts every other particle with a force of which you can define the exact magnitude,—that every hair of one's head, for instance, pulls at every hair on the head of any being on the planets of the great Sun Sirius (if there be planets of Sirius and beings with heads of hair on them), with a force varying inversely as the square of the distance? It is impossible to imagine a more mysterious fact than this. And two centuries and a half ago a man would have been thought a madman who pretended to know such a fact as that. Yet we do know it, and know the kind of reasoning by which we demonstrate the fact. Yet who can say that we can *explain* it? We can *methodise* all the phenomena which are due to this physical law, but we can do no more. The assumption itself is as much a mystery and as profound a mystery as ever. It is only pseudo-science which professes to *explain* it. And so again when you come to chemical laws. All the principles of elective affinities can be methodised and sorted, but cannot in any way be explained. They are mysteries, and mysteries which are not of the same kind as those of physics. The law of gravitation will not furnish the principle in which they are rooted. You cannot deal with them as you deal with the facts of physical astronomy. Oxygen and hydrogen fly together in one way, oxygen and iron in another, hydrogen and chlorine in a third. The mysteries of chemical affinity are mysteries of a new kind which are to be described and studied on quite new methods. But the "embracing force," as one of our poets has called it, relating to the various simple elements,—or what are supposed to be the various simple elements,—of the natural world, is quite a different embracing force from that which the force of gravitation exerts all over the universe. The mystery is as great as ever, but it is one which is to be methodised on new principles, and the processes of which can only be described in quite new language. So, again, when we come to magnetic and electrical phenomena. It is impossible to describe the leap of the iron filing towards the magnet, or of the straw to the excited amber, in terms of any of the physical or chemical laws which have methodised the principles of purely physical or chemical science. We are in the presence of a new region of mystery, the phenomena of which must be classified or sorted by its own methods. And so it is, as Professor Burdon Sanderson tells us, with physiological laws when you have exhausted the methods of physical and chemical classification. The diffusion of the blood you can explain in great measure by mere hydraulic laws. The constitution of the blood you can explain in great measure by chemical laws; but when once you come to the study of the distribution, say, of lymph in the building-up of the body, you find that neither chemical laws nor hydraulic laws will suffice. The cell which is placed at the door of many of the passages acts in a fashion of its own, which neither hydraulic nor chemical principles will explain. The cell stationed in one man's body at a particular point will play the porter and admit the lymph in one way, and the cell stationed at the same place in another man's body in another way, and so even the most accurately, and perhaps we might say the most pedantically, scientific of genuine investigators have come to admit a principle of life (neo-vitalism) which accounts for the difference on some quite new principle depending on the constitutional energy which the cells of each body put forth. There is certainly nothing unscientific in such a suggestion, when by close comparison it has been determined that there is some residual phenomenon which cannot be referred to any method known to either physics or chemistry. But would it not be simpler and much *less* mystifying instead of *more* mystifying if the new region of mystery were frankly admitted, without so much oracular pretence of solving all mysteries, whereas every new department of science is rooted in mystery, and rooted in a mystery which is as profound and inexplicable as creation itself? At every separate stage of scientific development we come to some new method, though it may be quite true that regions which were once regarded as distinct may be simplified and brought into one and the same province, just as the phenomena of eclipses have been really reduced to the same principles as those of motion when the shadows cast by any of the bodies of the planets are taken into account. The utmost that science can do in the way of simplification is to reduce two or more systems to one. But when it attempts to explain away all mystery it simply betrays itself. How can science, for instance, *explain* consciousness, or memory, or will? How are successive fields of new mystery, every one of which opens out problems deeper and more mysterious than the last,—fields of thought which cannot even be studied by the same method by which the processes of physics, or chemistry, or physiology, or organic assimilation can be studied with any prospect of success,—to be explained away? What science does is to generalise the order and process of different classes of phenomena, and sometimes to show that phenomena which at first seemed to be different are really the same under a new aspect. But science brings great and most unnecessary discredit on itself by professing to explain too much. It shows us what in a given region we may expect, what revolutions of the planets, what returns of the tides, what chemical effects light will produce on various chemically prepared tissues, what distributions of blood take place in the body under the action of the pumps in the heart, what nerves are necessary to sight and hearing, what are the laws of association, what are the motives which operate most powerfully on character, and what are the ordinary limits of self-control; but in none of these separate regions can we solve the ultimate mystery, or in any true sense explain chemical affinity from force, or life (why call it Neo-vitalism?) from chemical affinity, or consciousness from life, or memory from consciousness, or will from memory. We know the methods of many mysteries, but the ultimate mystery we cannot fathom at all.

XVI

INSTINCT AND DESIGN

1885

MR. MIVART, in the interesting article on "Organic Nature's Riddle," which he contributes to the March number of the *Fortnightly Review*, puts, in what seems to me a completely unanswerable form, the objection to Professor Haeckel's contention that the organs and organisms with which our world is peopled have not been produced or guided by anything resembling intelligent purpose. Mr. Mivart discusses at some length the operation of instinct and the operation of organic processes which, not being accompanied by any sort of animal consciousness (or "consentience," as he prefers to name the inferior forms of consciousness), cannot be called instincts, though they certainly produce results quite as remarkable as the most elaborate instincts; and he shows that in neither case is it possible to give any *rationale* at all of what occurs, without assuming the organisation of these processes by some power which deliberately adapts means to ends. Let me take his two most remarkable illustrations, the first from the well-known instinct of the sphex-wasp,—which is by no means a solitary case of this sort of instinct, Mr. Mivart showing that the mother pole-cat has been known to provide for the wants of her offspring in a precisely similar manner,—and the second from the wonderful healing agencies which have been known to restore completely the elaborate apparatus in a human elbow, after it had been removed by amputation. Here is the case of the pure instinct :—

"The female of the wasp, *sphex*, affords another well-known but very remarkable example of a complex instinct closely related to that already mentioned in the case of the pole-cat. The female wasp has to provide fresh, living animal food for her progeny, which, when it quits its egg, quits it in the form of an almost helpless grub, utterly unable to catch, retain, or kill an active, struggling prey. Accordingly the mother insect has not only to provide and place beside her eggs suitable living prey, but so to treat it that it may be a helpless unresisting victim. That victim may be a mere caterpillar, or it may be a great, powerful grasshopper, or even that most fierce, active, and rapacious of insect tyrants, a fell and venomous spider. Whichever it may be, the wasp adroitly stings it at the spot which induces, or in the several spots which induce, complete paralysis as to motion, let us hope as to sensation also. This done, the wasp entombs the helpless being with its own egg, and leaves it for the support of the future grub. . . . Even the strongest advocate of the intelligence of insects would not affirm that the mother sphex has a knowledge of the comparative anatomy of the nervous system of these very diversely-formed insects. According to the doctrine of natural selection, either an ancestral wasp must have accidentally stung them each in the right places, and so our sphex of to-day is the naturally-selected descendant of a line of insects which inherited this lucky tendency to sting different insects differently, but always in the exact situation of their nervous ganglia; or else the young of the ancestral sphex originally fed on dead food, but the offspring of some individuals who happened to sting their

prey so as to paralyse but not to kill them, were better
nourished, and so the habit grew. But the incredible
supposition that the ancestor should have accidentally
acquired the habit of stinging different insects differently
but always in the right spot, is not eliminated by the
latter hypothesis."

Still less, of course, can the explanation of instinct,
as a transmitted habit originally due to intelligence,
apply to such a case as this, unless the ancestral
sphex-wasp be credited with a far better knowledge
of anatomy than uneducated man has now,—in
which case the sphex-wasp would probably be in the
place of man, at the head of civilisation, and man
would be his slave. Again, in the case of the healing agencies at work in Nature,—which are, indeed,
only inferior forms of the original formative agencies
which first made those parts of our frame that they
are not always able to restore,—Mr. Mivart shows
what it is which is really effected, without even the
dimmest consciousness on our part of the nature of
the agency at work :—

"In the process of healing and repair of a wounded
part of the body, a fluid, perfectly structureless substance
is secreted, or poured forth, from the parts about the
wound. In this substance, cells arise and become abund-
ant ; so that the substance, at first structureless, becomes
what is called cellular tissue. Then, by degrees, this
structure transforms itself into vessels, tendons, nerves,
bone, and membrane—into some or all of such parts—
according to the circumstances of the case. In a case of
broken bone, the two broken ends of the bone soften, the
sharp edges thus disappearing. Then a soft substance is
secreted, and this becomes at first gelatinous, often afterwards cartilaginous, and finally osseous or bony. But not
only do these different kinds of substance—these distinct

tissues—thus arise and develop themselves in this neutral or, as it is called, "undifferentiated" substance, but very complex structures, appropriately formed and nicely adjusted for the performance of complex functions, may also be developed. We see this in the production of admirably-formed joints in parts which were at first devoid of anything of the kind. I may quote, as an example, the case of a railway guard, whose arm had been so injured that he had been compelled to have the elbow with its joint cut out, but who afterwards developed a new joint almost as good as the old one. In the uninjured condition the outer bone of the lower arm—the radius—ends above in a smooth-surfaced cap, which plays against part of the lower end of the bone of the upper arm, or humerus, while its side also plays against the side of the other bone of the lower arm, the ulna, with the interposition of a cartilaginous surface. The radius and ulna are united to the humerus by dense and strong membranes or ligaments, which pass between it and them, anteriorly, posteriorly, and on each side, and are attached to projecting processes, one on each side of the humerus. Such was the condition of the parts which were removed by the surgeon. Nine years after the operation the patient died, and Mr. Syme had the opportunity of dissecting the arm, which in the meantime had served the poor man perfectly well, he having been in the habit of swinging himself by it from one carriage to another, while the train was in motion, quite as easily and securely as with the other arm. On examination Mr. Syme found that the amputated end of the radius had formed a fresh polished surface, and played both on the humerus and the ulna, a material something like cartilage being interposed. The ends of the bones of the forearm were locked in by two processes projecting downwards from the humerus, and also strong lateral and still stronger anterior and posterior ligaments again bound them fast to the last-named bone."

Now that is but the imperfect repetition in later life of the process which first produces the elbow in every human frame; but it is impossible to account for it either by "natural selection" or by "lapsed intelligence." The former explains Nature as stumbling accidentally upon her greatest and most wonderful discoveries, and then persevering in and perfecting them by similar stumbles into a long series of improvements; and what could be more miraculous than such a knack of stumbling into a happy succession of stumbles? And why, if that be the explanation, should not a second attempt at an elbow on the part of the same organism which succeeded with the first, be even more likely to achieve success? The second view would explain the marvel of Nature as it is, only by assuming the intelligence of Nature as it was; and if we are to assume intelligence as the *origin* of structural laws, it is much easier to suppose that it is at work still, than that it has perpetuated and stereotyped itself in some organic habit, and then completely disappeared.

I hold, then, that Mr. Mivart has proved his case; but I must go on to ask what light his proof throws on the scope of design in Nature? What we have undoubtedly in such cases of instinct, and such cases of structural origination and renovation, as Mr. Mivart puts before us, is a very limited adaptation of means to ends,—limited, because, as he himself shows us, a very slight disturbance of the ordinary circumstances will suffice to put the agency at work entirely out of gear. For example, one of the species of wasps visits her grubs to provide them with fresh food, and finds her way with unerring instinct, though they are carefully covered up, to the place of concealment. But if the entrance is uncovered for her by man, the wasp is put out, instead of helped by the apparent assistance, and no longer recognises her young. Thus it is clear that the instinct is a general apparatus with which the species is furnished for adapting means to ends under such circumstances as are ordinarily to be expected, but is not, in any sense, a guidance vouchsafed to each *individual* insect by an intelligence prompting it at each instant to do that which would serve its purpose best. And again, in the case of the reparative functions of the human system, if the animal be young and strong, the injury is repaired effectually; if the animal be old, and the vital functions more or less exhausted, the injury is repaired much less effectually or perhaps not at all. Here again, then, it appears to be a strictly limited reservoir of resources for adapting means to ends with which the organism is supplied. No demands upon it in excess of these narrow limits will be honoured. What is pointed at, then, is not the immanent action of that unlimited store of force and design which we represent by the word Providence, but rather the existence of small, well-defined stores of organic capacity for adapting means to ends, easily defeated, easily exhaustible, though marvellous enough within their definite limits, and only intelligible at all as the handiwork of a larger intelligence. Just so the late Mr. Clerk Maxwell used to speak of the atoms of the chemist as highly "manufactured articles," full of specific quality and relation. Well, the qualities which Mr. Clerk Maxwell ascribed to the chemical atom, it seems that we must ascribe in a still higher degree to the animal organism, whether instinctive or merely structural It is a manufactured article of a higher kind than the chemical atom, fuller still of compressed specific quality and of elastic power to adapt itself to a very considerable range of circumstances, and this power is only intelligible on the assumption that it is provided by a higher intelligence, though it does not in any way represent the full resources and flexibility of that higher intelligence, since it is a power the limits of which are very easily reached. Mr. Mivart's argument seems to me to prove design to demonstration; but it proves design of a limited kind, design intended apparently to provide for only ordinary events, and not to be in any sense what instinct is sometimes called,—a lower sort of inspiration. And when I come to the consideration of design in its higher theological aspects, I am not sure that all these elaborate paraphernalia of stings and poisons and predatory instincts, and reparative forces more or less equal to what is wanted of them,—often rather less than more,—are at all easier to reconcile with the conception of a directly acting omniscience, than those unbending physical laws themselves, of which I suppose that these instincts and organic apparatus are more or less the outcome. As it seems to me, those highly "manufactured articles," —the ultimate atoms,—are at least as unintelligible without a creative intelligence as animal instincts themselves; while animal instincts, though they witness to some intelligent creator in every feature of their existence, suggest rather a limited than an unlimited store of resource behind them. After all, we have to fall back on the evidence of man's moral and spiritual nature for our belief in God the creator; and no evidence of organic nature, such as that insisted on by Mr. Mivart, would take us beyond a very secondary sort of "demiurgus." Design proves intelligence of a limited kind, not of an infinite kind.

And, therefore, natural theology will never be of effectual use for any purpose beyond the bare refutation of the Materialist and the Atheist. After they are refuted, the great problem of theology begins.

XVII

MR. FOWLE ON NATURAL RELIGION

1872

IN a remarkable article in the new number of the *Contemporary Review*, the Rev. T. W. Fowle takes up a somewhat striking position in relation to Natural and Revealed Religion. He argues that the tendency of modern science to lay more and more weight on objective facts as distinguished from the subjective hopes and aspirations of the mind, really tells in favour of what is called 'revealed' as distinguished from 'natural' religion—at least if the two are contrasted and not taken in conjunction,—because it makes appeal to fact as distinct from human dreams and hopes, and because historical revelation rests on such fact, if it has any solid basis at all. Mr. Fowle does not, however, deny, but justifies the great weight which intellectual and moral prepossessions or prejudices have in moulding our estimates of *evidence*. Indeed, his position is this,—that though the desires and hopes, and moral needs on which natural religion is apt to rely as the chief evidences of immortality, are worthless as evidences, in the face of the new philosophy, without such a fact as the resurrection of Christ to which to appeal, they have a most legitimate effect in determining how far we shall admit the credibility of a supernatural fact at all. He holds that, on the one hand, it is perfectly natural for an intellect educated solely in the spirit of the modern science to deny, with Hume, the credibility of any event which seems to run counter to the laws of Nature, and to demand for such an event as the resurrection of Christ evidence which it would require as great a miracle to disbelieve, as the miracle involved in the event itself; but that, on the other hand, to a heart which has always felt within itself the thirst for spiritual immortality, and the predisposition to believe in it, this miracle, miraculous though it be, is not *a priori* incredible, but perfectly credible, and credible on the same kind of evidence on which a surprising, but otherwise unmiraculous, event would be accepted. Mr. Fowle holds that if the resurrection of our Lord were an event short of the miraculous, nobody would think of rejecting it on the recorded evidence; and that it is rejected or accepted, and, as I understand him, legitimately rejected or accepted, according as the previous experience of the individual soul has led it to find an antecedent impossibility in a supernatural event or an antecedent probability therein. He thinks both kinds of previous mental experience,—that which renders such an event incredible, and that which renders it even probable,—likely to be associated with virtues of their own. The temperament, incredulous of any but natural events, will be associated, he thinks, with the virtues of strict and even austere intellectual scrupulousness, and that power to renounce the pleas of the affections which the highest intellectual sincerity seems to require. "Rationalism," he says, "will uphold the need of caution in our assent, the duty of absolute conviction, the self-sufficiency of men" (what, by the way, does he mean by that?) "the beauty of love, the glory of working for posterity, and the true humility of being content to be ignorant where knowledge is impossible." On the other hand, the predisposition to believe in the supernatural will be associated with large insight into the affections of men, with a keen sense of sin, with "a passion for life and duty which death cuts short"; in a word, with the emotional virtues rather than the intellectual virtues. Mr. Fowle holds, then, that the scientifically sceptical and the religiously believing temperaments will have to contend together till it appears which of them, on the whole, is the more completely in accordance with man's nature and destiny; and that whichever of the two proves itself, on the whole, the better and the stronger will sway men to accept or reject the evidence for Christ's resurrection, which is sufficiently proved for all who live in the supernatural, and insufficiently proved for all whose minds are trained solely by the study of natural laws. I need hardly add that Mr. Fowle himself evidently thinks that the naturalistic class of prepossessions, though they have been unfairly suppressed in former ages of the world, are now taking a position which would lead to a distortion of human nature and a cultivation of the intellectual at the expense of the highest moral virtues;—that the spiritual aptitude of man for a divine revelation is such that, with the historical evidence of the resurrection of Christ before it, this faith will take firmer root, as the great scientific reaction of the present age subsides, and the equipoise between the human intellect and the affections is re-established.

With the general tendency of Mr. Fowle's doctrine

I heartily agree. Nothing is clearer than this, that our estimate of specific evidence must vary according to our antecedent assumption of what is probable or improbable,—that a man with a deep sense of duty and sin, for example, will entertain a very different presumption as to the existence of God and the immortality of the personal life from one who has a difficulty in realising what sin is,—and that a man whose mind is saturated with the principles of the laws of nature will entertain a very different presumption as to an asserted resurrection from the dead from one who has studied man much and natural laws little. Nor can I doubt for a moment that a true balance of mind must owe much to both these elements of experience, and not rest exclusively on either. But for all that, I hold that Mr. Fowle, in asserting that 'revelation' alone furnishes any objective fact sufficient to justify a rational belief in immortality, and that the so-called evidences of natural religion weigh only in preparing the moral temperament by which the truth of revelation is to be judged, has been quite unjust to natural religion, —the case of which he has stated to my mind most inadequately.

In the first place, he deals with the widely-spread religious desires, hopes, and presentiments of mankind exactly as he would with the once widely-spread desire, hope, and presentiment of the alchemists that some process could be discovered for transmuting all substances into gold. Such interior prepossessions are of importance, he thinks, directly an actual fact with adequate objective evidence for it is produced which answers to them, because then they obtain a legitimate opportunity for their exercise, but not before; till then, you have no right to deny that some other purely subjective explanation of their origin may not be the right explanation. Admit that men in general, when past the savage stage and short of the scientific stage, have yearned after immortality and after communion with God, still that would only show,—in the absence of any historical proof that the gratification of their yearning was possible,—that the mysterious question of origin and destiny interests men deeply, and that the answer of the mind to it, in the absence of specific evidence, is apt to be that which would be least alien to our present experience and most agreeable to our feelings. But Mr. Fowle does not seem in this matter to have done any justice to the scientific character of the facts. Would he, or any naturalist, deny for a moment that the possession of a physical organ by a race, even though in some members of that race it were deficient, was the best possible evidence either that it has a real objective use, and serves the body's welfare now, or that at any rate it has done so at some time or other, in the case of the ancestors from whom we have inherited it? No doubt there are organs, as Sir W. Gull suggested the other day, with regard to which it may perhaps some day be decided that they are physiologically obsolete in the human race as it exists at present; but no physiologist even of the most thoroughly Darwinian school would doubt for a moment that organs common to the great majority of any race either are or formerly were correlated with external uses, and would not have existed but for those external uses. I say that such an argument is strictly *scientific*. Admit if you please that the spleen (say) has no visible use now in the human body. Yet any physiologist, however sceptical, will be ready to maintain vigorously that it must formerly, if not now, have had some objective use, or it would not exist. As the eye is correlated with light, so is every specific organ correlated with some external arrangement without which it would not have existed. Now apply this doctrine to that moral or spiritual faculty which in the majority of men acknowledges the presence of a spiritual observer and judge of absolutely secret thoughts and motives. Can we suppose that this sense of shame without the presence of any bodily observer, this sense of peace and even joy which streams in from outside just as it would do, though in larger measure, from the sympathy of a friend, is a mere imaginative overflow from the conception of ourselves as we *should* feel if our mind were transparent to the eye of those we wished to please? Surely the quiver of the whole nature to observation *from within* bespeaks as distinct an organ of our minds, as the sensitiveness of the eye to light bespeaks an organ of our bodies. If the structure of the eye implies light, if the structure of the ear implies sound, then the structure of our conscience as certainly implies a spiritual presence and judgment, the access of some being to our inward thoughts and motives. Of course, it is open to the sceptical psychologist to try and explain this experience in some other way, by the laws of association, or how he will. Of course I do not maintain that such an argument, without any examination of the possible replies to it, is final and unanswerable, though I believe that it will hold water after all the multitude of replies to it have been heard and strictly examined. All I maintain is, that when Mr. Fowle speaks of the argument as coming simply to this,—that because we wish something to be true, therefore it is true, he is grossly understating the case of natural religion. As a matter of fact, 'hunger,' which is no more than one of the desires, does practically attest, not certainly that the particular person who feels it can find food to satisfy his hunger, but certainly that the race from which he has descended have had food to eat. Hunger could not have benefited the body unless there had been food to which it had prompted our ancestors to have recourse, and therefore could not, even on Darwinian principles, have grown into a steady accompaniment of the need of food. So, too, unless there had been usually milk for the child, the instinct of sucking would not have been one of the primary instincts of human nature. In like manner, I maintain that though nothing can be less scientific than to say that every man's wishes are prophecies of fruition, nothing can be more scientific than to say that the existence of any *generic* appetite or desire is a clear evidence of the former existence, at all events, of conditions that satisfied that appetite or desire. It is possible, of course, that an appetite may survive the conditions which gratified it, as we see in the case of savage or brutal desires surviving the states of society in which they had habitual nourishment. But no one will apply this explanation to the structure of the conscience. No one will say that it is an heirloom derived from ancestors for whom it had an objective use which it has lost with us. From all we know of the lower animals, and even of the lower races of men, this apprehension of a spiritual presence to which their thoughts and hearts are open, is certainly not an inheritance derived from them, but an acquisition of man himself in his higher stages of being. If then it is a real function of the mind, if this sense of not being alone with our thoughts, but of being judged by a higher Being than ourselves, is generally a characteristic of the human race at all, there is a scientific case for the existence of some real ground for the impression. It would be surely very wonderful if this deep-rooted apprehension of spiritual observation and interference had grown up without any cause at all. The natural thing for a being of merely physical organisation would be to believe in life only where there was evidence of another physical organisation; and the almost uniform response of the conscience to the presence of an invisible and intangible Being seems as good a scientific ground for believing in such a Being, as the response of an Æolian harp to the wind is for believing in the wind. Certainly the truths of natural religion,—of the existence of some righteous and invisible Being ever present with us, and of the existence of a spiritual part of us which *may* at least be quite independent of our physical organisation, and *must* be so if that invisible relation is to continue, —are quite as scientific a kind of inference from the facts of conscience as the existence of iron in the sun would seem to be from the facts of the spectroscopic analysis. I do not say that there is no adequate reply to the argument, though I think that all the replies may be effectually replied to, but I do say that Mr. Fowle confounds a fallacy with a very sound argument, when he identifies the hasty inference from a wish to the necessary gratification of the wish, with the inference from a specific function (whether of mind or body) to the reality, either in former times or now, of a real object of the function. In the case of the conscience, the possible obsoleteness of the function is not one of the alternatives; and hence, unless it can be maintained that a false superstition has indefinitely benefited the race,— which Mr. Fowle does not seem inclined to admit,— I think, while agreeing with his able paper on many points, that he has done great injustice to the strength of the argument for the truths of natural religion.

XVIII

MR. JUSTICE FRY ON MATERIALISM

1882

It is a pity that the interesting and thoughtful lecture of Sir E. Fry on the Victorian era has been so poorly reported. There was at least one passage in it which I should have liked to have had in full, and which contains an argument that has always seemed to me of the greatest possible force against what is called the materialistic view of Creation. "There is, of late," said Mr. Justice Fry, "a tendency towards Materialism in many minds, a tendency to exalt matter beyond intellect or soul. For himself, the lecturer felt at least as certain, if not more so, from his own consciousness, of the reality of intellect, as of that of matter. Scientific men talked about molecules and atoms—things, by the way, which even to them were, so far, matters of simple faith, that they had never seen an atom, though he (the lecturer) did not deny their existence. But he felt it a striking fact that he, like others, was conscious of the same personality, the same individual consciousness, now that he had thirty years ago, although, meanwhile, according to the physiologists, the material portion of his being had completely changed every seven years. Hence, there was to be experienced a being within us separate from matter." That sense of personal identity in man has always been insisted on as one of the great strongholds of the spiritualist's case, and very justly; but I doubt if anything like as much has ever been made of it, as the strength of the case really requires. Even the greater Germans —like Dr. Weismann, for example, whose valuable and lucid book, *Studies in the Theory of Descent*, with a preface by the late Mr. Darwin, has recently been translated into English,—admit freely that the materialistic explanation of the universe only applies to its external forms; that unless you assume the ultimate atom or molecule to have some inner qualities analogous to those which we call mental,—qualities such as the late Professor Clifford used to speak of as those of mind-stuff,—there is no explaining how the mental universe is developed out of the physical. And Dr. Weismann himself goes so far as to say that the whole process of evolution, the whole mechanism of the universe, may well be conceived as having an interior and mental aspect, corresponding to its external and self-complete framework, which interior aspect is probably nearer to what we mean by "purpose" than to anything else of which we can conceive. Therefore, though he earnestly protests against the insertion of purpose as a modifying link between any of the external changes in the process of evolution, and maintains that the method of physical Creation is wholly explained by strictly physical laws, yet he grants, and even seems to contend, that there is a mental aspect to the whole, as there is a mental aspect to every part,—a mind-stuff for the whole, as there is a mind-stuff for the parts, —the interior view of which may correspond, more or less, closely to the general conception of a ruling intellect. But though I quite understand the point of view from which this is granted by evolutionists, —it is the only way, indeed, in which it is possible for physical evolutionists to explain the extraordinary intellectual and moral flowering of so much physical mechanism,—I believe that it suggests a very much less reasonable, and, indeed, very much less scientific, key to the riddle of the universe, than the key on which Mr. Justice Fry lays his finger, when he speaks of the evidence afforded by the consciousness of personal identity that there are some things besides our bodies which are concerned in the administration of the life we live.

The fact to which Mr. Justice Fry appeals,—that in some real sense a man who has lived for thirty years can pronounce himself with absolute certainty to be the same being, who has gone through an infinite number of changes, bodily and mental, of the greater part of which he can recall nothing whatever, though both the many and quite different bodies, and the many and very different states of mind and character, to which he thus lays claim as his own, could be identified as his own by no material test in the world, indeed by no test except the test of his own profound conviction of having passed through them, does seem to be explicable only on a spiritual theory of the origin of Man. The mere assertion of personal identity of any kind is an assertion not even expressible at all in terms of material things, nay, so positively inconsistent at first sight with the facts of change and variation which are also implied in this assertion, that it sounds more like a paradox than a truth, though it is a truth so true, that without it as a starting-point, there would be no possibility of paradox. What does it imply? As I maintain, it implies this,—that the spiritual laws of the universe are far deeper rooted in the universe than they could be, if they were either the mere reflex or the mere evolution of physical laws. Physical objects cannot establish their own identity with the physical objects of other days, still less with quite different physical objects of other days, and even if they could they certainly would not get their claim at once allowed, and made the ultimate basis and starting-point of a whole world of action. The power of our spirits to achieve this magic feat of memory, and identify ourselves with the children of a generation ago, is a wonderful assertion of the supremacy of mind over matter, but an assertion not by any means of the supremacy of any human mind over matter, but only of that Mind—for only a mind it could be—which so regulates the laws of the universe as to compel us all to make about ourselves this assertion, which we do not half understand, which we cannot explain, and which yet is at the root of all our actions, and part and parcel of the structure of every human society. If man's intellect were the highest intellectual phenomenon of our world, it is inconceivable that a truth so startling and so paradoxical could force itself upon us. Paradox is the partial glimpse which a lower mind gains of the truths strictly comprehensible only to a higher mind. The very firmness and absoluteness with which we grasp a paradoxical truth, and make it the light of all our being, is evidence that it is really imposed upon us by a higher Mind, to which it is a truism. We should be unable, by our own unassisted light, quite to believe in our own personal identity, so intrinsically paradoxical is it, were it not pressed down upon our minds by the final authority of the creative laws themselves. Nor can it be pretended that mere material forces could create any sort of belief at all, much less a belief in spiritual things almost contradicted by the evidence of the senses. This marvel of unquestioning faith, which every sane man carries from his childhood to his grave, that he is identical with, though different from, himself at all previous stages of his own career, is utterly inconceivable as a result of physical evolution, or as a result of pre-established harmony, or as a result of anything but spiritual laws far wider and deeper than any which we can comprehend, but which, none the less, so completely control our thoughts, as to hide entirely from the greater number of us the seeming contradictions which lurk beneath the truth, and to impress on us, as irresistible certainty, what the senses alone would declare to be nonsensical and incredible fictions.

Now, let me turn to the hypothesis which represents mind as never interfering in the course of physical events, but at best representing a mere inner aspect of the outward frame of things, a sort of backwater from the stream of physical laws and forces. It is of the very essence of that evolutional explanation of mind which assumes either, with Professor Clifford, that "mind-stuff" is one aspect of *all* matter, but that the highest mind-stuff in the universe is, so far as we know, the human mind-stuff,—or more reverentially, with Dr. Weismann, that there is a mind-stuff on the great scale, consisting in the whole mechanism of the universe, and bearing the same sort of mental fruit which our mind-stuff on its small scale, *i.e.* the human body, bears in what we call the mental life,—it is of the very essence of this theory of mind, I say, that mind is a phenomenon which varies in exact parallelism with the magnitude and scale of physical organisation, but which does not interfere between one link and another of the physical development, though it corresponds to it. Now, is that, so far as we have the means of judging, in any sense true? I should say, judging by that portion of the universe which is within our own observation, that it is absolutely untrue. I am conscious, say, of being in a true sense the very person who was at a given school on a given day, translating a particular passage from Homer, thirty years ago. But amongst the occurrences of those thirty years, for how few can I still answer. How little real parallelism is there between the mind-stuff and the mental flower or fruit of it. Of the events of nearly one-third of the time,—the time occupied in sleep,—my memory is probably a total blank; for a very great proportion of the rest of the time,—of the mechanical acts of walking, dressing, perhaps eating and drinking,—I am as little able to give any personal account as I am of my sleep. Of the few points of bright or intense consciousness, indeed, distributed over those thirty years, I can almost always explain the secret. Either a joy, or a sorrow, or a hope, or a fear, or a great effort of resolution, or some exciting cause which fixed attention vividly on the momentary attitude of my own mind, accounts for my personal self being so absolutely identified with that instant of life. But wherever attention was deficient, there memory, and consequently the power of self-identification, is certain to be deficient too. I can run back, even over my own history, only from point to point of lucid memory, knowing little about the intervals, except that there did live through them, somehow, a being whom I now identify as myself, and who gradually came to think as I think now, and feel as I feel now. But it is as far as possible from being true either that the mind varied precisely with the development of the physical organisation, *i.e.* the "mind-stuff," or that it never directly interfered in that development. On the contrary, the mind, so far as I can represent it by consciousness at all, was often most vivid when the "mind-stuff" or physical organisation was most exhausted; and again, great changes in the physical organisation or mind-stuff were due, and due entirely, to the direct interference of the mind. One illness, for instance, was directly caused by an ambitious attempt to do something beyond my powers; another, by running deliberately a risk of infection; a third, by overstraining my eyesight. Well, then, the self-consciousness on which alone we rely for our knowledge of our own identity absolutely assures us, first, that through a great part of our past lives the fulness of the development of our bodies was no index at all of the vividness of our mental life; next, that very great changes indeed in the development of our bodies were brought about solely by the direct interference of our minds in the circumstances of our bodily development. In other words, instead of that perfect correspondence or "pre-established harmony" between physical and mental development which is the only resource of the mere evolutionist who starts from a physical basis, the most critical of all the facts of our spiritual consciousness,—that which insists on connecting together with a thread of personal identity a long series of different bodies always in a state of flux and change,—asserts that it is only through our acts of attention, that is, voluntary states for which we have no physical names at all, that we can recognise ourselves surely as having existed in the past, and, further, that many of these acts were the causes of very great and sudden transformations of the physical conditions of our bodily life, which altered altogether the order and conditions of our physical development. Nothing, then, can be less like the theory of a mind-stuff exhibiting mental phenomena corresponding exactly to the elaborateness of physical organisation, but which only run parallel with it, and never intervene in the chain of physical causes which mould it, than this. Our minds, we find, have had crises of their own which were certainly not determined solely, or even chiefly, by bodily crises, but rather by the intensity of the feelings and the will; and further, those crises have constantly produced crises in the development of our bodies of the most important kind; so that neither does the development of the mental life reflect in any way the development of the bodily life, nor is the latter independent of the former, but is very greatly indeed influenced and modified by it. Indeed, it is clearly false to say either that the mental life is a function of the bodily life, or that the bodily life is a function of the mental life, or that there is a preconstituted harmony between the two. Each acts and reacts powerfully on the other, but neither is independent of the other. Instead of showing us any exact parallelism between the physical organisation and the mental life, the curious consciousness of personal identity, on which the whole structure of our life is founded, presents us with the story of a few vivid memories linked together by a mysterious conviction of sameness, of which we can give no account without involving ourselves in contradictions. Does not this suggest most powerfully that so far from the Mind, which is in the truest sense the Mind of the universe, being in any sense a reflex of the physical structure of that universe, it controls and overrides it, giving us this strange and fitful insight into ourselves which we find it so difficult to reconcile with the facts of our external existence; lifting us by glimpses of the unseen world into a certain limited command over the seen; and, in short, maintaining the order of this physical life by flashes from the illumination of a higher and larger life?

XIX

PROFESSOR STOKES, M.P., ON PERSONAL IDENTITY

1890

I HOPE that the President of the Royal Society intends to publish at length the lecture delivered at the Finsbury Polytechnic Institution on Sunday, of which the *Times* gave a short report in its Monday's issue. It is obvious that the lecture was one of great interest, though a great part of its drift has been so much condensed in the *Times*' notice of it as to diminish very much its value for those who were not present. Professor Stokes's main thesis seems to have been that neither is the intellectual part of man the mere product of molecular changes in the brain, nor, on the other hand, is physical organisation the mere cage or prison of the soul. Professor Stokes holds both the materialist hypothesis which makes the consciousness a blossom of the material organisation, and the psychic hypothesis which makes the material organisation a sort of bondage or confinement for the free spirit, to be inconsistent with the facts of life. He illustrated the error of the former view by remarking that after a great physical shock, such as a bricklayer is said to have received who was struck down and rendered unconscious for a time by a falling brickbat, the first thought on recovery of consciousness has been to complete the sentence which had been begun before the blow was received. Now, said Professor Stokes, the blow must have caused a great variety of important physical changes in the brain, yet the moment consciousness returned, the mind went on working in precisely the same groove of continuous purpose in which it was working before the blow fell. Could this be if the mind were nothing but the product of the molecular action of the brain? On the other hand, the notion that the body is rather a dead-weight than otherwise, which limits and confines the action of the soul, was regarded by Professor Stokes as subject to difficulties quite as great as the materialistic theory. We are not told in the report what these difficulties are, but I think I could suggest some of Professor Stokes's objections. If it were so, there would, one would think, be a greater approach to freedom and activity of mind during the decay of bodily power which precedes the dissolution of the tie between soul and body, than there is in the full vigour of the mature body; yet this is found not to be the case. The health and strength of the body implies a more favourable condition for the vigorous action of the mind than its frailty and decay. It is not in extreme old age nor in illness that the mind usually acts with most freedom and power, but, on the contrary, in the maturity and highest vitality of the body. The *mens sana* is found more perfect *in corpore sano*, than in any decadent state of the body; nor have we any evidence worth mentioning that at the approach of death the mind can take a more lofty and stronger flight. All this suggests that the relation between mental power and physical power is

not one either of mental effect to physical cause, or
of a spiritual cause in a phase of conflict with an
obstructing agency, but rather is the relation resulting from some deeper agency which contains in it, if
I understand Professor Stokes's drift rightly, the
principle of individuality, and determines both the
form of character and the physical frame as well as
the connection between them. Professor Stokes said
that there were indications in Scripture "of a sort
of energy lying deeper down than even the manifestation of life, on which the identity of man, and
his existence, and the continuance of his existence,
depended. Such a supposition as this was free from
the difficulties of the two theories he had previously
brought before them, the materialist theory and
what he had called the psychic theory. It represented the action on the living body as the result of
an energy, if he might say so, an energy which was
individualised; and the process of life, thinking
included, was the result of interaction between this
fundamental individualised energy and the organism.
The supposition that our individual being depended
on something lying deeper down than even thought
itself, enabled us to understand, at any rate to conceive, how our individual selves might go on in
another stage of existence, notwithstanding that our
present bodies were utterly destroyed and went to
corruption." It would be impossible, I think, to
doubt that our individuality, that is, our character,
depends on something "lying deeper down than
thought itself," for all that determines the direction
and the drift of thought, the passions, the affections,
the purposes, the will, must be conceived as preceding, or at all events as coexisting with, thought, and
giving it, so to speak, its sailing orders. It is not

thought which usually determines character, but, in an immense majority of cases, character which determines thought; and it is impossible to conceive that which determines otherwise than as preceding that which is determined. And I quite agree with Professor Stokes that the individuality includes more or less the physical organisation. The desires, the tastes, the ambitions, the affections, the spiritual yearnings, are more or less profoundly involved in the character of the senses and the physical organisation. It is impossible to make the individuality depend solely, or even chiefly, upon the will itself, though that is the one element of character which is self-determining, and which can more or less modify and change the set of the whole stream of tendencies and aspirations. Let any man consider in what the individuality of himself or any of his most intimate friends chiefly consists, and he will very rarely find that it is solely, or even mainly, the set of his purposes, the attitude of his will. That enters very deeply, of course, into his individuality, but it is very seldom the most conspicuous feature, and never the only conspicuous feature in it. The individuality depends still more on the bias of nature, the proportion between a man's feelings and his intellect, the vividness of his sensations, the tenacity of his memory, the vehemence of his passions, the eagerness of his curiosity, the depth of his sympathies,— all matters which are more or less determined for him, and which his will, though it has the power to regulate and guide, has no power to revolutionise. Thus individuality is something far wider than thought, or even "will;" and though "will" enters into it, almost as the direction of the helm enters into the course of the ship, nobody can deny that individuality includes elements which involve deeply the physical organisation no less than elements which are purely mental. Hence I agree with Professor Stokes that individuality lies deeper than either the purely mental or the purely physical elements of life, and I should be very willing to find reason to think that the individuality *moulds* both the mental and the physical organisation and the relation between them, rather than that it is the product of the mental and physical organisation and of the relation between them. But as no one was ever conscious of the moulding of his own or any other mental and physical organisation, and of the relation between them, it must be more or less matter of inference from more general considerations, whether the individuality was first conceived so as to precede and determine the mental and physical conditions under which life commences, with the relation between them, or whether these conditions, and their reciprocal influence on each other, *constitute* the individuality. Of course those who believe that there is something more in human life than any materialist hypothesis will account for, —especially those who believe in free-will,—will be very much more inclined to take the former view, than those who accept evolution as explaining not only the method but the absolute causation of human life. It is impossible to believe in free-will without believing in a divine mind, for it is clear that material forces could never have broken loose from their own fetters and blossomed into freedom ; and the moment you believe in a divine origin for the will of man, it is impossible not to believe that the divine purpose has placed the evolution and training of human character as a whole above all the other purposes of our human life. So much, I think, then, may safely be said, that if the human will is free, as Professor Stokes evidently believes, the evolution of the physical part of our life must have been more or less subordinated to the evolution of the moral and spiritual part of our life; so that it is not unreasonable to conclude that there is some individualised energy, deeper than life itself, which has more or less controlled the development both of the mental and the physical organisation of every man, and the relation between them. I say "more or less controlled," because no one, of course, can say how far the laws which regulate the evolution of social relations may not interfere with, or even supersede, what we should regard as the evolution of individual character. No man in his senses denies the lineal transmission of good and evil tendencies from parent to child, or even the contagion of good and evil between mere companions and friends, which has so astounding an effect as well on the regeneration as on the corruption of social groups; and our knowledge of this truth renders it quite impossible to say that the divine purpose contemplates the evolution of individualised characters as a thing apart from the evolution of the whole social character of which they will form a part. Professor Stokes therefore would not dream of regarding the individualised energies in which he finds the probable basis both of mind and of physical organisation, as formed without reference to the ancestors from whom those who were about to be brought into existence had sprung, and the society and nation in which they were to be developed. Still, I think it may be said by all who believe in the free will of man and the providence of God, that human character cannot be regarded as the mere product of circumstances and organism, but must be treated as stamping a new individuality on the life and the organism, by which in no small degree the character of that life and the power and elasticity of the organisation are controlled and directed. Professor Stokes believes that this individuality more or less evolves the bodily organisation, and cannot be left without a bodily organisation, even after our present bodily organisation falls into ruin or decay. To him the body is a constituent element of the individual, which will express itself in another, perhaps a less imperfect body, so soon as the old body disappears. That is certainly the suggestion of revelation, and appears to be quite consistent at least with reason, not to say of something which looks rather like the beginning of experience.

XX

THE RESURRECTION OF THE BODY

1895

I PERCEIVE with some surprise that many of the correspondents to the *Spectator* believe that the body which is to clothe the soul after death is identically the same as that which clothes the soul in this world, and is not, what St. Paul calls it, a spiritual body,— as different from that which died, as that which springs from the germinated seed is from the seed which gave many of its constituent parts to the soil and the air and the water with which it was watered, —but in some sense as much the body which passed through death as the soul is the soul which passed through death. One of the *Spectator* correspondents, whose letter is published to-day, declares this expressly, and makes light of the difficulty as to *which* body it is of the multitude of those with which in the course of life we have been clothed, by asking whether the soul too does not equally change in the course of a long life, and whether the soul or ego with which an old man dies is not very different from the soul or ego which he had as a child or a youth or a man. Undoubtedly it is; but that surely is an answer to his own assertion that there can be any *physical* identity between the dying body and the resurrection body. Does he suppose for a moment that because in some sense there is an identity of nature and character between the dying man and the man who survives death, there is no great spiritual change and sublimation of the mental powers which survive death? Does the memory survive in the same enfeebled state as that in which the failing powers of the brain leave it at death? Is it the exhausted and flagging imagination, the faltering and weakened judgment, the relaxed and hesitating purpose, the blanched sympathies of the aged, which survive death, or mental powers all transformed and exalted in the glow of a true resurrection? If the latter, as I suppose all men believe, and as St. Paul certainly believed, then surely it is neither the material body,—if, indeed, any body is properly speaking purely material,—which we bore in youth or in middle age, or at the moment which preceded death, which survives death, but something quite different, though it springs from the same origin and is governed by the same law of personal development by which the character of the renewed and restored life is connected with the character of the submissive and disciplined yet enfeebled and exhausted life. What St. Paul describes as the body of the resurrection can by no possibility be the very body of any previous time of life. "It is sown a natural body, it is raised a spiritual body." The man dies with all sorts of diseases upon him. The soldier dies with all his scars, with perhaps an arm lost and an eye blinded by a splinter of shell. The paralytic dies with his power of controlling his own motions gone. Nine aged men out of ten die with enfeebled sight and hearing, and other great traces of the destruction which time brings to a frame never meant to survive for more than a century at most. Does any one suppose that these marks of gradual decay survive after death? If so, Death is indeed the conqueror, and not the conquered. And if they do not, if the life that renews all the functions of both spirit and body be a spiritual life, is not the body even more fundamentally changed by the resurrection than the spirit itself? Does not our Lord say distinctly that in the spiritual world there is no marrying nor giving in marriage, but that the life of the immortal is as that of the angels in heaven; and does not that imply some great transformation of the physical into the spiritual body? Indeed, is not such a change involved necessarily in the description repeated many times of Christ's own resurrection-body as passing easily through closed doors and appearing at will, now in one place and now in another? It seems to me perfectly certain that though *character* survives death, and survives it in the very attitude and form into which life and responsibility had moulded it, a great spiritual change must pass over both the failing mental and the failing physical powers, and that the physical are even more vitally changed than the mental, for the very reason that they were less spiritual at the moment of death, and that the baptism of a great spiritual change brings them therefore a greater access of new vitality. It is simply childish to talk of any more *physical* identity between the body which breathes its last breath in pain and weakness, and the body which responds easily to the renewed and immortal soul, than there is between the apparently rotting seed and the flower or tree which springs from it into beauty or even majesty. There is a vital connection between the two, no doubt. The mustard-seed yields a different herb from the mignonette-seed, and the acorn from the beech-mast. But the "body that shall be" is just as different from, as impossible to identify absolutely with, the body that withers and dies, as the mind which expires in all its mortal weakness is different from, and impossible to identify absolutely with, the mind that begins its new career in the eternal world. The spiritual renewal beyond the grave is needed for both, and certainly even more for that side of man's nature which is least spiritual and most thoroughly used up in the "sundry and manifold changes of the world," than is the moral and spiritual essence of his character. It is impossible for us to analyse what makes the sameness between the child and the man. Partly, no doubt, it is a particular principle and law of self-generated mental evolution, partly a particular principle and law of involuntary physical evolution; but whatever it be, it is not the sameness of the physical atoms constituting his body which constitutes that identity. If it were, millions of men would have to compete for the same atoms which have at various times passed through millions of different bodies, and constituted parts of millions of different personalities.

The simple truth is that we are not in a position to say what is body and what is soul, or what is the distinction between them. No man feels that he has lost any of his personality when he loses even a hand or an eye, to say nothing of a foot or a lock of hair, yet he has doubtless lost something which was very intimately connected with his bodily life, and which more or less affects the impression which he makes on others. We cannot say with confidence whether there may not be something essentially material in a finite soul, nor whether there may not be something essentially spiritual in a human body. The only distinction we know with any certainty between the two is that the soul is *more* essential to the personality, and the body less so; but we cannot deny that there is much of the soul in the habits of the body, nor that there is a good deal of the body in the affections and emotions of the soul. What St. Paul seems to teach, and what it seems reasonable to believe, is that the whole nature of the change which we call death, is in the direction of making the dispositions of the soul and will relatively more important to the whole personality,—whether their dispositions be good or evil,—that death involves a change in the direction of giving new life to those dispositions which we have, ourselves by our own habits and actions, fostered and formed within us; and that when God "giveth us a body as it pleaseth him," that new body will be more under the control of the soul,—whether good or evil,—and more perfectly expressive of its inward dispositions than the body which we leave behind us here. But that the constituent particles of the body which we leave behind us here, will be reassembled in the body of the resurrection, seems to be inconceivable, in the face of what we know both of what we call physical law and of what we mean by moral personality. If there is and can be no physical or atomic identity between the body of the child and the body of the aged man, there is no conceivable reason why there should be any such identity between the body of the aged man and the body of the immortal. The identity lies hidden somewhere in the law and principle of growth, not in the material identity of the atoms of which we are at each successive moment made up. As the identity of the book does not depend on the identity of the paper or the binding, so the identity of the body does not in any sense depend on the chemical elements which constitute it, but only on the general drift of that expression and those powers which it conveys and commands.

XXI

THE MODERN EASTER DIFFICULTY

1891

DEAN BRADLEY, in his Easter Day sermon at Westminster Abbey, put his finger on the very centre of the contrast between ancient and modern feeling concerning Easter, when he said that while it was the crucifixion of Christ which was to "the Jews a stumbling-block and to the Greeks foolishness" in the great day when Christianity first came into the world, it is no longer the Crucifixion but the Resurrection,—which to both Jews and Greeks, though a great marvel, was a marvel which attracted rather than repelled them,—that seems to modern pride and scepticism a stumbling-block and foolishness. We feel no difficulty where the early believers felt most difficulty, in accepting the tremendous humiliation and sorrow and shame of the cross. On the contrary, as Dean Bradley told his hearers, the story of the Man of Sorrows is wholly credited by the sceptical world of to-day, and is accepted with even eager reverence and gratitude. It is the suffering, the forgiveness, the resignation, the peace, the calm, the fortitude, the sympathy, the "Daughters of Jerusalem, weep not for me, but weep for yourselves and for your children," the "Father, forgive them, for they know not what they do," the "Peace I leave with you, my peace I give unto you; not as the world giveth give I unto you; let not your heart be troubled, neither let it be afraid," in which we all believe,—even sceptics and those who are more than sceptics, who assert positively that "miracles do not happen." The shame does not humiliate us; we can see through it to the infinitely greater glory behind; whereas the Jews found it a sore stumbling-block to their pride of race, and the Greeks looked down upon it as radically inconsistent with that intellectual caste to which they ascribed the sole possession of "the good and beautiful" in all its perfection. To them the asserted resurrection seemed that which alone gave a glimmer of probability to the bold assertion that God had manifested Himself in human nature only to die upon the cross, and submit to the jeers and scoffs of Jewish and Roman ridicule. To us there seems something intrinsically convincing in the assertion that this great death was died, that that majestic calm and that magnanimous sympathy prevailed even over the torture of the cross; we only come to our difficulties when we come to the assertion that He who died that supernatural death really lived again to be recognised by those who saw Him die and heard Him foretell their own discomfiture and dispersion. The early disciples found it all but impossible to believe that a divine nature could go through physical and moral humiliation. Our difficulty is not in the least in believing in that which is divine enough to overcome any combination, however overwhelming, of physical and moral humiliation. What we find difficulty in believing is, that that which is **morally**

and spiritually supernatural, involves even any power at all of controlling or overruling what we suppose to be the fixed necessities of physical law. Our minds are jaded and hag-ridden, as it were, by the physical fatalities of modern science, and yet modern science itself might, if we only used our eyes, warn us of the extraordinary blunder we are making in thus depreciating the true power of mind over matter. It is generally supposed that physiology is the one department of modern science which has done most to shake the belief of man in the resurrection from the dead; and certainly Professor Huxley has used its teaching with extraordinary skill for that end. But let any one who thinks that modern physiology has disposed of the supremacy of the mind over the body, turn to the last *Lancet*, and read the review of a great German physician's (Dr. Albert Moll's) book on hypnotism; and what will he find there? Such sentences as the following:—
"It is quite impossible to assign any limit to the influence of mind upon body, which is probably much more potent and far-reaching than we are usually prepared to admit." (*Lancet*, 28th March 1891, page 722.) And this is not an assertion due to any *a priori* theory, but to the hard facts of actual observation,—an inference drawn from such evidence as this, for example, that real blisters,—to take a very petty detail,—will rise on a patient's skin as a consequence merely of persuading him to believe (when it is not true) that one has been applied to him. And this is one of the least remarkable of all the phenomena of what is now called hypnotism. I do not hesitate for a moment to say that the superstition which modern physical science has promoted, that the mind cannot seriously alter the effect or

modify the operation of the physical laws of the universe, science itself, carefully interrogated, has swept away; and that physiologists do not exaggerate when they say, as the *Lancet's* reviewer said last Saturday, that "it is quite impossible to assign any limit to the influence of mind upon body."

Yet we cannot well recognise with the Dean of Westminster that the modern world no longer sees any "stumbling-block," any "foolishness," in the story which so deeply offended both Jews and Greeks, of the death on the cross of the most divine of human beings, without also recognising the truth of the Dean's assertion that the resurrection from the dead has become a much greater stumbling-block, a much greater depth of foolishness, to that same modern world, than the Crucifixion itself appeared to the world nineteen centuries ago. There seems to be no capacity at all left in us to measure the power of the morally and spiritually supernatural against the power of the physically customary and habitual. We can believe in what we have never seen the least hint of in the one region, and yet cannot believe what we have seen many hints of in the other region. Where can we find any trace of experience to render it possible for us to conceive the nature which could spend the last hours of suspense before approaching death, and the first hours of the keen anguish of betrayal, in strengthening others for the shock and the suffering they were about to undergo, and which could lose all sense of the injustice and cruelty and cowardice and terror around, and the torture within, in the passion of pity and the might of forgiveness? Surely no experience that this generation has had has rendered it easy to conceive of supernatural goodness such as this. And yet we do not stumble at it; it is not a stumbling-block to us; it is not "foolishness"; it is not even difficult to believe. So much as this the modern world will believe without even asking to see anything like it. Yet to me it seems far more wonderful, a far more inconceivable marvel in human life, than any which is involved in the Resurrection. Look at the way the very best men pass through the little trials and struggles of this world. Read Dean Church's account of the Oxford Movement, of the bitterness, the jealousy, the alienation, the soreness, the resentment which followed on *both sides* the very natural and excusable excitements of that great movement, and then ask how far this age has had any experience of the kind of suffering through which our Lord passed on the cross without manifesting any trace of any of these feelings, and yet with all the physical agony to bear which must have intensified the pain and shame and sorrow to an extent which it is impossible for us even in the least degree to measure. To my mind, the spiritual miracle of the Crucifixion was an infinitely greater miracle than the physical miracle of the Resurrection, —a much more impressive evidence of the actual mingling of the divine with the human. It is strange that a world which can accept heartily the one should find it so difficult, and in some cases so impossible, to accept the other. This implies, I think, that what it does accept it accepts without any true insight into the wonder and majesty of the personal manifestation the reality of which it professes to recognise. Certainly ours is a superstitious age, though superstitious rather in the excess of its respect for the physical energies of the universe, than in the excess of its respect for the spiritual. Only on the day before Good Friday, there appeared in the *Echo* this wonderful letter, which seems to me as astounding an evidence of the physical superstition of our age, as any belief in table-turning or witchcraft could be of superstitions of another species:—

"OXFORD AND THEOLOGY

" TO THE EDITOR OF THE 'ECHO'

"SIR—Is it after all true that the only sane folk live in Colney Hatch? That question is apt to arise when we read of the public subscribing £10,000 to endow three studentships 'in order to stimulate the study of theology in Oxford.' (See the Dean of St. Paul's letter in yesterday's *Echo*.) Just think! The idea of devoting the laborious fruits of human industry to the 'study of theology,' when the very existence of a God is a matter of yes or no, whichever you please; not the faintest gleam of light being available, or even possible, upon the subject. And this while the burden of life becomes more insupportable day by day for the great majority, owing to the lack of the merest bodily necessaries. When I look at that £10,000 given for the 'study of theology,' and think of the empty bellies that want filling, I am ashamed of the weakness of my indignation which saves me from a fit or something. Upon my word, there would be more reason in endowing a chair for the 'study' of the habits of the man who resides on the 'off' side of the moon.—Yours, etc., J. FRANCIS.

"*Camberwell, 25th March.*"

Could that intensity of superstition be easily surpassed? For a thinker who knows what faith has done, and has done for the poor, to ridicule the expenditure of £10,000 on theological education as compared with its expenditure on doles of bread and meat,—which for the most part go to increase the number of hunger-ridden paupers,—does seem to me a bewildering depth of superstition. Of course I do not say that this gentleman is wrong in being profoundly sensible of the difficulties which stand in the way of our highest theological beliefs. That is a totally different matter. But that any man of the world even, should suppose that these difficulties are so overwhelming as to render the prosecution of all theological studies a simple absurdity, appears to me to show that he has never had the capacity to enter into the foundations of religious belief, or even to measure the significance of the latest evidence of science on the subject of the relations of the mind to the body. That a small mind, under the influence of a *false* belief, can be made to suffer all the effects of a physical burn, without any application that physical science recognises as adapted to produce such consequences, and yet that a mighty mind possessed by a true belief could not be conceived as controlling the issues of life and death,—though we have quite as good evidence that it did control those issues as we have for what are termed the phenomena of modern hypnotism,— seems to me a paradox which far exceeds the paradoxes of the great mediæval superstitions. That there is a mind expressed in the order of the universe, and that that mind controls the order which it constituted, is surely far more certain than that the influence of belief,—true or false,—over physical life, is a fact of daily scientific experience.

XXII

DR. ABBOTT ON NATURAL AND SUPERNATURAL

1879

In another column of the *Spectator* an interesting criticism by Dr. Abbott is published on the remarks made in that journal last week concerning his conception of Liberal Christianity. To a good deal that he says in that letter I have no reply to make. I do not know that I differ from him substantially in relation to his definition of worship, and am glad to find that he wishes to express by the term something much deeper and larger than that purely spontaneous and instinctive sentiment to which some of the language of his book appeared to confine it.

But as regards the latter portion of his letter, I fear that the better I understand him, the more widely I differ from him; and as there can be no doubt but that Dr. Abbott's view is widely spread, and perhaps becoming more widely spread every day, I do not think it amiss to offer a few more remarks on the subject which he there touches. I had questioned how far a thinker who denies altogether what is called miraculous power to Christ,

could consistently attribute to Him the "divine power" which is a condition, of course, of human faith and worship. If I understand aright Dr. Abbott's reply, it is this,—that there is no real connection between control over the outward physical processes of nature, and divine power,—that he attributes to Christ all the divine power which is usually attributed to God, except the power to alter these uniform relations of physical phenomena,—and that even this exception is not in any sense a limit on Christ's power, since, in the same sense, he would attribute the same positive changelessness, the same fixed will against change, to God Himself, so that there is no denial of the so-called power of miracle to Christ, which he would not, in one sense, be willing to extend to God Himself. His words are these:—
"We believe (in a sense) that Christ could have turned the stones to bread, just as we believe (in a sense) that Christ *could* have listened to the voice of the Tempter; but, as a matter of fact and history, we believe that He did *not* thus 'mould nature,' and hence we infer that it was not His will to do so. Perhaps we may go still further, and say that as He *could* not commit sin, so neither *could* He mould nature contrary to nature's recognised laws." Take this in connection with Dr. Abbott's assertion that Christ had "power enough to redeem a seemingly fallen world; to introduce and keep current among men the hitherto non-existent or latent faculty of forgiveness; to discern the deepest needs of human society and the fittest and most natural means for satisfying them, to foresee and plan the triumph of life over death by self-sacrifice, of righteousness over sin by repentance; and to purify by His spirit not only the comparatively insignificant fraction of

mankind called the Christian Church, but ultimately the whole human race"; and I suppose it means that Dr. Abbott attributes to Christ all the moral omnipotence needful to hear and answer human prayer in the only sense in which, in his belief, it ought to be answered,—and of course, therefore, without any deviation from the strict uniformity of physical nature, — including the omnipresence necessarily implied in such omnipotence. If this interpretation of mine be correct, Dr. Abbott holds that Christ has access to every human heart and every human will in every age, knows all our wants and wishes, inspires us in proportion to our needs, and is gradually renovating the whole universe of spiritual being in His own likeness. If such be his meaning, he has sufficiently answered my doubt as to the foundation he would lay for the worship of Christ. If he really holds that whatever God can do for men, Christ can do, and that whatever limits there are on what Christ *will* do, there are also on what God will do,—namely the moral limits of what is fitting, and no others,—then, however much he may differ from me in ascribing to the physical uniformities of nature a sort of spiritual sacredness which makes it morally impossible even to God to change them, he undoubtedly has in his own faith an ample justification for using of his attitude towards Christ, the word "worship."

But then, by this explanation, Dr. Abbott has only shifted the ground of my difficulty concerning his view of Christianity. He earnestly asserts that what he ascribes to Christ is an infinite moral power, involving that omniscience without which even such power would be all but impotence; and yet the evidence on which he believes this is precisely the same, and no other, than the evidence which he finds wholly worthless when it is brought to prove certain physical facts far less marvellous. If Christ forgave the paralytic's sins, He coupled His forgiveness with the saying,—"But that ye may know that the Son of man hath power on earth to forgive sins,—Arise, and take up thy bed, and go thy way into thine house." Dr. Abbott, if I rightly understand him, accepts the unverifiable half of the story, the insight into the paralytic's repentant heart and the forgiveness of his sins, and casts the other half, the half that was within the observation and verification of a human witness, away. Again, in the case of the multiplication of the five loaves to feed five thousand, and the seven loaves to feed four thousand people, Dr. Abbott rejects both stories as pure myth or legend; but accepts with enthusiasm the statement that Christ is still feeding, by His direct, personal, spiritual influence, the hearts of millions who never heard His name uttered by any human being. If I have understood him rightly, he thinks our Lord's prediction of the destruction of Jerusalem unhistorical, and regards it as an interpolation after the event; but he thinks His prediction of the complete triumph of His teaching over the world perfectly historical, and accepts it, though as yet ages from its fulfilment, as one of the evidences of Christ's divinity.

Now, this state of mind is to me hardly intelligible. I do not say it is wholly unintelligible, for I do not believe, as the old writers on the Evidences used to assert, that the evidence of the physically superhuman is so much easier to get and to test than the evidence of the spiritually superhuman, that in the absence of the former we have no measure of the latter. On the contrary, I hold with Dr. Abbott that the evidence of the spiritually superhuman is the first step, and the clearest; but then it does seem to me most unreasonable that when you have satisfactorily established the spiritually superhuman character of Christ's life and work, you should be greatly offended and surprised at miracle, and induced to regard with great distrust the element of the physically superhuman closely combined with it. On the contrary, it would be rather reasonable, in the absence of any direct evidence on the matter, to expect the manifestation of physically superhuman power in the person of Him who has already manifested spiritually superhuman power. Dr. Abbott, so far as I understand him, declares that he is not in any way prejudiced against the evidence of physically superhuman power in Christ, if it is forthcoming (though he is quite clearly not prepared to expect it), but that it is not forthcoming. And his reason for this very curious statement is,—that the more you examine the structure and growth of the Gospels, the more you see that the miraculous element in it is of later growth. I can only say that I have given a considerable portion of my life to this study, and that I cannot conceive a proposition which seems to me more utterly without foundation. Why, two most stupendous miracles,—the two multiplications of the loaves, with the conversation with the disciples in which our Lord refers to each separately, and reminds His disciples of the number of baskets of fragments taken up in each case,—are both recorded in what Dr. Abbott regards as the earliest of all the Gospels, St. Mark's, and both recorded without the smallest suggestion of any mode of explaining them as an event that might have occurred in the ordinary course of nature. The rebuke to the storm on the Lake of Galilee, and the impression produced by the sudden sinking of the wind and waves on the minds of the disciples, are also recorded by the same Evangelist, with the same brief and earnest simplicity. So is the walking on the sea. And if there be several miraculous events not recorded in St. Mark which are recorded in the other Evangelists, the explanation lies in the extreme compression of the Gospel, not in the slightest evidence that St. Mark told in germ what the other Evangelists expanded into leaf and blossom. It seems to me that the natural effect of rejecting as untrustworthy the story of the visible side of Christ's life, is to inspire a great doubt of the higher interpretation of the invisible side of that life. And that this will be the practical effect on those who accept Dr. Abbott's view of the Gospels, I feel entirely assured. It is impossible to conceive the discrediting of something like one-quarter of the story of our Lord's life, as it is now given to us, without the discrediting in an almost equal degree of the other three-quarters.

But then Dr. Abbott will tell us that the teaching of science runs directly counter to the story of miracle, and that unless we accept God's teaching humbly on the physical side, we shall not succeed in getting His teaching humbly accepted by physicists on the moral and spiritual side. I quite agree; but what I utterly dispute is that the teaching of science concerning the uniformity of nature, properly studied, goes to discredit miracle, any more than it goes to discredit the spiritual divinity of Christ. There is a direction in which the teaching of science goes to discredit both,—the direction in which it confines the attention to a class of purely physical phenomena in intimate conversance with which a habit of mind is apt to be formed far from favourable to the admission of any sort of superhuman power, either physical or spiritual. There is a direction in which the teaching of science goes to discredit neither,—the direction in which it discovers the secrets of new powers which it can neither explain nor deny, and which are totally inconsistent with the theory of an ultimate control exerted by physical agencies over the moral and spiritual agencies of the universe. Keep to the science of the intermediate links between the well-established physical phenomena of the universe, and you will contract the former habit of mind; immerse yourself in the science of controlling causes, of such phenomena as mesmerism, somnambulism, and all the strange phenomena of specially simulated and so-called clairvoyant states—what Dr. Carpenter and others have rather audaciously included under the term "mental physiology"—and you will have no reason to complain that your belief in the uniformity of natural laws seems in any degree inconsistent with that belief in the complete subservience of matter to spirit which is all that is involved in miracle.

For what is implied in miracle, as it is brought before us in the Bible, is not, of course, any caprice in nature, but a subservience of physical to spiritual agencies in exact proportion to the closeness of communion between man and God. Even Dr. Abbott appears to believe in this so far as it concerns the healing agency of faith, and Dr. Carpenter and other great physiologists go so far as to say that the power of emotion over the body is even sufficient to produce from natural, but as yet entirely hidden, causes the "stigmata" as seen, for instance, on the body of St. Francis of Assisi and many of the modern Extaticas. Well, if that be possible,—as men of great authority tell us it is,—what more would be needed than such divinity as Dr. Abbott attributes to Christ, to involve mental control over physical nature of an immeasurably higher kind,—a power rising to what we have hitherto called miracle,—a power of conveying signs of specific meaning, that is, of divine purpose intelligible to finite minds, through phenomena which usually embody only a mere fragment of an infinite purpose? Establish as you will the moral divinity of Christ, but however you establish it, your conclusion will imply the strongest possible probability that Christ must have also had a spiritual control over physical nature. Undermine as you will the belief in the spiritual control of Christ over physical nature, and your result will imply the strongest possible probability that the moral divinity of Christ, so far at least as it implies omnipotence or omnipresence, must have been a dream. Dr. Abbott apparently thinks physical miracle, though a question of fact, one of complete moral indifference to spiritual faith. I cannot agree with him. I believe that there is but one step from thinking the system of physical law so absolutely fixed by divine will that it never has been, or ought to be, "violated" as the phrase goes, to doubting whether it was a divine will at all, or anything like it, to which that rigidity of system is due. The people who believe to-day that God has made so fast the laws of His physical universe, that it is in many directions utterly impenetrable to moral and spiritual influences, will believe to-morrow that the physical universe subsists by its own inherent laws, and that God, even if He dwells within it, cannot do with it what He would; and will find out the next day, that God does not even dwell within it, but must, as M. Renan says, be "organised" by man, if we are to have a God at all.

XXIII

MR. LLEWELYN DAVIES ON CHRISTIAN MIRACLE

1888

In the new number of the *Fortnightly*, Mr. Llewelyn Davies has written a thoughtful and impressive article to explain what he holds to be the true avenue to Christian faith as it was understood by Christ Himself, though he has laid himself open to various misunderstandings by saying at the very opening of it, what is certain to mislead many readers as to its true drift :—" I believe that it will be entirely to the advantage of Christianity that we should dismiss the idea of 'the miraculous' from our contentions and our thoughts. The claim made in the name of miracles has had a pestilent effect upon the Christian cause." From this it will be inferred by those who do not carefully study the latter part of Mr. Llewelyn Davies's article, that he thinks that the highest kind of belief in Christ can exist without belief in the Christian miracles, and I am quite sure that no more mistaken inference could be drawn. Mr. Llewelyn Davies only wants to express strongly his belief that Christ discouraged, and even severely condemned those who were drawn to Him not by the spiritual spell of His own character, but by the wonder and awe with which they were impressed by His superhuman cures, or by His control of winds and waves,—to emphasise his deep conviction that the one great miracle in which all Christians are bound to believe first, and which if they believe, they will have but little difficulty in believing any other, is the stupendous miracle that Christ was given authority to declare to man the nature and character of the Eternal Power to which we owe our existence, and especially the will of that Power to forgive us our sins, and to renew us with a spirit which will reconcile us to Himself. Mr. Davies asserts that it was not Christ's plan "to announce Himself as a supernatural being, and to perform miracles as His credentials; on the contrary, He was deeply displeased by the demand for miracles, and repelled the support which men were willing to give to a miracle-worker. But from the beginning to the end He assumed authority as having come from the Father; He taught, and gave commands, and organised His followers, and made plans for the future as one having authority. The adherents He desired, and whom alone He expected to win, were those who were childlike and ready to believe in a heavenly Father. To these He offered pardon, guidance, grace, and help of all kinds. The Galileans He selected and appointed as His envoys were simple, truthful men who believed in Him because they could not doubt His assurance. And when these envoys went forth after His death to proclaim Him as Lord, they still made the same remarkable offer,—that of forgiveness and reconciliation to the Father. He was exalted, they said, to give repentance to Israel and remission of sins. The word committed to them was: 'God forgives mankind,—be ye reconciled to God.'

And St. Paul, the chief founder of the Church, was accustomed to protest that he stood on the self-commending power of this message, which was as light to those of his hearers who had eyes to see." In other words, Mr. Llewelyn Davies, so far from dismissing "the idea of 'the miraculous' from our contentions and our thoughts," as one which has had "a pestilent effect on the Christian cause," begins from the true miracle, the supernatural in Christ Himself, and His authority to declare the very mind of the Eternal. "If we are to believe," as he puts it in a subsequent page, "that the man Jesus of Nazareth had a special commission to reveal the heavenly Father, we are admitting what every agnostic would repudiate as a stupendous miracle; and I cannot imagine that if an agnostic were persuaded to believe this, he would obstinately stumble at smaller miracles as incredible." Very true. Then why does Mr. Llewelyn Davies give room for misunderstanding by professing to wish "to dismiss the idea of 'the miraculous' from our contentions and our thoughts," when what he is really aiming at is to get men to see that it is easier to leap at once to the belief in the supernatural life of Christ, that is, in the greatest of all miracles, the miracle which assumes the moulding power of the spiritual over the natural, and the revealing power of the natural, when so moulded, than to begin by believing in one or two astounding interferences with the natural order, and to build up on this, inductively, a belief that Christ must have derived this power to interfere with the natural order from his command of supernatural resources? What Mr. Llewelyn Davies really maintains is that we must be prepared by the spiritual power working in our own minds to accept the divine authority of Christ, before we pass any judgment on His physical miracles, and that it will be easier to believe His physical miracles because we believe in His divine nature, than it ever could be to believe in His divine nature because we are convinced that He effected astounding changes in the order of Nature. I heartily accept his position as a whole that,—man being what he is,—faith in the spiritually supernatural justifies belief in the physically supernatural, much more effectually and permanently, than any amount of astonishment at the physically supernatural is ever likely to justify faith in the spiritually supernatural. I believe, with Mr. Llewelyn Davies, that this was, on the whole, our Lord's own teaching, and that we should be rash and presumptuous in attempting to exchange His doctrine for what looks like,— though it is not,—a humbler and more inductive process. But though I accept Mr. Llewelyn Davies's position as a whole, and think it a matter of no little importance that this method should be followed, I cannot at all agree in Mr. Llewelyn Davies's strong assertion that "it was not His [Christ's] plan to announce Himself as a supernatural being, and to perform miracles as His credentials." That is precisely what He did, though He did it only as verifying by actions of infinitely less moment than those which warranted the great faith He demanded, the conviction that there was that in Him which did not merely impose on the imagination of His disciples, but which wielded real forces, and forces quite outside the region where illusion was easy. When He said to the paralytic, "Thy sins be forgiven thee," and the standers-by asked who it was that assumed a power to forgive sins, He added,—"But that ye may know that the Son of Man hath power on earth to forgive sins, Arise, take up thy bed, and go unto thine house." This is surely exactly what Mr. Llewelyn Davies denies, a claim to supernatural power of the highest order; and then, in order to prevent men from thinking that the power to which they had surrendered themselves could be founded on mere illusions of the imagination, He gave evidence that He could thrill the body,—a much less wonder, and yet one less liable to imaginative misapprehension,— with the same health-giving power with which He claimed that He could thrill the soul. And it is just the same when John the Baptist sends his disciples to ask if Jesus were "He that should come," or whether they were to look beyond Him, and our Lord replies,—"Go, and show John again those things which ye do hear and see; the blind receive their sight, and the lame walk, the lepers are cleansed, and the deaf hear, the dead are raised up, and the poor have the gospel preached to them; and blessed is he whosoever shall not be offended in Me." How could Christ have said more plainly,—'Yes; I claim to be the true and ultimate object of your hopes and expectations, and though I can only appeal to your spirits to prove that great claim, I can give you these further evidences that I am not bewildering your imaginations, for I will do in the physical world what I claim to do in the spiritual world,—fill you with new life?' Christ's rebuke to the mere craving for signs seems to me to be directed not to the very natural and human self-distrust which was expressed by the two disciples in the walk to Emmaus when they confessed that the crucifixion had shaken their hope that Christ was He who should fulfil the desire of Israel, but to the state of mind which had no disposition to believe in the spiritual origin of the natural, unless that disposition could be engendered by the contemplation of a number of preternatural occurrences which they would not be able to account for except by some sort of omnipotent interference. Even the passage which Mr. Llewelyn Davies refers to, when our Lord says, "Except ye see signs and wonders, ye will not believe," appears to show this. For when the nobleman answers simply, "Sir, come down ere my child die," Christ accords to the implicit belief in Him so expressed what He would not have accorded to the mere craving for a sign, and yet makes it a sign as well, as is shown by the exact accordance of the hour of the crisis in the disease with the hour of Christ's assurance, "Thy son liveth." There was here, therefore, a distinct purpose to let the sign produce its effect on a mind which had already felt the attraction of our Lord's goodness. It was only to those who, while they asked for signs from Him, were apt to ascribe them, when they saw them, to evil powers, that Christ sternly refused to show any sign. To those who could understand, and trust in, the physical "signs of the times," but who could not understand or trust in the spiritual signs of the times, He refused to exhibit His divine power. But to those whose hearts were stirred deeply by His influence, but who hardly knew whether they ought to trust the deeper impulses within them or not, He seems to me to have been most willing and anxious to prove that it was no illusion of the imagination to which they were giving way. "The wicked and adulterous generation" which sought after a sign, and to which no sign was to be given but the sign of the prophet Jonah, were not those who were yearning to believe in Christ, but who, like the Apostles themselves, found their faith oozing out with every discouragement. He denounced those who yearned for prodigies only, and even when they had prodigies, saw no spiritual meaning in them, but rather an unspiritual meaning. But even St. Paul insisted that if the great sign of the Resurrection were untrustworthy, the whole Gospel which he had declared was a dream.

I cannot but regret that Mr. Llewelyn Davies has put his protest against the old and unspiritual use of miracles to force belief on sceptical hearts and consciences, with what appears to me more energy than discrimination. For while I heartily agree with his main drift, I am quite sure that the physical miracles of the New Testament add a majesty of their own to the whole effect of the great spiritual miracle in which Mr. Llewelyn Davies very justly demands our faith, and are not, as it has lately been the custom to represent them, a mere dead weight on the spiritual grandeur of the Gospel, rendering it more difficult to believe than it would have been without them. Yet there are passages in this interesting and powerful article which, if taken alone, would certainly convey this false impression, though I do not think that Mr. Llewelyn Davies in the least intended to convey it.

XXIV

CARDINAL NEWMAN ON INSPIRATION

1884

CARDINAL NEWMAN, in the very interesting paper which opens the February number of the *Nineteenth Century*, has carefully defined what Roman Catholics mean by the inspiration of Scripture, so far as an individual Roman Catholic can define what the Church to which he belongs has not yet fully drawn out. He only glances at the difficulties to which Protestants are liable, when they accept a divine revelation on the one hand, but deny, on the other hand, that there is any sure and unerring external guide in the discrimination of what the limits and scope of that revelation really are, for his subject is not in any degree controversial, but solely expository of the obligations to which, as he understands, every one who joins the Roman Catholic Church subjects himself. But he does glance at the difficulties of our side of the case, and it is worth while to recall what these are before dealing with those which appear to me to attach to the hypothesis of an infallible Church. The difficulty of accepting as divine, a revelation of which the books of Scripture contain the history, but a history which may be understood in one way by one interpreter and in another way by another interpreter, and a considerable portion of which may be rejected on external or internal evidence as inaccurate by a third interpreter, is obvious enough. As the Cardinal justly enough says, nothing is more difficult than to combine the belief in a divine superintendence of the whole history with the admission that its record is contained in miscellaneous fragments by all sorts of different persons, some of whom tell you that they have constructed their narrative out of previous documents of which they say nothing more, and do not tell you that they have been divinely guided in their selection; while others are given with either wrong notes of authorship, or, at least, notes of an authorship so difficult to reconcile with the known facts, that the most orthodox scholars profess their belief that the authorship assigned is mistaken. It is no easy matter, I say, to combine a profound belief in a communication by God of matters the most important that can be imagined to the soul of man, with the recognition of this fragmentary and apparently almost accidental record. Cardinal Newman, for instance, lays it down as more than probable that the original Scriptures of the Jews suffered much loss and injury during the captivity and under the persecution of Antiochus, so that even of the divinely inspired record some portion has been permitted by Providence to be lost. It is clear, then, that this divine treasure is preserved to us in earthen vessels, which are liable to be broken and the contents spilled. If this be so, what is to prevent these documents from being regarded even by believers in the Revelation, as other works of literature are regarded,—as something quite unfixed, to which one man may assign one drift and another another, so that even of the believers in Revelation no two shall entirely agree as to what that revelation really is? Cardinal Newman argues that,— "Surely, if the revelations and lessons in Scripture are addressed to us personally and practically, the presence among us of a formal judge and standing expositor of its words is imperative. It is antecedently unreasonable to suppose that a book so complex, so unsystematic, in parts so obscure, the outcome of so many minds, times, and places, should be given us from above without the safeguard of some authority; as if it could possibly from the nature of the case interpret itself. Its inspiration does but guarantee its truth, not its interpretation. How are private readers positively to distinguish what is didactic and what is historical, what is fact and what is vision, what is allegorical and what is literal, what is idiomatic and what is grammatical, what is enunciated formally and what occurs *obiter*, what is only temporary and what is of lasting obligation? Such is our natural anticipation, and it is only too exactly justified in the events of the last three centuries, in the many countries where private judgment on the text of Scripture has prevailed. The gift of inspiration requires as its complement the gift of infallibility." Of course, that does state a great difficulty. Protestants and Anglicans alike admit that as a matter of fact, men who are equally impressed with the belief that God exists, and has revealed Himself in the story of the Hebrew people, differ in the most startling way, where they accept no final human authority on the subject, as to what the burden and drift of that revelation is. Some reject one book of Scripture, and some another; some one doctrine which appears to be assumed in Scripture, and some another; some believe our Lord to be God, and some a mere human being with supernatural endowments; some believe Him a human being without supernatural endowments; some reject the Old Testament miracles, and some reject all miracles; and very many reject a large proportion of the history with which these miracles are interwoven, and there is no authority amongst us who can say, 'There you are wrong; you are rejecting revelation itself; you have no right to be called a believer in divine revelation, and ought to associate with those who reject it.' This is all quite true, and no honest Protestant or Anglican will deny the fact that this is strange and mysterious, and does threaten the very existence of the Christian Church as an institution formed to spread the knowledge of God.

But now look at the difficulties on the other side, which seem to me to be still more, I might truly say *far* more, overwhelming. What has the Roman Catholic believer to hold? He has to hold that though the Church is infallible, it has to gather its first evidences of what Revelation means from the testimony of those fallible Christians whom it calls "the Fathers." "Though the Fathers were not inspired," says Cardinal Newman, "yet their united testimony is of supreme authority." Well, but what does united testimony mean? The Cardinal has himself told us, in another place, that on the question of baptism some of the weightiest Fathers of the Church took for generations together the wrong side, the side that Rome afterwards adjudged to be erroneous, and contrary to Revelation. So that the first duty of the infallible Church, in deciding on what is and what is not Revelation, is to go over the evidence of a number of fallible witnesses, some of the weightiest of whom may be wholly in the wrong. In the next place, the Church has decided that writers are inspired who, if inspired, have been inspired to suggest to all ordinary judgments that they are *not* inspired,—surely a very difficult conception, which almost presents to us the inspiring spirit as directly tempting us to doubt. "Ecclesiasticus" is one of the inspired books of Scripture, according to the Roman Catholic Canon. But Cardinal Newman himself quotes the author of Ecclesiasticus as entreating his readers to "come with benevolence" to his work, and "to make excuse for coming short in the composition of words." "Surely," says Cardinal Newman, "if at the very time he wrote he had known it, he would, like other inspired men, have said, 'thus saith the Lord,' or what was equivalent to it." That seems to me unanswerable. And yet the Roman Church is bound to hold that the author of Ecclesiasticus was, because really inspired, inspired to suggest to those who should read him, doubts of his own inspiration. Again;—the Church has never decided that the accuracy of all the smaller items of fact, such as what concern the dog of Tobias, or the cloak of St. Paul, or the wine recommended to Timothy, is guaranteed, and some of the best Roman Catholic authorities, though they will not justify the suspicion of error even in such minute facts, do not incline to condemn all who regard these minutiæ as purely human enclaves in an inspired book. But what can better represent the difficulty of the position than that after insisting on the inspiration of Scripture as regards all matters of fact which touch faith and doctrine, the Church should admit that Scripture may err on smaller matters of fact which may or may not involve either? For the difficulty of this position is that it must be extended even to chronological order,—which may very well involve faith and doctrine. Cardinal Newman admits that the order of events in St. Matthew's Gospel is not generally regarded by Catholic critics as the true order; in fact, they suppose that St. Matthew, though inspired, paid little attention to the order of the events which he narrated, and often massed them in groups which would mislead us as to the chronology. Surely that is a very great concession, indeed, as regards the difficulty of maintaining the inspiration of the *book* in any sense, as distinguished from the inspiration of the author; yet Cardinal Newman admits that the Church has ruled that the books, no less than the authors, are in some sense inspired.

On the whole, is there not far less difficulty in assuming that God, in revealing Himself to fallible beings, has left us with no human guide better than our own consciences, our own judgments, our own collective efforts, as they are overruled by Him, in all sincere efforts to reach His truth and to find out what He has and what He has not revealed, and that gradually He will overrule those efforts so as to enable us to attain a sufficient clearness and certainty for all purposes of duty and trust,—than in assuming that there is a human power which has final authority in these matters, but which has so exerted that authority as to rule that the most glaring apparent contradictions have been separately inspired? For, on this assumption, it must be the very first principle of a true interpretation of Scripture to lay down that divine inspiration may intentionally put the most serious difficulties in the way of unsophisticated minds, otherwise eager and anxious to submit themselves to its guidance.

XXV

LOSS AND GAIN IN RECENT THEOLOGY

1881

Dr. Martineau, whose genius has done more to mould the religious philosophy of the present day, especially in its conflict with empiricism and materialism, than that of any other thinker of our time, has just delivered an address to the students of Manchester New College, in which he estimates, from his own point of view, the "Loss and Gain" in recent Theological developments. His title reminds me of a very different book, Cardinal Newman's estimate of the "Loss and Gain" which the hero of his remarkable tale had to balance when he left the English Church for that of Rome. Dr. Martineau, of course, in a very brief address, cannot go over the ground which his own mind must have travelled with anything like the elaboration of Dr. Newman, and only touches the heads of the great subject with which he deals. But it is obvious that the two estimates of "Loss and Gain" made by these two very different men of genius are nearly opposite; that nearly everything which Dr. Martineau regards as gain, Dr. Newman would have regarded as loss, and that nearly everything that Dr. Newman regarded as gain, Dr. Martineau would have regarded as loss. It is curious enough to contrast the general conclusions of the two men. "Englishmen," said Dr. Newman, through the mouth of one of his characters more than thirty years ago, when near his summing-up of the loss and gain of conversion, "have many gifts; faith they have not. Other nations inferior to them in many things still have faith. Nothing will stand in place of it; not a sense of the beauty of Catholicism, or of its usefulness, or of its antiquity; not an appreciation of the sympathy which it shows towards sinners; not an admiration of the martyrs and early Fathers and a delight in their writings. Individuals may display a trusting gentleness or a conscientiousness which demands our reverence; still, till they have faith, they have not the foundation, and their superstructure will fall. They will not be blessed, they will do nothing in religious matters till they begin by an act of unreserved faith in the word of God, whatever it be,—till they go out of themselves; till they cease to make something within them their standard, till they oblige their will to perfect what reason leaves sufficient indeed, but incomplete. And when they shall recognise this defect in themselves and try to remedy it, then they will recognise much more; they will be on the road very shortly to be Catholics." That, of course, is the form in which the case against the tendencies visible in recent theology would be presented by a Roman Catholic, but the Romanising element in it is not that with which I have any concern. Of course, Dr. Newman regarded the Catholic Church as the representative on earth of God's revealed will, but the argument I have quoted was not an argument for trusting that or any other

Church, but for trusting God's revelation as something higher and worthier than man's own sense of fitness, for fixing the mind on something outside men, and ceasing to make "something within them their standard." Dr. Martineau's estimate of loss and gain in recent theology is a computation conducted on the most opposite principle conceivable as to what is loss and what gain. He congratulates his former pupils on "the disappearance from our branch of the Reformed Churches, of all *external authority* in matters of religion,"—and what he means by external authority, he tells us clearly enough. He goes so far, indeed, as expressly to condemn the attempt "to extract a proof of eternal life from the records of Christ's resurrection," which he speaks of as one of a class of mistakes justifying a feeling of moral "humiliation." And he explains himself further as follows:—

"The Catholic prediction, so often made when Luther threw off the restraints of ecclesiastical Tradition, has at last come true; and the yoke of the Bible follows the yoke of the Church. The phrases which we have heard repeated with enthusiasm,—that 'the Bible and the Bible only is the religion of Protestants,' that 'Scripture is the rule of faith and practice,'—are, indeed, full of historical interest, but for minds at once sincere and exact, have lost their magic power. I need not remind you how innocently, and how inevitably, this has come about: how completely the conception of a *Canonical* literature that shall for ever serve as a divine statute-book, belongs to a stage of culture that has passed away; how widely discrepant are the types of doctrine and the conceptions of morals and the recitals of fact, in different parts of this supposed uniform manual; and how, if you disown these human inequalities and insist on artificially filling up its valleys and levelling its hills, you destroy a region glorious in beauty, and doom its running waters to stagnate in unwholesome fens. It is simply *a fact* that *dictated* faith and duty are no longer possible, and that, by way of textual oracle, you can carry to the soul no vision of God, no contrition for sin, no sigh for righteousness. The time is past when a doctrine could save itself from criticism by taking refuge under an apostle's word, or a futurity authenticate itself by a prophet's forecast, or a habit become obligatory by evangelical example. To our function, as witnesses for divine things, this seems at first a disastrous change, little short of a loss of both the credentials and the instructions which legitimate our message. We naturally think how easy was the preacher's task when he had only to exhibit the sacred seal, and make clear the sentences it covered, and the reason of men would accept them as truth and the will would bow before them; when doubts of Providence fled from the sufferer at the mere sound of the words, 'The hairs of your head are all numbered'; and the shadows of death vanished before the voice, 'This mortal must put on immortality'; and the guilty conscience shuddered to hear, 'There shall in nowise enter therein anything that is unclean, or that maketh abomination and a lie.' In our moments of weakness, when we cry, 'Ah, Lord God, behold I cannot speak, for I am a child!' we may long for some infallible support which may bear our burden, and relieve the strain of thought and love. But it is just in order to bear this burden, to sift out the eternally true and good from transient and tempting semblances, and make the divine light glow amid human things, that we have girded up our wills and set apart our lives for spiritual service. And if there were a book-theology ever so perfect, the verbal quintessence of all transcendent truth, the more we spared our own souls and depended upon it, the less should we pierce to the seats of conviction, and rekindle sight for the blind. Religion is not the truth of any stereotyped propositions, but the highest life of the moving spirit, nor can it be conveyed from mind to mind, except by the vibration of harmonic chords."

So that the very tendency which Dr. Newman, when he left the Anglican Church, selected for special condemnation,—the tendency, I mean, to lean on a purely human and subjective standard of truth, Dr. Martineau selects, thirty-three years later, as a matter for special satisfaction,—and, if so, no doubt one in respect of which the modern Unitarians are justly entitled to very special congratulation.

How are we to explain this absolute and violent contradiction between two men of high religious genius, each of whom has done much to fortify the religious spirit of the age against the materialism of the day, in Churches far removed from the sphere of their own special influence? Or shall we infer that one at least of the two was entering on a wholly false and misleading track? No doubt, the one had entered definitively on the track which led to a recognition of an infallible authority for the definition of divine truth, while the other has long ago chosen that track which leads to an ideal and religious rationalism indeed, but still to pure rationalism,—in other words, the recognition of the human conscience and reason as the final and only index of the law and reason of God. But what I want to consider is this, whether either of them is, so far as I can judge, wholly wrong or wholly right. And the answer I should give is this,—that while Dr. Newman and the Catholics go much,—I might almost say demonstrably,—too far in assuming for those elements of revelation which stretch beyond the verge of our utmost "verifying faculties," whether of reason or conscience, the same degree and kind of authority which belongs to those elements reflected and echoed in our own minds, Dr. Martineau goes quite as much too far in congratulating himself and his brethren on their having thrown off the yoke of external authority altogether, and having learnt to limit revelation by the area of the strictly natural religion in their own hearts and minds, and to deny it all extension and all authority beyond that which those hearts and minds can give. I will explain my meaning rather more at length.

The Catholic Church, as it seems to me, accustoms her children to look habitually for a degree of certainty in relation to the most incidental and, as I may say, arbitrary regions of religious speculation, which is not really to be got, if only for this reason, —that if you lay down your dogmas in these matters so absolutely, they react on you so as to suggest doubt as to the authority of the organisation which speaks so confidently and precisely on questions on which our reason and conscience do not speak confidently at all. For instance, in the very conversation from which I have quoted, Dr. Newman makes his Roman priest say, " I understand what a Catholic means by going by the voice of the Church; it means practically, by the voice of the first priest he meets. Every priest is the voice of the Church." Now, that view is, I think, a very natural consequence of the excessive importance attached by the Catholic Church to external authority. But the effect of it is that the Church in all ages has spoken through priests what in the next age it had to correct as false. In one of the earliest centuries, numberless priests of high authority maintained that no layman, still less a heathen, could baptize effectually; and yet soon that opinion was formally condemned. In century after century, up to our own time, priests of the highest authority have preached, with the most earnest belief in their own absolute authority to declare divine truth, and have even published to the world "consensu superiorum," doctrines of hell which are now declared by equally high authorities to be quite unauthorised by the Church, and which it is at least not impossible that within our own time the Pope may *ex cathedra* condemn. No wonder, then, that Protestants distrust a Church which has so accustomed her children to rely on infallible external tests of truth, that the very organs of the Church preach century after century, without in the least doubting their own right to do so, dogmas which the Church herself, on reflection, finds herself compelled to modify, to soften, to limit, in reality and substantially, to retract and deny. Full of the sense of her own infallibility, the Roman Church thinks that on all points of theology she ought to have a clear judgment, and the consequence is that her priests have often declared as truths of revelation what were not even decisions of the Church, but only their own private opinions, moulded in the atmosphere of a particular country and particular age. This results, in my opinion, from relying too much on the Church's power of understanding and interpreting those aspects of revelation which range far beyond the scope of the reason and moral apprehension of man.

On the other hand, I cannot in the least enter into Dr. Martineau's position that there is, and can be, nothing in revelation worthy of our reverence and acceptance which does not demonstrate itself to our moral and religious intuitions,—in other words, that natural and revealed religion must in effect mean the same thing, since a truth once revealed to the reason and conscience becomes virtually a truth of natural religion, while a truth not so revealed cannot be, to the man whose moral or intellectual faculties have not grasped it as truth, a truth at all. What I should say is this,—that all who believe in God at all as a Being whose ways are not as our ways, nor His thoughts as our thoughts, ought to expect to find, in His revelations to us, first, that which we can discern to be absolutely true; next, that which we can discern to be full of difficulty, but still, on the whole, impressing us as coming from above, and not from beneath us; and lastly, that which we could not discern to be true at all, did it not come in close connection with truths which encompass and overwhelm us, and from that close connection derive an authority of its own, to which it is only right to accord a definite share of influence on the conduct of our lives. I do not think that the authority of these different classes of truths can ever be identical, for this simple reason,—that the moment we get out of our depth in the world of truth, that moment we are in danger of defining wrongly, if we define too much at all,—are in danger, in fact, of undermining the very evidence on which we accept all divine truth, if we insist on translating into our definite human dialect the mysteries of God. That revelation which reason and conscience clearly understand and accept, is necessarily of the highest possible authority, because we know exactly what it is, where it begins and where it ends. That which reason and conscience only recognise as coming from above, though lying, more or less, beyond our grasp, is of less authority, so far, and only so far, as there are a great many different ways of interpreting its significance, and the character of its divine origin. That which derives its authority solely from its close association with what really controls and rules us, has necessarily an authority of a vaguer and less definite kind. But it is to me almost unintelligible how a theologian who believes as strongly as Dr. Martineau in a self-revealing God, should seem to identify all authority in religion with that which has fully and finally incorporated itself with human nature, so that it involves a direct disloyalty to reason and conscience to doubt of it at all. This seems to me just as unreasonable as for a child to take nothing on its father's authority, except what that father can demonstrate to the undeveloped reason and conscience of its tender age. When, for instance, Dr. Martineau writes as follows, he seems to me to take for granted at one and the same time, first, that Christ was so immeasurably our moral and spiritual superior as to be able to regenerate our nature; and next, that we are so immeasurably His intellectual superiors, that we can disentangle all His illusions from His truths, can see through His dream of supernatural power, and strip Him of all the disguises in which partly His own and partly his disciples' imagination dressed Him :—

"Take the measure of another great change which, though gradual and timid in its advance, has for us reached its completion within our own memory, the disappearance from our faith of the entire *Messianic mythology*. I speak not merely of the lost 'argument from prophecy,' now melted away by better understanding of the Hebrew writings, or of the interior relation, under any aspect, of the Old Testament and the New, but of the total discharge from our religious conceptions of that central Jewish dream which was always asking, '*Art thou He that should come, or look we for another?*' and of all its stage, its drama, and its scenery. It no longer satisfies us to say that Jesus realised the divine promise in a sense far transcending the national preconception, and revealed at last the real meaning of the Spirit which spake in Isaiah. Such forced conforming of the Jewish ideal to the Christian facts, by glorifying the one and theorising on the other, was inevitable to the first disciples, and could not but colour all that they remembered and thought and wrote; and the imagination of Christendom, working with undiscriminating faith on these mixed materials, has drawn upon its walls a series of sacred pictures, from which art has loved to reproduce whatever is tender and sublime, and which have broken silence in the *Divina Commedia*, in the *Paradise Lost* and *Regained*, in plaintive Passion Music, and the kindling popular hymn. All this is of intense interest to us as literature, as art, as the past product of devout genius; nor will I too rigorously question those elements of it which fairly admit of symbolic use in setting forth the truths we really mean and the affections we deeply feel. But, as objective reality, as a faithful representation of our invisible and ideal universe, it is gone from us; gone therefore from our interior religion, and become an outside mythology. From the person of Jesus, for instance, everything *official*, attached to him by evangelists or divines, has fallen away: when they put such false robe upon him, they were but leading him to death. The pomp of royal lineage and fulfilled prediction, the prerogatives of King, of Priest, of Judge, the Advent with retinue of angels on the clouds of heaven, are to us mere deforming investitures, misplaced like court-dresses on 'the spirits of the just'; and he is simply the Divine flower of humanity, blossoming after ages of spiritual growth,—the realised possibility of life in God. And if he is *this*, he has no consciously exceptional part to play, but only to *be* what he is, to follow the momentary love, to do and say what the hour may bring, to be quiet under the sorrows which pity and purity incur, and die away in the prayer of inextinguishable trust. And, to see him thus, we go to his native fields and the village homes of Galilee, and the roads of Samaria, and the streets and courts of Jerusalem, where the griefs and wrongs of his time bruised him and brought out the sublime fragrance of his spirit. All that has been added to that real historic scene,—the angels that hang around his birth, and the fiend that tempts his youth; the dignities that await his future,—the throne, the trumpet, the great assize, the bar of judgment; with all the apocalyptic splendours and terrors that ensue, Hades and the Crystal sea, Paradise and the Infernal gulf; nay, the very boundary walls of the kosmic panorama that contains these things,—have for us utterly melted away, and left us amid the infinite space and silent stars."

If all this Messianic side of Christ is mythology, where is His truth? M. Havet is far more reasonable from this point of view than Dr. Martineau. He strips off all that Dr. Martineau strips off; but then, after doing so, he does not hesitate to speak frankly of the narrow and ignorant Judaism which he finds beneath. Those who see what Dr. Martineau sees in Christ are surely marvellously rash in assuming that no true supernatural power over nature, and no true vision of the eternal past from which, in our Lord's own belief, He issued, and of the eternal future into which He passed, was combined with that marvellous spiritual might. It seems to me one of the most wonderful characteristics of religious rationalism, that while it finds what it truly finds in our Lord's history, it is so much offended as it is at finding other tokens of divine life and power, and other visions of truth which are not accorded to ordinary men. To pare away revelation to the dimensions of natural religion, seems to me to imply something like a latent doubt that it is revelation, — *i.e.* truth revealed to us by one above us all,—and not rather the spontaneous divination of the human mind, opening by its own intrinsic energies to a sudden augury of its origin and destinies.

XXVI

DR. MARTINEAU ON SPIRITUAL AUTHORITY

1890

Dr. Martineau's new book on *The Seat of Authority in Religion*, published by Longmans, is not one that it is easy to read and master in a few days, or even in a few weeks. It has compressed into it the laborious studies of a long lifetime, all skilfully marshalled with the sharply outlined and masculine vividness, and the imperious confidence of a historical judgment singularly decisive, singularly keen, and, I should add, singularly and quite unreasonably sceptical. Indeed, nothing is more remarkable than the contrast between the vividly sceptical bias of Dr. Martineau's historical judgment and the still more vivid devoutness of his spiritual nature. In the region of conscience, there is no more truly religious writer in England, and certainly none at once so powerful and so devotional. In the region of historical criticism, there is hardly any with so iconoclastic a bias towards pulling to pieces all that the religious sentiment of mankind has slowly built up. The scorn with which Dr. Martineau treats the beliefs of all the Christian ages is, I suspect, expressed with a force that he himself has no power to realise.

It has never occurred to him, I should think, that the same spirit which inspired the spiritual and moral revelation of which he thinks so highly, may have guided with as much providential care the impression produced on the mind of the universal Church by which that revelation was received. Is it not a very arbitrary treatment of history, to insulate the divine revelation as Dr. Martineau supposes it to have been given through Jesus Christ, and to ignore entirely, as if it were quite irrelevant and without any bearing on the divine meaning and purpose of that revelation, the impression produced by it on the minds of generation after generation, as if that were really no essential part of the phenomena of Christianity? To me it seems an essential part of the supernatural course of the Christian religion that the theology of St. Paul took so profound a hold of the Church, and that the theology of St. Paul was so soon developed into the theology of St. John. It is about as strange a feat for a thinker of Dr. Martineau's force and rank to treat all these fresh and natural testimonies to the character of Christ's nature and teaching in the Church, as if they were mere refractions and exaggerations of human loyalty to an exceptionally pure human being,—a mere nimbus, as Dr. Martineau calls them, encircling his head in their imagination,—as it would be for an astronomer to treat the corona and the red prominences of the sun as if they were mere subjective phenomena that had no interest except as throwing light upon the mind of the observer. I can understand such a contention on the part of those who do not believe in Jesus Christ as a special revelation of God at all; but for those who, like Dr. Martineau, do so believe, to treat the steady development of the mind of the Church concerning Him as a mere growth of human error that bears no likeness at all to the divine significance of the real figure concerning whom all this halo of illusion (as Dr. Martineau holds it) sprang up, is like giving an explanation of the rainbow which dispenses with the sun. The real difference between Dr. Martineau's conception of spiritual authority in these matters and my own, is this, that Dr. Martineau attributes to God's revelation only the very few residual phenomena of Christ's life which his destructive and very arbitrary analysis leaves us after it has done its fatal work; while I attribute to it not only the great majority of the facts of our Lord's life as recorded in the Gospels, but the great majority of the impressions produced upon the minds of His disciples and followers as they grew and shaped the traditions of the apostles and the disciples who constituted the Church of the primitive age. Dr. Martineau regards the divine revelation as limited to the life of Him who first removed the veil. I regard it as extending to the minds and lives of those from whose eyes the veil was removed, and as shaping the growth of their faith and love. Nor can I conceive an authority limited as Dr. Martineau would seem inclined to limit it. He brings us to a great tree, tears away its leaves, hews down its branches, strips off its bark, and then tells us to regard the naked and fatally injured wreck as the true life of the whole. I say that we must look for the life of the whole in the collective phenomena; not only those of Christ's life (though I regard Dr. Martineau's analysis of that life as one of the most wonderful achievements of destructive criticism with which, from a man of great genius, and,—in a sense too,—of great religious genius, I ever met), but also in the life of the community chiefly affected by it, in the faith in which it flowered, in the actions in which it bore fruit, in the devotions which it generated, in the institutions to which it gave birth,—in a word, in the whole results which it evolved, though not in any thing which can be shown by reasonable criticism to be a mere excrescence on, or a parasitic growth upon, that life. It seems to me that Dr. Martineau's conception of authority, as limited to the conscience alone, is infinitely too narrow. The conscience, no doubt, is the centre of authority over the life of man. But the conscience lays hold, by all sorts of delicate filaments, of the tastes, of the imagination, of the affections, of the social system; and in all these its manifestations, the divine inspiration appears to me as real a shaping power while it moulds the confessions and attitudes of the whole society towards Christ, as it is even when it first manifests itself through Christ Himself. It would be as easy for a child to pick out everything in the conduct of its parents that it might safely disregard, and so to lay bare the only justification for true filial reverence, as for a critic to discharge historical Christianity, as Dr. Martineau does, of nine-tenths of its actual contents, and to fix upon the one-tenth which is supposed to give all its vitality to the remainder. He seems to forget that the same "authority" which appealed to the conscience of man through Christ, spoke no less in the gradual development of the Christian worship and the gradual growth of the confessions of the Christian creed. I can hardly understand how a thinker so great as Dr. Martineau was capable of writing down, for instance, such a canon of criticism as the following, which he calls "the rule for separating the divine from the human in the origin of our religion":—"The former will be found, if anywhere, in what Jesus of Nazareth *himself was*, in spiritual character and moral relation to God. The latter will be found in what *was thought about* his person, functions, and office. It was the Providence of history that gave us *him:* it was the men of history that dressed up the theory of him: and till we compel the latter to stand aside, and let us through to look upon his living face, we can never seize the permanent essence of the gift." That is a canon conceived just as if God did not kindle the faith, as truly as present the object of faith. There is no real antithesis corresponding to Dr. Martineau's. No doubt we must look, as earnestly as we may, at the living face, but does it appear a likely mode of doing so, to prepossess ourselves, as Dr. Martineau does, with the strongest possible prejudice against the legacy left us in the life and teaching and traditions of those who were the earliest gazers on the living face? And if looking at the living face means, as it means in Dr. Martineau's book, looking at a Christ who never once predicted His death and resurrection, though it is admitted that He must have had sad forebodings of the former, who never claimed to be the Messiah at all, but only imposed a stern veto on Peter's disposition so to proclaim Him, instead of solemnly pronouncing Him blessed in having received God's own revelation of the truth, who, in fact, claimed nothing further than to continue John the Baptist's message of an *approaching* kingdom of God of which He Himself was not to be the central figure, who never worked a miracle, and after His death on the Cross, never communicated to His disciples anything but a spiritual impression of His resurrection, who had no sort of connection with the mythical Christ, as Dr. Martineau regards Him, of the Fourth Gospel, —a figure, according to Dr. Martineau, first conceived in the middle of the second century,—and, in a word, who can be safely credited only with such acts and words "as plainly transcend the moral level of the narrators,"—if this is what "looking at the living face" is to signify, I would just as soon look at the living face in a dark room, and fancy myself after doing so vastly more familiar with its features than those who had only studied them in a well-lighted mirror.

As a specimen of Dr. Martineau's scepticism, I may take his reasons for believing that Christ only professed to repeat and continue the message of John the Baptist, an assumption contradicted by every Gospel we have, and of which Dr. Martineau persuades himself on the slenderest conjectural evidence which it is possible to imagine. This evidence is derived from the statement in the Acts of the Apostles that upwards of twenty years after the Crucifixion, a body of disciples was found at Ephesus under the teaching of Apollos, who had "taught carefully the things concerning Jesus, knowing only the baptism of John." This Dr. Martineau interprets as meaning that "for *neither* prophet did the Baptist's sect assert a higher claim than that of *herald* of the kingdom, but regarded both as warning messengers to prepare the world for meeting its Judge." That is a fair conjecture, though it is little more, and the fact might be susceptible probably of twenty different explanations, if we had fuller knowledge of the history ; but how does it show that the Baptist sect which held this, if they did hold it, knew anything adequate of the teaching of the disciples of Christ? We know, if we know anything, that John the Baptist, before his own death, either for his own sake or for that of his disciples, sent messengers from his prison to elicit from Christ what His own claim was; and it is easy to suppose that disciples who had been separated from John the Baptist by his imprisonment, and who had afterwards migrated to Ephesus, would have gone on teaching that, as Jesus had accepted John's baptism, He was merely one of the greatest of his followers, and had never even claimed to be the Messiah. Yet Dr. Martineau builds upon it the astounding inference that all the express assertions of the Gospels in a different sense are *ex post facto* inventions, and that before the visionary appearance of Christ to His disciples after His crucifixion, they had never heard from Him of any claim to be the founder of the new kingdom, and that that claim rested wholly on the inferences which they drew from their newly-formed impression of His spiritual existence and restored energy. Surely it is hard to find an instance of any great man's more credulous incredulity. What would Dr. Martineau have put into the mouth of Jesus as the reply to John's messengers? Surely it would have been this: 'Go and show John again the things which ye do hear and see: the blind do not receive their sight; the lame do not walk; the lepers are not cleansed; the deaf do not hear; the dead are not raised up; and least of all have the poor had the Gospel preached to them'?—for such an edition of the Gospel as Dr. Martineau alone authenticates, a Gospel of beauty without power, of promise without performance, would have had no chance of startling, or eliciting blessings from, the poor.

To my mind at least, Dr. Martineau's conception of divine authority as manifested in the whole development of the Jewish and Christian revelations, seems a conception of failure to express itself adequately, instead of a conception of revealing power. If there is one thing more certain than another in that history, it is that the belief in God's supernatural power, as manifested *both* in the sharp struggles and conquests of the inner life and in the wonderful signs given in the external fields of history and nature, was the one connecting thread of their history, and moulded the steadily expectant character of their anticipations of the future. If Christ's life, death, and resurrection did not fit into this long line of supernatural manifestation, it was not the future for which the people of Israel had been disciplined and prepared; it was only a half-and-half supernaturalism, and not of a piece with the long traditional development of which, in almost all Christians' belief, it forms the consummation and the crown. Divine authority which is shut up in the conscience exclusively, and extends to no other part of life, may suit a purely philosophical system like Dr. Martineau's, but it does not represent in any sense the drift of the teaching of either the Hebrew or the Christian Church.

XXVII

THE HEAD MASTER OF CLIFTON COLLEGE ON THE THEORY OF INSPIRATION

1883

THE Society for Promoting Christian Knowledge has seldom done either a better or a bolder thing than its publication of two remarkable lectures by the Head Master of Clifton College,—the Rev. J. M. Wilson,—on *The Theory of Inspiration*. It has never done a bolder thing, because these lectures face the difficulties of the Bible in a much freer and franker spirit than the Councils of our various Religious Societies can usually persuade themselves to sanction and approve. It has never done a better thing, because these lectures do not rationalise and explain away Revelation into a mere human evolution, but are well calculated to vindicate the faith in a divine power in almost the only way in which in our day it can, as I believe, be triumphantly vindicated, as a faith justified and even required by the study of history—which contains constant proofs of a power perpetually conversing with man, and sustaining, indeed, as one of the minor prophets terms it, "the Lord's controversy" with him,—a power especially reflected in the history of the Jewish people, and receiving at last its perfect human embodiment in the life of Christ. Mr. Wilson begins by contrasting the extreme reticence not of one Christian Church only, but of nearly all the greater branches of the Christian Church, as to the true definition of Inspiration, with the desire of Secularists and Agnostics so to define it that they may confute the Christian revelation, as it were, out of its own mouth. He contrasts impressively the language of two different authorities on this question. One of these says, "The purely organic (*i.e.* mechanical) theory of Inspiration rests on no Scriptural authority, and, if we except a few ambiguous metaphors, is supported by no historical testimony. It is at variance with the whole form and fashion of the Bible, and it is destructive of all that is holiest in man and highest in religion." The other authority says, "It will not do to say that it [the Bible] is not verbally inspired. If the words are not inspired, what is?" And then Mr. Wilson explains that the former authority, who protests so strongly against verbal inspiration as inconsistent with historical testimony and fatal to what is highest in religion, is Canon Westcott, of Cambridge, one of the most learned of our living Biblical critics; and that the latter authority, who is eager to tie the Bible down to verbal inspiration, is the well-known American Secularist, Colonel Robert Ingersoll, who really contends for verbal inspiration as the only intelligible kind of inspiration, in order that he may explode all inspiration altogether. "Do you, then, ask me," says Mr. Wilson, "can I become a Christian without having first believed in the divinely-guaranteed accuracy of the Bible? A thousand times I answer, 'Yes.'" And then he proceeds, in a passage of great beauty and wisdom, to explain himself:—" The truth is, that the belief in inspiration is not the portal by which you enter the temple: it is the atmosphere that you breathe when you have entered. You may become a Christian,—most men do become Christians,—from finding in the life and sayings and death of Jesus Christ something that touches them, something that finds them, something that is a revelation of divine love to the human heart. Men find that there is something in them dear and precious to God. And then love springs up in them, and a new life begins. They look out on the world with larger and more loving eyes. They see God in their brethren, God in Nature, and God in their Bibles. In their Bibles they read of the Christ whom they love. Those pages are filled with power that moves the soul; never man spake as this man; never book spake as this book. And this, and this only, is the theory of inspiration that Christians must needs possess. It is primarily an internal question among believers, not an external question with the world. It has little or no relation to the convictions which make and keep a man a Christian. It is not a question which I or any one would care to talk about to one who is not already drawn to Christ. It is premature to talk with others of the exact limits of inspiration. Let them first read the Gospels, read them as they would read any other book, with any theory of inspiration or with none, with the one aim of learning the truth about Jesus Christ, of finding in the book what is pure, and noble, and elevating; let them first learn to admire, to love, to copy, to serve Jesus Christ, and I care not what theory they may form of inspiration; they will have got the thing, and then they will not be over-anxious to define it." In a word, to be a Christian, all you have to believe is that a real power infinitely higher than man manifested itself to man through the series of historical causes which prepared the way for Jesus Christ, and most perfectly of all in Jesus Christ himself. Believe this, and the antecedent improbability of miracle vanishes at once, while the mind is prepared to accept as historical events, physical marvels which are plainly asserted to have happened in close association with what is super human on the spiritual side; but as regards all individual miracles, you are free to weigh the evidence for them individually and on their own basis; they do not all "stand or fall together," but, so, at least, I should interpret Mr. Wilson's meaning, though I am now speaking for myself, and not for him,—those miracles which are most closely implicated, most absolutely in harmony, with the spiritual marvels of revelation, will stand most firmly; while those completely separable from those spiritual marvels, and standing in what may seem accidental relations with them, will remain on a distinct plane of evidence of their own, and we shall feel perfectly free to say in our own minds, 'Whether that really happened exactly as it is there declared to have happened, is a question on which we do not feel called upon to profess any decided opinion, nor are we even capable of forming such an opinion. We can only say that the sufficient evidence on which we should be ready to believe it is hardly in existence; and that whether it was a miracle or a natural event glorified by the halo of popular tradition makes absolutely no difference to the substantial truth of the history of the divine education of Israel, or to the culmination of that education in the life and death and resurrection and ascension of Christ and in the descent of the Holy Spirit on His disciples.'

Thus far goes the drift—as I understand it—of Mr. Wilson's first lecture. The second lecture, on the moral difficulties of the Bible, insists on the view that the divine inspiration of man is necessarily relative to the actual historical condition of the race by whom that inspiration is received. All that is needful to compel the belief that a divine agency external to man is engaged in his education and purification, is the evidence that whatever his actual condition, he finds within him, and especially within the hearts of his best religious teachers, a power which constrains him, against the grain of his nature, to become holier and purer than he is;—no matter whether that which to one century is far holier and better than the spiritual life of that century, seems to us looking back, after the better experience of thirty or forty centuries more, less excellent than the best spiritual life of our own day. "We must judge of a divine command in the Old Testament by the following considerations. The voice spoke in the heart, not outside it, and was but the voice of the conscience enlightened up to its then standard, and receiving from the ever-present, ever-acting Spirit of God, such fresh enlightenment or inspiration as it could bear. Did the voice seem wrong to them? Was it not in general a call to something higher, to some fresh duty? Could it have been intelligible, if given in the modes of thought of this century, so widely separate as they are? and why of this century rather than of any other, past or to come? To my mind, the only intelligible revelation is the gradual, historical, accommodated revelation. Such commands or permissions are only so far given to us as they are applicable to our conditions of society and morals; and here is the function of intellect, an ample sphere for our keenest moral judgment and most trained insight." And Mr. Wilson illustrates his meaning by saying of the command to Abraham to take his son Isaac and to offer him as a burnt offering:—" I, for one, can only interpret this as in any sense a command from God by the help that I get from the historical view of revelation that I have been setting forth. The inner voice of God in our hearts and later revelation, tell us this command is wrong to us; if the outer voice tells us that it is right to us, the contradiction is intolerable, and even maddening. But the question is not what the inner voice in *our* hearts *now* says, but what it said in Abraham's, nearly four thousand years ago. And to understand this we have only to reflect that, strange as it may seem, the offering of the first-born was then common; that it was no moral shock, only a sorrow and trial to Abraham; and that the command was used,—its importance is that it was used,—not to sanction, but to abolish human sacrifices, and to look forward by a long series of types to the perfect sacrifice of will and life that Christ made on the Cross." That is finely put, and I wholly agree with the view expressed, but I should like to add to what Mr. Wilson says, that the only reason, so far as I can judge, why the command addressed to Abraham is " wrong to us," and would be simply incredible to us as a divine command, is not in the least because we may not be required rightly, and in numbers of cases, to give up to death at least as certain as ever Abraham destined for Isaac, those who are as dear to us as ever Isaac was to Abraham, but solely because in His revelation of Himself as a father, God has taught us to cherish the deeper human affections, and what they suggest to us, as truer and more decisive revelations of Himself than any sort of external voice which would merely and blankly command the severing of those relations. We may be, and often are, commanded by the interior voice of duty to do what hazards the continuance of these relations on earth, and what ends, perhaps, in as complete a severance of them as that for which Abraham showed himself to be willing at God's command. But the difference is that since Abraham's time anything like a direct outrage on the sacredness of these affections has been forbidden, and that we have been taught, what Abraham till then had never been taught, that God reveals to us more of Himself through the life of these affections,—and by that reverence which the Fifth Commandment especially enjoined,—than through any outward teaching of any other kind. Instead of representing,—as the religion of the Phœnicians represented,—the jealousy of God as if it were a jealousy felt by Him of the *existence* of human affections, as if it were a jealousy felt by one who regarded Himself as competing with human love for the exclusive devotion of His worshippers, —His revelation has explained the true divine jealousy as requiring the highest fidelity and purity in human relations, for the very purpose of educating us towards fidelity and purity in our relations to God. The relations of father and son, and of wife and husband, instead of being depreciated as in rivalry with religious worship, have been surrounded by His revelation with infinite mystery, and treated as training us to the truest conceptions of what our love for God Himself ought to be. It is not that Abraham's lesson as to God's claim upon us for the willing surrender even of our dearest earthly treasure has ever been cancelled or reversed, but that it has been taught in a different manner,—first, by the careful forbidding of everything which outrages those deeper affections and tends to lower and degrade them; and next, by teaching us to consecrate these affections with all the mystery and glory of religious associations. The sacrifice of Isaac, seemingly accepted, but really forbidden, and thenceforward made the starting-point of a new teaching as to the fatherhood of God and the revealing character of the higher affections of man,—a teaching developed till, as Mr. Wilson says, it culminated in the sacrifice of the Cross,—seems to me to furnish one of the noblest illustrations in history of the evolution of the highest religion out of a creed which, once significant but rude, was rapidly falling into a corrupt and cruel superstition when it was suddenly rescued from that degradation and expanded into the highest of all religions, by the supernatural providence of God.

XXVIII

PROFESSOR JOWETT'S QUESTION

1890

PROFESSOR JOWETT concluded his Sunday evening lecture at Westminster Abbey on Robert Browning and Professor Hatch by the remark: "If asked where, among all the Christian Churches of the age, the Gospel was to be found, he would answer, 'Where it always has been found, in the Christian life.'" That this is a large part of the answer is perfectly true; that it is the whole of the answer is certainly false. It always has been true, and always will be true, that the "good news" of the most thoroughly Christian life actually lived in this world is the tidings best adapted to spread in the world the fascination of the Christian life; but it is certainly not true that the Christian life could be actually lived without the help of any other tidings to sustain it except the tidings of other lives actually so lived. One might almost as well say that the life of a plant which is propagated by the dropping of its own seed, is dependent on nothing else for its propagation except the formation of its own seed. Now, we know perfectly well that a plant which thrives and flourishes in the most luxuriant manner in one soil and one climate, will dwindle to the poorest and most meagre vegetation in another soil and another climate, and will absolutely die off and vanish altogether in a third. The inherent vitality of the plant is enormous under one set of conditions, feeble under another, and completely disappears under a third; and yet it is no less true that even under the conditions under which it flourishes best, the growth of the plant is needed to spread the plant, and that it will be impossible to spread it except from a living germ of its own kind. Just so it is, I take it, with the Christian life: without the Christian life, the Christian life will not spread; but under one set of conditions the Christian life will spread itself freely and rapidly, and under other sets of conditions the Christian life will spread itself slowly and meagrely, and under other sets of conditions again, it will not spread itself at all, but will die out altogether. Now the Gospel has usually been taken as the name of those good tidings which promote its growth and vitality most, *apart* from the inherent force of its own organic structure. It is quite as true that until you get a germ of Christian life there can be no propagation of that germ, as it is that until you get a germ of physical life there can be no propagation of that germ. But even when you have got a germ of physical life, there is no free or luxuriant reproduction of that germ without favourable conditions, and this is equally true of the spiritual life of Christianity. As Christ himself said, you may strew it on the hard ground, where it lies perfectly unfruitful till it is carried off by some accident; or you may strew it on a light and stony soil, where it cannot make root enough to grow; or you may strew it amongst thorns, where it is choked by the greater vitality of the thorns; or you may strew it on good ground, and yet even on the good ground there will be differences of condition which show themselves in the rate of fertility, some bringing forth thirty, some sixty, some a hundred-fold. It has been usual to regard the Gospel, "the good news," as describing not so much the Christian life itself, as the revelation of truths which tend to foster and guard and stimulate the Christian life; and it seems to me a great mistake to suggest that there are no such intellectual and spiritual conditions without the general acceptance of which the Christian life will cease to spread at all events with any freedom and luxuriance, even if it does not vanish altogether. We must remember that the Christian life, in a very limited and maimed sense, is the subject of enthusiastic praise even among the Positivists. The late Mr. Cotter Morison, in his book on *The Service of Man*, spoke with the utmost appreciation and admiration of the highest type of character which Christianity had produced, though he thought that it had failed in greatly raising the level of the character of the average Christian. He held that the conditions under which the saintly character had been nourished, involved the acceptance of a series of spiritual and intellectual illusions which tended, however, to foster a high kind of idealism in the finer and more sensitive natures, though they failed to impress deeply the coarser and tougher specimens of human nature. Yet even Mr. Cotter Morison did not, so far as I can judge from his book, imagine that the spiritual type of the Christian saint could have been fostered and developed *merely* through the charm which it exerted,—which it exerted, indeed, even on those who regarded the faith under the influence of which it was produced as a mere dream. Nothing in the world is more certain than that the Christian saint could never have existed at all without the Christian faith and hope on which his character was nourished,—that his detachment from worldly motives, for instance, and his heartfelt exultation in suffering for his devotion to Christ, would have been utterly inconceivable without his absolute belief in the "things above," where his heart "was hid with Christ in God." Some fragments and scraps of the Christian morality might, indeed, reproduce and multiply themselves without the belief. Apparently there is something in what is now affectedly called the "altruistic" doctrine that fascinates men on its own account, and without relation to the beliefs and hopes with which it is connected in the minds of Christians. But the altruistic agnostic is separated by as wide a chasm from the Christian saint, as the Buddhist or the Pantheist. The life of worship is for him a folly; the inward scrutiny and purification of motive is a waste of power; the humility, the submission, the obedience, the gratitude, the patience, the aspiration, are all unmeaning to him. If he spends himself in labour and care for others, it is with a restless heat and urgency which are not trained to await God's slow and sure processes of preparation. Not working for God, but for man, he cannot see beyond the bitter disappointments which work for man too certainly involves; he cannot escape the pessimism, the cynicism, the despondency, the exhaustion which fruitless work for a finite creature who seldom understands, and hardly ever repays it, almost inevitably produces. If the Christian life itself is the whole Gospel, then the Christian life must include the Christian creed as part and parcel of the Christian secret of success in living it. You might as well plant in your vineyard the wild vine in place of the vine which has been cultivated for centuries, and then expect grapes from which you could distil a fine wine, as plant mere altruism for Christianity, and look for Christian fruits. Matthew Arnold tried to show that the wild grape and the cultivated are essentially the same; that we might get rid of the very idea of God and yet possess "the secret of Jesus"; but he failed lamentably, and left in the world to which he appealed a strange impression of spiritual Quixotism applied to a field in which he had no real experience, and had, of course, never attained even a partial success.

And nothing can be plainer than that the Gospel, as it was originally preached, was a message which put new power and life into man, by enabling him to believe in a new power and life outside him. It was the proclamation of a kingdom,—of a king who could enable the blind to see, the lame to walk, the deaf to hear, the dead to live, which was the gospel preached to the poor. Without the proclamation of a new kingdom, there would have been no springing of a new life. It was the advent of a new power in the world, and the belief in that new power, that constituted the conditions of the new life. The announcement that both the outward and the inward man was subject to the new power, that sin could be forgiven by Him who could command the palsied limbs to rise and walk, was of the very essence of the new life. What account does St. Paul give of the Gospel?—"I am not ashamed of the Gospel of Christ, for it is the power of God

unto salvation to every one that believeth." So
St. Peter blesses God for having inspired in him
"a lively hope by the resurrection of Jesus Christ
from the dead." And St. John makes the new
power to consist in the belief that "Jesus Christ is
come in the flesh," and that whatever He commanded, man has the power through faith in Him
to do. Nothing can be plainer than that the answer
to Professor Jowett's question in the first age of the
Church was something more than Professor Jowett's
answer to it now. The early Church did not deny
that the Gospel was to be found "where it always
has been found, in the Christian life," but it did
proclaim that what rendered the Christian life possible, what alone rendered it possible, was a new
belief as to the power by which it was sustained, as
to the divine nature which had revealed itself in the
order and principles of that life. And what was
true of the earliest age of Christianity is quite as
true of the latest. The Christian life is not sufficient to itself now, any more than it was then. It
is a life which can only be lived by those who have
living faith in the divine strength which supports it.
Its intrinsic beauty, its intrinsic fascination, are not
enough, because its intrinsic beauty and fascination
depend on its reality, and there is no reality in it,
unless the promise of spiritual support from within
is a true promise, a promise that can be verified by
the actual experience of life. There never was a
time in which a genuine belief in spiritual aid to
live the Christian life was more needed than it is
now. There is a sort of nihilism in the air which
shows itself nowhere more plainly than in the desire
to represent the Christian life as its own strength
no less than its own witness, whereas nothing is

more certain than that the Christian faith has always, and from the first, repudiated the notion that the Christian life is its own strength, and has exulted in reiterating with St. Paul, that when we are weak, when we trust ourselves least, then we are strongest, and have most reason to hope the very best. The Christian life is its own witness, but what it witnesses is that the power which sustains it comes from beyond itself, and that the whole faith is a delusion of delusions, unless such power flows freely into the soul from beyond.

XXIX

MR. GLADSTONE AND DR. LIDDON ON THE BIBLE

1890

IN *Good Words* for April, Mr. Gladstone has begun a series of papers in which he proposes to give popular reasons for the belief that the inspiration of Scripture will hold its ground, even if the specialists who are now attacking the different books of the Bible, and especially some of the most important books of the Old Testament, from the critical side, should establish their case. "It appears to me," he says, "that we may grant, for argument's sake, to the negative or destructive specialist in the field of the ancient Scriptures all which as a specialist he can by possibility be entitled to ask respecting the age, text, and authorship of the books, and yet may hold firmly, as firmly as of old, to the ideas justly conveyed by the title I have adopted for this paper, and may invite our fellow-men to stand along with us on 'the impregnable rock of Holy Scripture.'" Dr. Liddon, who has published a very eloquent sermon,[1] probably directed

---

[1] *The Worth of the Old Testament.* A Sermon preached in St. Paul's Cathedral on the Second Sunday in Advent, 8th

against the view taken of the Old Testament by
one of the writers in the volume called *Lux Mundi*,
a sermon which has just reached a second edition,
to one brilliant passage in which Mr. Gladstone
refers, does not apparently at all agree with Mr.
Gladstone; for he manifestly thinks that almost all
the objections directed by the modern critics against
portions of the Old Testament would, if accepted, be
fatal to Christian faith, partly on the ground that
the Apostles gave a general sanction to the teaching
of the Old Testament as they knew it, and still more
on the ground that our Lord Himself referred to the
Jewish Scriptures as a final authority for their own
time and place, and especially that He drew certain
inferences of His own from statements made in the
Old Testament Scriptures as if their evidence was unanswerable. Of course I am unable to judge from
Mr. Gladstone's preliminary paper what he regards
as the limits of that which a specialist can, "as a
specialist, by possibility be entitled to ask respecting
the age, text, and authorship of the books" of the
Bible; and it may turn out that he assigns to this
limit so narrow a significance, that destructive
criticism would hardly be entitled to its name at
all, since he might deny it all substantially destructive power. But of course this is not a very probable view. No one knows better than Mr. Gladstone that if the Fourth Gospel could have been
relegated to the middle of the second century, as
many of the destructive critics have maintained, it
would have had no authority at all as expounding
the theology of the Incarnation; nor even that if
the Book of Daniel could be shown to have been

December 1889, by H. P. Liddon, D.C.L. Second Edition,
revised, with a new Preface. London: Rivingtons.

written in the time of Antiochus Epiphanes, after many of the events predicted had really taken place, the prophecy, as a prophecy, would, as Dr. Liddon intimates, have been utterly untrustworthy, and, in fact, a deception. I feel sure that Mr. Gladstone cannot refer to such destructive criticism as is here involved, when he says that Christians could afford to "grant, for argument's sake, to the negative or destructive specialist all which as a specialist he can by possibility be entitled to ask respecting the age, text, and authorship of the Bible, and yet may hold firmly, as firmly as of old, to the ideas justly conveyed" by "the impregnable rock of Holy Scripture." Destructive criticism of the kind I have mentioned may, and in the case of the Fourth Gospel I believe that it does, utterly break down; but if it did not utterly break down, if it could establish anything like what it professes to establish, I believe that it would, as Dr. Liddon maintains, go to the root of the Christian revelation, — at all events, as the Christian revelation has been understood by nine-tenths of all existing Christians.

On the other hand, if we take Mr. Gladstone's qualification of the limits of havoc which the destructive critical specialist may possibly work, as signifying the limits within which there is at the present time any weighty reason to suppose that the destructive critical specialist may succeed, I should be much more disposed to agree with Mr. Gladstone that he cannot really strike any serious blow at Christian faith, than with Dr. Liddon's more alarmist view. I hold, indeed, that the historical school might very possibly succeed in upsetting the view that the Book of Daniel dates from a period long before

Antiochus Epiphanes,—a point on which Hebraists tell us that the philological evidence of the language itself is virtually decisive,—and yet that no serious blow would be struck at the truth and power of the chief part of the historical revelation contained in the Bible. Again, if the view of such critics as Robertson Smith as to the date of Deuteronomy in its present form were regarded as established, I do not think that any serious blow would have been struck at the truth and power of the chief part of the historical revelation contained in the Bible. So far as I can judge, the whole weight of Dr. Liddon's argument depends on one assumption, that our Lord in taking a human nature, and in speaking from the centre of that human nature, was yet virtually so dominated by the divine omniscience, that except on one subject, His human knowledge, —the knowledge derived from His human nature, —was unlimited. "Our Lord has told us," says Dr. Liddon, "that on one subject His knowledge was limited. We have no reason for supposing that it was limited on any other. But if our Lord, *as Man*, did not know the day and the hour of the Judgment (St. Mark xiii. 32), He did not as Man claim to know it. Had He told us that the real value of the Books of the Old Testament was hidden from Him, or had He never referred to them, there could have been no conflict between modern so-called 'critical' speculations and His divine authority." Surely this is going a great deal beyond the true significance of the evangelists' teaching as to Christ's human life. It seems to me that that life implies the limitation of His human knowledge on various different occasions. What is the meaning of "How is it that ye sought me? wist ye not that

I must be about my Father's business," if our Lord was perfectly aware all the time that Joseph and Mary were searching for Him for parts of three whole days, while He was attending in the Temple to ask questions of the doctors of the Jewish law? What, again, was the meaning of His "asking them questions" at all, if all the time He not only knew the answers far better than those who answered Him, but knew also what the answers He was to receive would be, before those whom He interrogated had opened their mouths? Surely our Lord did not "as man" claim to know the answer to *any* question which He appeared to ask for the sake of instruction. I cannot even conceive the scene of our Lord's boyhood as described by St. Luke, except on the hypothesis that our Lord's human nature was genuinely human, that He really desired to know the interpretation put by the Jewish doctors on the Jewish Scriptures, and that He had not anticipated the anxiety felt concerning Him by His mother and her husband. Again, take the prayer in Gethsemane. What is the meaning of the prayer, "If it be possible, let this cup pass from me, and yet not as I will, but as thou wilt," if He in His human nature knew perfectly well that it was God's will that He should drink the cup? The whole meaning of that hour of anguish, the whole depth of that spiritual cry, depended on the human limitations of the nature the agony of which escaped in that cry. And the same impression is derived from the Gospel which may be called the Gospel of the Incarnation, in its account of what I may fairly speak of as the foretaste of the agony. When our Lord says: "Now is my soul troubled, and what shall I say? 'Father, save me from this hour.'

But for this cause came I to this hour. Father, glorify thy name,"— can any one doubt for a moment that such a deliberation as that with Himself, was a deliberation simply impossible to divine omniscience conscious of its omniscience, and that its profoundly touching and impressive character is derived only from its frank expression of human determination to accept as God's will what He would fain have deprecated? I admit and assert, of course, that our Lord's human nature was frequently pierced by flashes of divine insight and divine power; that, as St. John says, He knew "what was in man," as none other could have known it; that He stilled the tempest and multiplied the loaves as none other would even have attempted to do in His place. But even His power as man was limited, as His rebuke to the disciples who would have used force to resist His capture shows, where He speaks of His power to "pray to his Father" for angelic aid, had He thought it right to offer such a prayer, not of any power inherent in His human nature to summon such aid. The mystery of the two natures in one person is seen, indeed, at many points in His career; but Dr. Liddon's view of our Lord's human intellect as absolutely unlimited in all but a single direction, appears to me to solve this mystery in a sense which almost destroys the humanity, instead of taking it up into God. And why, if it be admitted, as every one admits, that our Lord suffered all the grief which lacerated human affections suffer, all the sense of desolation which human weakness involves, all the consciousness of an almost intolerable burden under which unassisted human effort so often succumbs, should it be thought necessary to deny that He also suffered in His human experience from the limitation of His human knowledge? It is surely not reasonable to suppose that even that constant communion with God which theologians express under the name of the beatific vision, could have removed from the genuinely human nature which He had assumed on our behalf, the human limitations which are of its very essence.

But if Dr. Liddon is mistaken in thus disposing of almost all the limitations of our Lord's human intellect, if this would falsify the very deepest pathos of the Gospel narrative, then surely it would be right and natural to assume that our Lord's human knowledge of the Jewish Scriptures was just the knowledge which the best teaching of His time, linked to true spiritual perfection, would confer, and was not the sort of knowledge which modern philology and modern studies would secure, —was, in short, consistent with such a view (say) of the Book of Daniel as the best Jewish doctors of His time could have imparted, even if that view were erroneous. So far as I can see, Dr. Liddon's conception of our Lord's nature tends as much in the direction of denying His humanity, as the Unitarian view of our Lord's nature tends in the direction of denying His deity. But if I am right the force of Dr. Liddon's argument disappears, and then I should certainly hold with Mr. Gladstone that whatever (within reason) the negative school of criticism may establish, it will not really injure the essence or diminish the impressive historical effect of the revelation so wonderfully and so gradually communicated to the Jewish race. Even if some of our canonical books turn out to have been rashly accepted, and some that are deutero-canonical prove to be more authentic and more weighty than those supposed to be of the highest authority, the Anglican Church at least is committed to no view of inspiration that will make it difficult to confess the errors of the past and to rectify the teaching of the future.

XXX

THE SACRAMENTAL PRINCIPLE

1872

THE judgment of the Judicial Committee of the Privy Council in Mr. Bennett's case has given rise to the usual amount of small witticisms on the delicacy and evanescence of theological distinctions, —witticisms of that type of which Gibbon's ironical description of the vowel-modification which distinguished the Arian from the orthodox doctrine of Christ's nature as "this important diphthong," is perhaps the best specimen. One able writer has, with unnecessary coarseness, described the difference between Mr. Bennett's latest expressions about the consecrated elements and those for which he would, by the admission both of the Judge of the Court of Arches and of their Lordships of the Judicial Committee, be censurable, and if not willing to retract, liable to deprivation, as the difference between saying "hocus-pocus," and declaring that he had only meant to say "ocus-pocus" and that if he had pronounced the aspirate, it was rather from unfortunate habits of articulation than from real intention. That is a forcible though, as I have said, a coarse expression of contempt for the minutiæ of distinctions which the writer apparently regards as distinctions not only without a real difference, but also without, what is still more important, a sincere belief in any difference. And for my part, I confess that I cannot at all grasp Mr. Bennett's distinction between "adoring and teaching the people to adore the consecrated elements, believing Christ to be in them," which was admitted to be a flat contradiction of the Anglican teaching forbidding any adoration of the consecrated elements, and "adoring and teaching the people to adore Christ present in the Sacrament under the form of Bread and Wine, believing that under their veil is the sacred Body and Blood of our Lord and Saviour Jesus Christ," which is now declared by the Judicial Committee to be dangerous and rash language, but not expressly contradictory of the Church's statements, and therefore of course entitled to the benefit of the doubt. I should have thought that any evidence which would justify the former statement, — supposing there to be such evidence, — would better justify the latter, and that the two are hardly practically distinguishable to ordinary human intellects. But for all that, I feel no sympathy at all with the spirit of the 'hocus-pocus' witticism, which really means that the Sacramental principle is pure nonsense, and the various refinements of which it has been made the theme are mere variations in the mode of expressing nonsense, — in other words, nonsense of a higher order, nonsense in form concerning nonsense in substance. Nothing seems to me less surprising than that all religions with any vitality in them should show that vitality in an attempt to help the spiritual through the material life, as well as to transform the material life through the spiritual.

And whatever ought in point of fact to be surprising or otherwise, certainly no one can have the smallest acquaintance with the teaching of Christ and His Apostles without seeing that thoughts of this kind lay at the very basis of their doctrine, that in that teaching the material world is often treated as spiritual, and the spiritual world as material; that spiritual food is spoken of as Bread, and physical Bread is treated as the means of spiritual health; that water is treated as the instrument of regeneration, and spiritual teaching is called living water; that sometimes the physical touch is regarded as healing the spirit, and sometimes the spiritual touch as healing the body; in short, that Christ discerned a most intimate alliance between physical and spiritual agencies, in virtue of which the physical were often spiritual and the spiritual often physical; that He claimed the power to make the most ordinary constituents of the human body channels of spiritual life, and the most marvellous spiritual teachings equivalents for ordinary rest and nutrition. He recognised not only the working of the spirit on the flesh, but of the flesh on the spirit, and promised not only spiritual aid to overcome physical passions, but physical aid to overcome unspiritual passions. And in so doing, Christ did but follow the track of the natural life of man. What is more common than to find pure air restoring health to the spirit as well as pure social influences restoring health to the body? Does not the beauty of mountain scenery give a new zest to the very food we eat, and make it go further in nourishing the bodily tissues? Does not pure food give a new activity to the mind, and make it keener even in the life of prayer and of duty?

But most men will admit at once that the reciprocal action of the spiritual on the material and of the material on the spiritual is the most certain and, perhaps some will say, the least mysterious of human phenomena, since if Mind creates matter, all material forces are but mental energies in disguise; and if Matter constitutes mind, mental energies are but material forces in disguise. In such apparently reciprocal influences of material and spiritual agencies, then, it will be said, there is not the vestige of the alleged Sacramental principle, which is not supposed to consist in the natural influence of the material on the spiritual, but in a supernatural transformation of material agencies which, while leaving them to act in their old material way, yet infuses them with a new life that not only affects the mind directly, but affects it also by purifying or refining the bodily organs. What rationalists deny is not the effect of material agencies in stimulating the spirit,—which they would of course steadily assert,—nor the effect of spiritual agencies in exciting the spirit,—but the possibility that by any spiritual process whatever a material agency could have its material effects so modified as to make the body a more pure and perfect organ of the spirit, in other words, as to make it respond more easily to the government of the higher Christian impulses. They would admit that the habit of self-control would make the body a more manageable organ for the spirit; and again, that healthy physical habits would make it a more efficient instrument of every kind; but they would deny that the particles of food could be made to have any different effect, as particles of food, through any conceivable religious rite which might be performed, though they might concede that any high excitement of the nerves would probably disturb the bodily functions, and make their action *different*,—probably not healthier,—than it otherwise would be.

But is not that mere attempt to state the case accurately, as it is conceived by the rationalists, full of evidence that it is exceedingly difficult so to state it as to exclude all room for the proper sacramental principle? They have to admit frankly that the same material substances act in most different fashions under different spiritual conditions;—only they would maintain that the changed spiritual conditions act through the nervous system of the recipient, and not through any transformation of the elements which pass into the body. Admitted, but is not this in its turn a distinction as refined and intangible as almost any theological distinction? Could any physiologist distinguish between an effect produced on the assimilation of food by the higher tension of the nerves due to spiritual feeling, and an effect produced by the modification of the substance received? An element once in the body, the discrimination between what is due to its action on the bodily organs and what is due to the action of the bodily organs on it, is surely almost inapprehensible, and quite evanescent? Supposing the body be really made a finer organ for the spirit by any internal change, suppose the inflammability of evil passions were diminished, and the impressibility to spiritual impulses were increased, is it not almost as childish and as unverifiable a refinement as any of which theologians have ever been guilty, to maintain that you can distinguish between what is due to the physical action of the food on the body, and what is due to the nervous action of the spirit or spirits on the food? No doubt it may be very fairly said that if anything of the sacramental influence supposed to be exerted were really due to the bread and wine received, it would be only reasonable to assume that that influence would depend, as it does in the case of the air breathed in beautiful scenery for example (which doubtless has a more salutary effect on the body than equally good air breathed in uninteresting scenery), in great measure on the physical *amount* so received, whereas, as everybody knows, most of the believers in the Sacramental principle regard the minutest portions of the sacred elements as amply adequate to convey the new stream of spiritual life, and hold, therefore, that even though no material substance were taken at all, if the recipient *believed* that he had received the symbols of Divine life, the rite would have precisely the same physical and spiritual effect upon him as if he had really received them. Nor can I, of course, doubt that this is true. But the question which suggests itself is this,—whether, supposing it to be true, as of course it is, that it is not the elements received which effect anything, but only the divine influence of which they are such vivid symbolic channels, it may not yet be quite as much a physical as a spiritual change through which that divine influence operates. If beauty both of sight and sound acts, as it does, on the body by modulating the organs of sense, why may not the highest divine life mould the body directly, as well as through the slow influence of the mind upon it? The real essence of the Sacramental principle is, I imagine, contained in the assumption that the divine life enters us by physical as well as by spiritual channels;

and for this purpose, of course, it matters not at all whether the sacred elements be but living symbols to our minds of that belief, or the actual channels of it. There seems to me, at all events, no sort of superstition in holding that,—independently of course of all sacerdotal conditions,—the rite which treats Christ's body as the bread of life, does exert a very strange and spiritually-renovating influence on the human *body*,—does make the body, that is, a more perfect and delicate instrument of the human spirit. It is quite certain, at all events, that no Church, in which the Sacramental principle,—the principle that the spirit is spiritualised through the divine influence acting on the body as well as on the spirit,—has been deficient, has ever avoided at once the dangers of too exciting and fanatical a doctrine of conscious "conversion," and also the danger of too cold a reliance on "good works." The Sacramental principle and it alone has brought home to religious people the many different avenues, involuntary and unconscious as well as voluntary and conscious, physical as well as spiritual, by which the Spirit of God must enter man, if the character is to be really pervaded with divine influence. That principle alone guards adequately against morbid Calvinist broodings over the evidence of special grace, and cold Pelagian reliance on moral goodness. That exaltation of the common things of nature, which results from the teaching that divine life enters through the daily bread into the very tissues of the body, no less than through the Spirit of God into the conscience, prevents the relative over-rating of the Spiritual life as such, besides exerting a unique influence on the affections by the strictly personal relation to Christ into which it brings us.

XXXI

PRAYERS FOR THE DEAD

1881

In Mr. MacColl's paper, published in the *Fortnightly* for July, on the Princess Alice,—the depth of pathos in whose letters, by the way, he brings out with singular success,—he touches a weak article in the theology of some of the Reformed Churches,— namely, the condemnation of prayers for the dead. This has always seemed to me to admit of only one kind of justification, and that a justification which it cannot plead.—I mean the plea that the condition of the dead is unchangeable, that by death they are turned, as it were, to stone. The Princess records in one of her letters, after the loss of her youngest boy, that the eldest "always prays for Frittie"; and as Mr. MacColl justly remarks, this is simply natural, and is even shown to be so by the practice of the unsophisticated child. Mr. MacColl declares that "to forbid prayers for the dead is to undermine the doctrine of prayers for the living." And there I agree with him most completely, since the dead, if their spirits are what they were at all, cannot be unchangeable, cannot be beyond the power of God, cannot be beyond the reach of prayer. Of course I know the sort of ground on which prayers for the dead have been held to be superstitious and heretical. This is held by those who think that "probation" is strictly limited to this life, and that an alternative of absolute blessedness or absolute misery is hereafter certain. Such persons hold that the habit of praying for the dead cannot even be innocent, since it must take the form either of a prayer for what is already granted,—which implies distrust of God,—or else a prayer for what is already refused, which implies rebellion of heart against Him. The answer, of course, is that we have no assurance in Revelation that probation is absolutely limited by this life for all alike;—the subject is not even explicitly dealt with in the New Testament. And even if that were so, and nothing seems more unlikely, none the less we could not be in any way assured that the state of those who are beyond the veil is unchangeable, that the blessedness of those who are blessed admits of no increase, and the misery of those who are miserable of no decrease. Except in the presence of a positive divine revelation to the contrary—of which no one even pretends to produce evidence—the natural assumption is, that whatever prayer tends to do for one who is living on earth, it equally tends to do for one who is living in the stage beyond. As Mr. MacColl says, those who make light of the efficacy of prayers for the dead are in a fair way to make light of the efficacy of prayers for the living. If it is argued that they are useless because God may be absolutely trusted to do the best for the dead without our prayers, why, that applies just as much to the living as to the dead. And if it is argued that after death their state is so absolutely unalterable that no prayers can avail them anything, the natural inference is that long before death that crystallisation of their destiny must have set in which turned to petrifaction afterwards. If the positive instruction to pray for each other is to apply to this life only, why was it not carefully limited to the domain of this life by those who taught us to pray? Is it not obvious that what was intended was to foster in man's heart the habit of pouring forth all his desires and wants freely to God? And if those desires and wants do not stop short at the grave, if they affect as much those who have passed beyond it, as those who are on this side of it, it can be nothing but the most artificial and unnatural of arrangements to teach us to divide our desires into two strictly separated classes, of which those belonging to one are never again to be breathed to God, while those belonging to the other are to be poured forth with all the old fervour. What teaching could be better adapted to make the invisible world unreal to us than this complete ignoring, in our intercourse with God, of all the affections which connect us with the world beyond, —this sedulous restraining of our thoughts to those who are still with us in the visible frame of things? If men once ignore the dead in their prayers, those who are gone will become dead to them in a quite new sense,—nay, the world of the highest life will become dead to them also. As it is the very highest effect of prayer to connect the unseen with the seen world, and to convince men that God has regard to the cry of man, when it is in accordance with His spirit, nothing seems to me more fatal to that highest use of prayer than to represent it as strictly limited in its scope to those who are still with us, and entirely without possible result on those who are gone from us. How could the conception of "the whole family in heaven and earth" be a true one, if the members of it who are on one side of the grave may properly pray only for those who are on the same side as themselves, but should treat those who are on the other side of it as beyond the range even of their intercessions? That is *not* one family, half of which may not even pray to God for blessings on the other half.

The horror felt of prayers for the dead in some theological circles is justified, I believe, by the argument that, if once we begin to think of the condition of any one who is beyond the grave as changeable at all, we shall get into the habit of thinking that even if we are as evil and selfish as we please in this life, even if we delay repentance till after all the evil enjoyments of life have been exhausted, we may yet rescue ourselves, or be rescued by others, from that misery we deserve, by change of heart in the world beyond. But the true answer to this is, not to assume a single arbitrary point like the moment of death, as the point when change for all alike becomes hopeless,—a doctrine which seems to me as little founded in Scripture as it is in the evidence of human nature,—but to show that whether on this side of the grave or on the other, a character once matured is so obstinate in its habits, so difficult to change, so moulded by its own former acts of choice, that the hope of any sudden revolution in its tastes and preferences is far more of a dream than of a reasonable expectation. It simply cannot be that a child who dies at ten or twelve has a character as formed as a man who lives to fifty or sixty; and if so, even the selfish child who dies at ten or twelve must be much more open to the higher spiritual influences which affect the next life than the man who lives to fifty or sixty, after a long career of steady resistance to those spiritual influences, can be conceived to be. The true teaching surely is, that prayer for others can never hurt, and may often help them; but that it can never help as much those who have set the grain of their own characters steadfastly against doing that for which we pray on their behalf, as it can those who are yet in the stage of growth in which every influence tells. Prayer for those who, with numberless faults, have died young, must, I should think, always be far more hopeful than prayer for those who, though they are still living, are living with all their faults hardened into the rigidity of habitual sins. Neither prayer may be wasted; both may do good; but the reasonable thing certainly is to hope more from the prayer for those,—whether living or dead,—who are not yet confirmed in evil, than for those, whether living or dead, who are so confirmed. It is not death that makes the difference. If the earnest prayer of a good man avails much, it yet avails more for those who have not hardened their hearts against the drift of such a prayer, than for those who have; and this even though he who is so hardening his heart to the influence of such prayers be still in the body, while he who is opening his heart to the influence of such prayers has been delivered from the burden of the flesh. It is not death which makes the difference: it is the life of him for whom the prayer is breathed. On the life which is growing more and more intractable to such prayers, whether it be embodied or disembodied, the prayer can have little effect, just as a touch will have but little effect on the course of a landslip. On the life which is growing more and more sensitive to the influence of such prayers, whether it be embodied or disembodied, a prayer may have, under the providence of God, great effect, and may even form the turning-point of a career. But that is a doctrine which does not open any very sanguine hope of the effect of intercessory prayer on the future of those who have used ill a long probation here, though it may open much hope of the effect of prayer on those who have had here the mere shadow of a probation, with hardly any experience of the fascination of good, and with the fullest experience of the attractions of evil.

But the great danger of forbidding prayers for the dead is, as Mr. MacColl says, that it must tend to discourage prayer altogether. If the heart may not pour itself out to God freely, it will soon cease to pour itself out at all. And clearly it cannot pour itself out freely unless it can say its say about both worlds, about those who are wholly in the one world, as well as about those whose life is partly in the one and partly in the other. "Where the treasure is, there will the heart be also;" and if the treasure is in the other world, to forbid the heart to be there too is fatal. And how can any one pray to God except for that for which his whole heart craves?

XXXII

CANON KINGSLEY ON REASONABLE PRAYER

1873

CANON KINGSLEY preached last Sunday at Westminster Abbey on a part of the subject which seems to have agitated so much the Presbyterians of Dundee,—the right we have to expect an answer to prayer. If I may argue from the imperfect report of his sermon which I have seen, it must have been a very fine one. At least he put with very great force one point which people in their worldly and corrupted view of spiritual things almost always lose sight of, and that is, that when prayer means, and is, nothing but a selfish wish launched into the invisible spaces around the heart, on the chance, as it were, of its over-persuading a spiritual listener who has power to give that wish effect, there is no kind of reason, on either Christian or natural grounds, for hoping that it will be granted. The first condition of prayer is that it shall be really offered to *God*; and God can mean nothing less to any one who prays than the highest and purest Will of which he can form any apprehension. Now the very meaning of prayer to that Will is that the being who offers it desires to be brought closer to him to whom it is offered, does not desire to overrule, but to be overruled by him. Hence the launching of a selfish wish into the unseen world, in the dim hope that it will become operative through the good-nature of a Being who has infinite power to do as he will, is not in any sense prayer at all, for it is not offered to God as God;—it does not seriously profess to desire that God should be more and more in the universe, and selfish creatures less and less; it is not, in short, addressed to the perfect righteousness and perfect love, but only to the most potent of all administrative agencies; it is directed, not to the infinite purity, but to a mighty Executive of the universe, and would be addressed to that mighty Executive much more hopefully if infinite good-nature instead of goodness were his essence. Now this is certainly not, in Christ's sense, prayer at all. In His sense, it is of the very essence of prayer that it aims at the establishment of the Divine will, and the annihilation of all that is inconsistent with that will. It is not to God's omnipotence primarily, but to His spiritual nature, that Christian prayer is addressed; the whole purport of it being that the unity of the Divine Kingdom may be asserted and its laws established. If this be not the first condition of any petition, then in the Christian sense that petition is not prayer at all. Prayer is not a short and easy cut to the thing next your heart; but the chief method by which the eager and shortsighted and imperfect mind gradually learns to purify itself in the flame of divine love. People talk and think as if prayer only meant bringing *pressure to bear for private purposes* on the power which touches the secret springs of life. Certainly, in Christ's teaching, it does not mean that at all. It means, on the contrary, bringing divine influences to bear on these private purposes, so as to extinguish or transform them;—to obtain the means of giving full effect, *not* to the latter, but to the former. "If ye then, being evil, know how to give good gifts unto your children, how much more shall your Heavenly Father give the Holy Spirit to them that ask him." In other words, the central idea of all prayer is the Holy Spirit, and all other petitions are to be asked and are likely to be granted only in strict subordination to that. The disciples were to believe that if they had "faith in God," they might say to the mountain on which the Jewish Temple was built, "Be thou removed and cast into the sea," and that it should be done,—as it virtually was done,—but only because that faith of theirs was faith *in God*, because its essence was the belief in the kingdom of God as revealed in Christ, not because the drift of it coincided with a private wish of their own, so that the request would be, if granted, an astounding example of the power accorded them to pull the invisible strings by which the universe is moved. All this Canon Kingsley evidently must have explained with his usual force. He told his hearers very plainly that most men who cry to God to save them are expressing a mere selfish desire to be saved from pain and discomfort, which there is no reasonable hope that God will grant. They do not want to be blest, but to be comfortable. And God, who wills to bless, but by no means wills to make us merely comfortable, is much more likely to refuse to save, in their sense, what only cumbers the earth, and promises, here at least, no good fruit. "Why should Christ save you? What use is your life to

God or to any human being? Why should Christ keep you alive, if you are not doing your duty? Why should He not take you away, if you are an offence, an injury, nay, a nuisance to Him and His kingdom, and put some one else in your place?" The only conceivable answer is that there may be, perhaps is, something in every man which admits of saving in the higher sense, which admits of being united to God, and of being expanded till it swallows up all that is evil and selfish in the man,—which is therefore really worth salvage, and in the infinitely minute and tender economy of God will not be allowed to perish in the wreck of the lower nature.

But may it not be said that this doctrine is too high for the simple, affectionate, and, so to say, confidential character of prayer, as illustrated by revelation, and would have prevented Abraham's praying for Sodom on condition that ten righteous men could be found there, and St. Paul's praying for the lives of those who were in the ship with him on his voyage to Rome? How could either of these know that the divine law did not require the prayer to be rejected, and how could it be right to attempt to sway the infinite Good away from its perfect purposes, for the sake of a mere sinking at the heart which distressed a shortsighted man when he contemplated the apparent tendency of those purposes? If all prayer is in essence a yearning for the triumph and prevalence of the divine Will over life, where is the room for those specific petitions which embody little but the natural and kindly feelings of a tender-hearted man, expressed, perhaps, in wishes that may be the blindest in the world? The answer seems to be that though the highest prayers are prayers for the fulfilment of

God's will, whatever it be, even by the drinking of the cup that human nature shrinks from, there is so much of spiritual education in the habit of intimate communion with God,—that is, of constantly bringing our human desires into a presence in which nothing merely selfish can long remain,—that we are induced to pour out our hearts even to their most childish wishes before Him, by the assurance that it is often His will to give what we ask *because* we ask it, even where it would not have been God's purpose to give it, had we not asked it. Is there anything necessarily inconsistent between this belief,—that there are some human prayers which God grants in order to draw closer the tie between Him and man, which He could not grant if they were never prayed,—and the belief that the true object of prayer is to lift man up to God, to subdue the human will to the Divine, to dissolve the arbitrary dictation and ignorance of our self-will? Does the belief that God grants to prayer what is not so necessarily good in itself that He would grant it without prayer, really lend any sanction to the petty interference of human caprice in the providence of the universe, or restore under the form of a divine compromise what had been virtually forbidden by the teaching that all true prayer centres in the divine will, and demands the perfect surrender of the anarchy of human wishes? I do not think so, and for the following reason. The whole purpose of Christian teaching is to impress upon us not that man must be extinguished in God, but that he must be utterly willing and desirous to surrender himself to God. Hence he is to have a self to surrender, a permanent self, which he is to mould more and more into the divine image, but never to lose. The very difference between Christianity and the various Pantheistic systems is that in it this human self is sedulously respected, even, so to say, by God. One great reason, according to the Christian teaching, why God became man in Christ,—emptied Himself of divine glory to take up human infirmities,—was to make man feel that he really is more than a mote in the divine sunlight, that he has a life and freedom of his own which is the object of God's infinite love, and if not worthy, at least treated as if it were worthy, of divine suffering and sacrifice. Now this same doctrine seems to me to be virtually repeated and reaffirmed in the teaching that there are things which God will grant to prayer which He would not have granted without prayer, though they must be of course perfectly consistent with the overruling laws of His holiness. It is not Christian to regard even redeemed humanity as a mere inner circle of the divine life. Man is to have affections of his own, the independent life of which God approves, and to which He gives what He would not give without the cry of human love imploring it. Granted, that this really involves the admission that the prayers of other men may make our own lots other than they would have been had they been moulded by God's will without relation to those prayers; that some men may live, for instance, longer, and wearier, and lonelier lives than they would have lived had none prayed for the prolongation of their lives, just because God chooses that human affection and human prayer should have a real weight in His providence, when they are subordinated to His will. Is there anything terrifying in that? So long as we are within the divine rule, and live under its love, is it so terrible to think that the prayers of shortsighted mortals may make our lives other than they would be without them? Why, that is what we all believe as to each other's outward *actions*. No one doubts that our lots are in matter of fact altered materially by the actions of those amongst whom we live; and so long as we believe the government of God to be over all, we do not shrink from the conviction that human wrong often makes our lives sadder, and human goodness sweeter, than they might otherwise have been. And if we hold that God thus gives human freedom of action a real moulding influence over our lives, why fear any the more the secret influence freely conceded to prayer by the divine love? It is as severely regulated, as much under control, in the one region as in the other; indeed it is hardly possible to believe in the real influence of human freedom over the lot of man in the outward sphere, unless it has a similar influence in the inward. I wish Canon Kingsley would add to his very fine sermon on the "reasonable" influence of prayer over the petitioner's own lot, another on the reasonable influence of intercessory prayer over the lot of others,—that is, over the divine government of society.

XXXIII

CANON LIDDON ON PRAYER AND MIRACLE

1874

IN the second edition to his thoughtful lectures on *Some Elements of Religion*,[1] reviewed in the columns of the *Spectator* a year and a quarter ago,[2] Canon Liddon has replied, in a very clear, careful, and interesting preface, to my criticism on his doctrine of prayer as sometimes at least involving prayer for a miracle, and so far as it does so, as being really open to the scientific objections which are so often unreasonably directed against all prayer. Dr. Liddon's reply makes it evident that he regards *all* answer to prayer as miraculous, in any sense in which he can attach an intelligible meaning to the word 'miraculous':—"It may perhaps be questioned," he says, "whether every real answer to prayer is not miraculous. Or, to speak more accurately, every such answer involves a certain departure from what, as we presume, would otherwise have been His mode of working who works everywhere,

[1] *Some Elements of Religion.* Lent Lectures, 1870. By H. P. Liddon, D.D., Canon of St. Paul's. Second Edition. Rivingtons.
[2] On the 21st September 1872.

in the physical as in the moral world. The difference between a resurrection from the dead at a prophet's prayer, and the increase of clearsightedness or of love, through the infusion of grace in the soul of a cottager, is a difference of degree. It is not a difference of kind. Each result is the product of a Divine interference with the normal course of things." And it is, I suppose, a development of the same idea, when he tells us in a subsequent page that he regards the reign of Law as extending to all regions of the universe equally, in all senses in which it extends to any, and not to be in the least inconsistent with the existence of free-will, though unquestionably "the activity of free-will in the moral sphere makes the laws which govern that sphere much more intricate and difficult to trace than are physical laws." Free-will, says Dr. Liddon, "cannot be held to annihilate all law in the highest region of created life, and therefore, if the presence of law be an objection to prayer anywhere, it is an objection to prayer everywhere. If it is an impertinence to ask God to vary His ordinary working in the lower regions of physics, it must be an impertinence to ask Him to do so, in the higher region of spiritual being,—of morals."

I cannot agree with this view of the matter, which seems to me not to be built on a distinct apprehension of the word "law" in its scientific sense. I understand the region of Law to be the region of practically invariable successions of phenomena,—phenomena in the order of which, when that order is discovered, thousands or millions of experiments have failed to discern any variation, and the order of which, so far as it is unknown, is assumed to present equally invariable lines of succession to the penetration of the investigator. Of course, I do not for a moment deny to God the *power* to vary, if He will, even the most uniform of all natural successions. I take the uniformity of Nature to be the sign and result of His will, not a controlling power of fate overruling His will; but the distinction is clear between successions in phenomena the order of which is assumed to be not only independent of every will but God's, but as a result of God's will fixed and knowable by man unless a miracle change it by way of sign to man, and successions in phenomena the order of which depends more or less directly on human wills, and varies constantly with human volitions. I quite understand necessarian thinkers, who hold that there is no such thing as free-will in man, asserting that the reign of law extends as much to moral as to physical phenomena. That has a definite meaning. It means that if we could but analyse the laws of character and circumstance, as, according to that conception, we may one day be able to analyse them, we should be able to forecast human actions of all kinds with as much certainty as that with which we now predict the revolutions of the planets or the results of chemical combination. But how can a man who believes in any human free will hold this? Such a belief implies that much, or at least something important, probably in every day of every human life, is left absolutely free to a man's choice; that his will *determines* the order of succession in all such cases, and, so far as there is freedom, that nothing external to his will determines his will. Of course, even in human life every rational man admits that the sphere of circumstance and necessity is large, and the sphere of freedom and real choice comparatively small. But so far as that sphere extends, to talk of the reign of law being still paramount seems to me to be using the same word in different and inconsistent senses. I mean by the reign of law the existence of an order so invariable, that given the proper antecedent, we can infer the consequent with as much confidence as we infer that if we place our hands near the fire we shall feel its warmth, or that if we divide an artery the blood will flow. But so far as free-will really obtains, how are we to conceive of such an antecedent phenomenon as will enable us to infer with certainty the moral consequent? Whenever the consequent comes, the cause of it, so far as the will was free, was an act which, by the very conditions of the case, might have been otherwise, not only without a miracle, but without a reason for surprise. If the will is ever really free to take either of two alternatives, compelled by no preponderant motive, by no involuntary inclination, in its choice, it is impossible to say that, given all the antecedents of the choice, the consequent could have been inferred as you infer that fire will warm the hands. To be suspended in anticipation between one of two or more consequents is not to be dealing with what comes under the "reign of law;" not to be so suspended, to be able to declare with certainty which of the two or more consequents will succeed, is to be dealing with the reign of law, but then it is also to deny real free-will. If God leaves anything really dependent on human will, so far He denies, even to the fullest knowledge, the certainty of scientific inference;—if more than one alternative is really open, no knowledge, however wide and minute, of human antecedents would enable us to select the inevitable consequent, and without an inevitable consequent there is no reign of law. God, who knows the inmost will, may foresee how it will act without controlling its freedom, but that is not after the manner of human foresight; it is not the anticipation of a consequent from a knowledge of such antecedents as are visible to human minds, but is due to a knowledge that goes far beneath anything that men can observe. Admit free-will, and you admit a number of cleavages in the rules of the uniform succession of phenomena which throw out science, in the human sense, altogether. Once admit that we may be able one day to predict volition absolutely from a knowledge of the laws of circumstance and motive, and you practically admit that volition is not a true self-determining power at all, but a mere name for one link in the chain of ordained successions.

And this is more than abstract theory. If free-will is more or less woven into the very substance of every day of every human life, and if prayer, being intended and declared by God to be the highest and most fruitful exercise of free-will, is also of the very substance of human life, resulting in answers to prayer, which involve, as Dr. Liddon justly says, "a certain departure from what, as we presume, would otherwise have been God's mode of working," then clearly such modifications and alterations of the order of life as that order would be without prayer, cannot be rare or wonderful—must, on the contrary, be among the most constantly recurring of human events, *i.e.* cannot be miracles, but must be a part, if not of the order of Nature in the limited sense, yet of human life as including something beyond Nature, namely, the regular and intelligible order of the supernatural. Now what I want to ask Canon Liddon is, whether there is any analogy between such regularly ordained alterations, introduced into what would be the merely secular or unreligious order of life, under the dispensation of prayer, and miracles, the very essence of which is something rare and stupendous, a deviation from God's ordinary rules of action? "The increase of clearsightedness and love, through an infusion of grace in the soul of a cottager," to use Dr. Liddon's own illustration, is, as I suppose he holds, in a Christian country at least, an event of every hour of every day. If that differs only "in degree," and not at all in any intelligible principle, from "the raising of a dead man at the prayer of a prophet," then surely there is no use in studying the divine order at all. It seems to me to be the most obvious teaching of constant experience, *i.e.* of science, that there are certain rules of succession among phenomena over which, as a matter of fact, our wishes and our prayers are not, as such, allowed the least control, or rather have never been allowed this power except in the great crisis of a divine revelation, when it was necessary to show once for all that God's power, even in the physical order, is guided by free love, and not by fate. On the other hand, in the sphere of free-will, in the sphere in which the sense of duty and of affection to God grows, there is a very large reserve of divine power which answers freely to human yearning and petition,— not of course always in the sense demanded, but always in some sense which makes us feel that human yearning and petition to God are not vain, but fruitful. Is it wise to ignore this difference? Does Dr. Liddon himself doubt that when death, for instance, has once happened, to pray for the resurrection of the dead in this world, however pure and pious the motive of the prayer, is to pray for what God has shown us by millions of proofs, through centuries of His government, that He will not grant? Is it pious to pray for what God has thus shown us that it is His better will not to grant? Can we for a moment let evidence of the uniformity of the divine action go for nothing, even in the sphere of prayer? Is it not all but certain that what God has never done but in one or two moments of unveiling, He has some great and divine purpose in refusing to do, which it is anything but pious in us to attempt to gainsay? Dr. Liddon says that my argument goes further than I intend,—that if we are to argue from what God does to what He wishes, we ought to limit ourselves to acts of resignation and praise, and not ask for any specific gift at all. But this is a complete misinterpretation of my position. I hold with Dr. Liddon that God does, both by the conscience and by revelation, teach us that prayer is both in the highest sense natural and also fruitful,—that He does habitually answer prayer for moral and spiritual help, and constantly also grants petitions for other blessings which perhaps we might have spared without any real spiritual loss, simply for the sake of encouraging the habit of communion with Him, and teaching us that there is a real sphere of life not beyond the moulding power of our requests, in which He meets us half-way, though He often denies what would hurt us. But I hold also, not, apparently, with Dr. Liddon, that this sphere is strictly limited, and that it belongs chiefly to the neighbourhood of that moral freedom in which the law of uniform antecedents and consequents fails. As a matter of fact, most men believe that they can more or less, mould their own lots by their volitions. If they can mould them by their volitions in any real sense at all, it is clear also that they can mould them by the prayers which influence volitions. And that, also, all who habitually pray, believe. But it does not follow in the least that because there is a real sphere within which the will is free, and prayer is efficient, there should be no sphere within which the will is not free and prayer not efficient. I may know that I have the power to do either this or that, but I know also that whichever I do, I cannot avert the natural consequences of the choice I make. I may believe that I shall obtain power to choose right, even though otherwise I should not have the power to choose right, by prayer. But I do not believe that if I pray that I may do wrong and yet suffer no ill moral result from it, the prayer will be answered. Just so, it may be of the greatest profit to pray that death may not come till a given work is done, and of no profit at all to pray that death may not come at all. When Dr. Liddon contends that, for a sufficiently high spiritual purpose, we are just as right in praying for a miracle as for an event which involves, indeed, supernatural gifts, but no miracle, because it involves nothing which is not asked and given every day, he seems to me to maintain that God does not teach us His true Will through the order of Nature at all. Suppose a man earnestly believed, as one of the Apostles, for instance, very well might have believed, that by continuing to live through all the centuries, he could give a witness to the facts of revelation such as would otherwise have been impossible, would he have been justified in praying for such an æonic life? Dr. Liddon would say yes, for he says that for a sufficiently high spiritual purpose, it would be legitimate to pray that an eclipse which was just on the point of beginning might be delayed. I should say no, on the distinct ground that to pray for miracles is to pray for what God has taught us by the simplest sort of teaching to believe contrary to His will; and I do not doubt that whenever prophets or apostles did pray for miracles, they did so only under the special illumination of a higher knowledge than any which ordinary men possess. My position is that the laws of the natural world, so far as they are known, are distinct lessons on the limits within which God's laws are practically immutable, and within which, therefore, our duty is absolute acquiescence, and not even humble petition. I should think a prayer for the restoration of the dead to life, as David apparently did, a prayer that God's will might *not* be done. So, too, I should think a prayer that fire might not burn, that a river might suddenly run dry, that the sun might not rise, or that gunpowder might lose its explosive power, a prayer that the Creator's laws might fail. If it is not permissible to judge of the divine purposes from uniform physical succession, in the absence of any higher illumination, these laws have no moral teaching for us at all. This is an error of the opposite extreme to that of science, which regards the physical laws as more really characteristic of God than His moral or spiritual laws. That, no doubt, is very false. But it is a bad remedy surely to teach that the physical laws of God are so little divine that every well-intentioned human wish may so far impugn their wisdom, as to beset God with entreaties to change the principles of His government and repent the never varied decrees of generations and of ages.

XXXIV

MAURICE AND THE UNITARIANS

1884

THE early portion of Colonel Maurice's Life of his father contains what has been regarded in many quarters as the most interesting section of the book,—the story, I mean, of the break-up of a heartily pious Unitarian family into its elements, some turning to the Church of England, some to Calvinistic Nonconformity, all except its head rejecting the Unitarian interpretation of the Bible, and he contemplating with a pathetic dismay, and an equally pathetic resignation, the sudden tumult of heart and intellect around him. The "notes,"— I use the word in the diplomatic rather than the homely sense,—in which the daughters conveyed to the elder Mr. Maurice their inability to worship in his chapel,—the tenderly-regretful tone in which the wife confided at length to her husband her change of faith, and her ardent desire to give effect to it in the way which would be least painful to him,—the perplexity of the old man at a state of mind which he so little understood, and the eagerness with which he evidently clung to the hope that his son,—of whose elevated nature they were all proud,—would adhere to what he regarded as the more reasonable faith, and vindicate him in his loneliness, are all so vividly laid before us, that even the reader who holds with Maurice, and not with his father, cannot help feeling a pang when he, too, confesses that if Revelation be a true name at all for the light given in the Bible, it must mean a great deal more than his father thinks; while if it be not a true name, the Bible cannot be made the foundation of a potent faith. Yet, undoubtedly, the change of faith, as it took place in the son, caused very much less of estrangement than the previous changes of the other children had caused; and for this reason, that the change in Frederick Maurice was in great measure the offspring of a yearning after a principle of unity, while the change in the other members of the family was, in form at least, little more than the substitution of one interpretation of Scripture for another interpretation which they had abandoned as poor and inadequate.

What, then, is meant by saying that Maurice's rejection of Unitarianism was the result of an ardent yearning after a centre of more perfect unity with others,—others generally differing from himself,—than he had ever been able to find in Unitarianism? It means just this, that Maurice regarded the self-revelation of a God within whose eternal nature there is something more complex and more mysterious than mere lonely will and lonely power, as the best guarantee of which he could conceive for the mutual affections and the mutual forbearances of a human society; and that he believed that such a gradual revelation was actually made to man in the Providential story of Jewish history as it culminated in the life and death and resurrection of Christ. It did not trouble him beyond measure that so many good men failed to recognise the truth of this revelation. It did not even trouble him beyond measure that so many failed to recognise any revelation, failed even to recognise the existence of any God at all. So long as he was sure that the history of the Jewish race was the history of a divine guidance tending steadily, and with ever increasing clearness, to the manifestation of the eternal Son of God in human nature, of one who knew and spoke the mind of the Father to the world, and came to reconcile the world to the Father, so long he regarded the blindness of those who recognised the truth inadequately, or who did not recognise it at all, as a very limited kind of calamity—one fairly comparable with the calamity of popular ignorance in relation to other beneficent agencies,—healing agencies like those of light, and air, and water, which are, of course, less beneficent while they are unrecognised than they are after they are recognised, but are beneficent in every phase, and so beneficent that the blessings they confer are sure to be recognised at last. The reason he was dissatisfied with Unitarianism was simply this,—that Unitarianism, even as his father understood it, explained away a great part of the actual revelation made by God to man, and therefore attenuated its importance and the trust and hope with which it inspired him. It was not that he thought himself any holier than Unitarians. On the contrary, he thought many Unitarians much holier than himself. But he held that the history contained in the Bible pointed to something much more mysterious and much more adequate to the need, and guilt, and passion of human nature, in the character of the divine life which it revealed, than anything which the Unitarians could find in that history, and therefore he held the Unitarian interpretation of that history to be a pallid one, which missed a good part of its true burden, and especially that part of it which is most essential to promote the true unity of men, and to add depth and intensity to the social relations. He admits in a letter to his father that Unitarianism is a much *simpler* account of the revelation given in the Bible than his own faith. But then, what it gains in simplicity it loses in adequacy, both as regards the actual language of Scripture, and also as regards that actual life in man in its appeal to which the language of Scripture is so potent. "It is simpler," he says, "to believe in a Great Spirit with the North American Indians, it is simpler to worship wood and stone; but what is the worth of simplicity, if it does not satisfy wants which we feel, if it does not lead us up to the truth which we desire?" The prophecies of the many predecessors of Christ were to Maurice unintelligible, if they represented nothing but the foreshadowings of a great "exemplar," and the life of Christ was still less intelligible as the mere life of that great exemplar. Either this long history, with its great catastrophe, meant something a great deal more expressive of that groaning and travailing of creation to which St. Paul referred, than the coming of an exemplar, or else a great deal less even than the Unitarianism of the elder Maurice represented it to be. Maurice believed that it meant a great deal more, and not a great deal less, than his father and the Unitarians generally understood by it; that it meant the deliberate unfolding of the nature and life of God with such power and passion as to inspire in man a transforming trust and a uniting love. Maurice did not, of course, expect that any theological belief could be the centre of unity; but he did expect that, if God were what he held that Scripture declared God to be, God Himself would be that centre of unity, because it showed God to be spending on the reconciliation of men to Himself the infinite stores of that divine passion of which we find our only adequate type in Gethsemane and on Calvary.

It is impossible to read Colonel Maurice's book without feeling that Maurice's change of faith was almost as much due to a passionate desire to find some centre of unity beneath the religious feuds of the world, which might prove to be an antidote to the poison of opinionative self-love, as it was due to the impression made upon his mind by the Scriptures themselves. And he held that he had discovered this centre of unity when he had discovered the evidence of a growing divine purpose, prosecuted for centuries, to draw man closer to God, a purpose effected not by any unnatural convulsion of human nature, but by the descent of God into human nature, and the taking-up of human nature into God. If such a purpose had been entertained and revealed to us, those who had caught a glimpse of it might, he thought, very safely trust Him who had entertained and revealed it to accomplish His own work in all good men, however little they might see what they were about, however much they might misunderstand it. He thought no worse of his father for remaining a

Unitarian, nor of his mother for believing herself beyond the reach of divine grace, nor of his sisters for their different and too vehemently-expressed religious convictions; he felt quite assured that in all of them, by different processes, the same divine work was going on which had engendered the new trust in himself; and that whether they saw it, or failed to see it, the God who had revealed Himself in the agony of the Cross and the glory of the Resurrection would reveal Himself through faith or doubt, through hope or despondency, through scepticism or dogmatism, to all who did not repel Him when they felt His prompting in their hearts. He did not think that Unitarianism could engender the same confidence, simply because he did not think that Unitarianism recognised the divine passion of love for man in the same clear and potent form— because he held that Unitarianism ignored the most significant and impressive of all the features of the divine life and character. Confidence must depend on the clearness of your vision of the power on which you lean. God is the same to the Unitarian as to the Trinitarian, but the confidence felt in God by Maurice when he was a Unitarian, and by Maurice when he became a Trinitarian, could not be the same, for this plain reason, that in the latter. phase of his life he saw evidence in God of a much deeper sympathy with man, and of a nature more assuredly capable of being engrafted on that of man, than he had seen in the former phase of his life. Maurice always said of the Unitarians that in their deep belief in the fatherhood of God they were founded on a rock. But he held that that belief would be in danger of fading away, if it were held, as it was by Unitarians, to affirm only the relation of the Eternal Being to finite creatures, and not rather to affirm a relation intrinsically belonging to the divine nature, and extended to include man only because the Son of God is the organic head and redeemer of the human race. And has not the development of Unitarianism, since the time when Maurice ceased to be a Unitarian, done much to verify his fear that the profound belief in the fatherhood of God for which Unitarians were once remarkable would fade gradually away into something like the faith or no-faith of modern Agnostics,—the disposition to worship laws of Nature, and vaguely adore the Unknown and Unknowable? Unless I greatly misread the recent story of the Unitarian Church, the ardent belief in the fatherhood of God entertained by Unitarians fifty or forty years ago has faded away in a great many of their congregations into Theism not always of a Christian type, or even into an ethical variety of scientific Agnosticism.

XXXV

MR. MAURICE AS HERESIARCH

1872

THOSE of my readers who may have known nothing of Mr. Maurice except what they found said of him in the columns of the *Spectator* last week, will probably have asked themselves the question how such a religious teacher as I have described could have been feared as he was,—could have been regarded as a great heresiarch, could have been condemned in these loose-thinking latter days by an obscure college council, and even to the last always held as a dangerous man unfit for Church promotion by the official scrutineers of Church opinion. I should be disposed even to think that the Dean of Westminster has been far less feared by those curious in the arts of safe ecclesiastical navigation than Maurice. The reason no doubt is, that while the Dean of Westminster is regarded as a latitudinarian whose teaching ignores all the finer distinctions of theology as not worth the study, Maurice teaches nothing that he does not teach intensely, and that his mind was so spiritual that when he seems to the anxious theologian to err at all, his error is a sunken rock on which the unwary voyager may not only strike, but stick. Even the *Guardian*, cordially as it writes of Maurice this week, is profoundly permeated by this feeling. It speaks of him as something high, and deep, and sweet, but for all that dangerous,— to be held a little in awe and fear for the depth of his errors, as well as in love for his noble personal qualities. "It is the work of the future to pronounce on his influence and teaching; at the present moment, almost over his grave, we shrink from the task;"—"there was much, very much in his teaching with which we could not sympathise, which we think unsound in itself and dangerous in the inferences which more logical minds will draw from it. But his career was remarkable, and in some sense so entirely unique in its influence on English thought and life, and the character of the man himself stands out so nobly, that," etc. Evidently the fear he inspired, as of a not only great, but *deep* heresiarch, whose fervour and intensity constituted the very danger of his fascination, survives him. The safe men still think of him as a sort of theological maelstrom, by which it is pretty certain that you will be sucked in if you go too near it. What is the warrant for this half-fearful wonder with which Maurice is still regarded by 'sound' Churchmen? No one ventures for a moment to deny the profound humility which made so striking a feature in Mr. Maurice's character, yet humility has never been the characteristic of any heresiarchs. No one denies the extreme and shrinking aversion which he felt to admitting the existence of actual error in Scripture, yet a deep and even mystical faith in the literal divinity of Scripture has certainly never been the characteristic of modern heresiarchs.

I believe that the real foundation for this fear of

Maurice as a great distracting force in the world of theological thought is caused by that intense inwardness of his spiritual faith which almost snatches away theology from the purview of the mere intellect, and makes men who are hardly capable of approaching it from any other than an intellectual side sensible that they are nowhere, as it were, in his writings;—nay, that the very essence of their mode of thought is almost branded by Maurice as "of the nature of sin," as something which he has often been "tempted" to acquiesce in, but which in the depth of his reverence for God's revealed truth he never "dared" to acquiesce in. Theologians of the ordinary type coming to the study of Maurice are not only apt to be bewildered as to his real meaning, but to feel themselves reproached for that external and "notional" view of things divine which they find him rebuking as the lowest element in himself, whereas *they* had rather taken a pride in their masterly speculative apprehension of matters so transcendental. Now this sort of impression that the intellectual and systematic view of theology was denounced by Maurice as a moral danger was very trying to men whose theological conceptions were saturated with speculative and logical ideas. They hardly knew how to deal with such a point of view. It embarrassed and it alarmed them. They thought theology would not often be studied by "such beings as we are in such a world as the present," if it was not to be learnt as a system and connected together by intellectual generalisations. Mystics, they did not deny, have their place in relation to any faith of which the whole cannot be adequately grasped; but here was a mystic who, not contented with his own province of thought, invaded theirs and made them feel unspiritual because they approached theology from the intellectual and not from the spiritual side. This is, I believe, in a great degree the real account of the distaste and fear with which safe Churchmen regard Maurice's teaching; but it was of course greatly increased and brought to a focus by his special heresy, as it was thought, in relation to the Eternal punishment of the wicked,—a point on which his doctrine was both profoundly misapprehended, and, so far as it was apprehended, dreaded and condemned. Mr. Haweis endeavoured the other day, in a letter to the *Pall Mall*, to define Maurice's true position on that subject; but as I have heard it remarked that the explanation was as difficult as the teaching itself, I will in my turn try my hand at elucidating the most critical point of this great religious thinker's teaching.

When Mr. Maurice was asked what he meant by 'eternal' as distinguished from 'endless' or 'everlasting,' he always replied in effect that it was related to 'everlasting' as the spiritual source is related to the outward form; as, for instance, the depth and truth of a principle are related to its durability and influence on human society; as the vital germ of a tree that lives for centuries is related to its length of days; as the inward character of a great man is related to his age-long ascendancy over human thoughts,—in a word, as the constitution of anything is related to its outward duration. 'Eternal' he held was properly applied solely to God. 'Everlasting' is simply our translation of the divine essence into the language of time. It is impossible for us to conceive God, if we conceive Him in time at all, as ever having had either beginning or end; He is at the heart of everything, so that nothing whatever is conceivable without Him; hence, if we do translate 'eternal,' which is applicable only to Him, into the language of time at all, we must translate it as 'everlasting,' as having neither beginning nor end. He preferred the word 'eternal,' because he did not think the time-view the original one, but a derivative one. 'Eternal' took you, he held, into the depths of the invisible life *behind* the world,—while 'everlasting' only bewildered the imagination with a futile attempt to strain back into the past beyond our reach, and forward into the future beyond our ken. Still, if time-language were to be used at all, 'everlasting' was the right translation for 'eternal.' He did not think it a very instructive translation; he thought we lost by not keeping to the qualitative essence of God, rather than insisting on the quantitive duration. But the word 'endless' he repudiated altogether, because it is applicable to things clearly *not* divine, —signifying duration which, though it *has* begun, will never cease,—and so losing the necessary reference to God which he regarded as embodied in the word 'eternal,' and not lost in 'everlasting,' since 'ever' goes back as infinitely as it goes forward, and is only applicable therefore to Him without whom all existence is inconceivable. Such being Mr. Maurice's view of these three words, he maintained that 'eternal life' and 'eternal death' meant nothing more or less than 'life in Him who is eternal,' and 'death from Him who is eternal,'—life in God, and death from God. His great Scriptural authority of course was St. John's report of our Lord's prayer, "This *is* life eternal, to know thee the only true God." If 'eternal life' were knowledge of God, 'eternal death,' he inferred, must be loss of the knowledge of God. If, therefore, any attempt were made to translate 'eternal life' and 'eternal death' into the language of time, we must remember that the everlastingness is only the attribute of God, not of the relation between the individual and God. A man may have 'eternal life' even in this world, and may again lose it, may fall from eternal life into eternal death, may cease to live in the divine righteousness, and be immured again in the hell of self. Mr. Maurice's most emphatic teaching was, that to be immured in self,— to have no vision of the source of life and redemption,—*is* hell, the worst conceivable hell, the most terrible of all tortures. In this world indeed he would say this hell can never be quite complete; there is always the sensible world at least to draw one out of oneself; but if any one gives way to the tendencies which make self supreme, the time may come when the self has not even this distraction, when, after death, it is immured wholly in its own ugly and impotent thoughts, when its perfect solitude becomes intolerable anguish. This was his notion of 'eternal death.' It did not mean everlasting death, it meant the loss of life in God. So eternal life did not mean everlasting life, it meant life in the everlasting,—in God,—but which might yet assuredly be severed from the everlasting,— from God. As to the duration of this death, Mr. Maurice would never express any opinion, except that it must last till the evil will was overcome, and that as God had expressed His will that all men be saved, he would not dare to affirm that the will of God would fail to triumph over all the evil wills that resisted it. Still he felt no wish to measure the enormous power which might be contained in the evil will of man. He admitted that God Himself could not triumph over that power without the willingness of man to submit, and he did not "dare" measure the power of resistance. His whole mind, however, revolted against the conception that God Himself ever casts any man's soul into the hell of self-imprisonment. He was horrified at that interpretation of our Lord's words in the Sermon on the Mount, which supposes him to represent God as killing and casting into hell. "I say unto you, my friends, be not afraid of them that kill the body, and after that have no more that they can do; but I will forewarn you whom ye shall fear: Fear him which, after he hath killed, hath power to cast into hell; yea I say unto you, fear him." "We are come," said Mr. Maurice, "to such a pass as actually to suppose that Christ tells those whom He calls His *friends* not to be afraid of the poor and feeble enemies who can only kill the body, but of that greater enemy who can destroy their very selves, and that this enemy is,—not the Devil, not the spirit who is going about seeking whom he may devour, not he who was a murderer from the beginning,—but that God who cares for the sparrows; they are to be afraid lest He who numbers the hairs of their head should be plotting their ruin." This interpretation horrified Maurice. He always asserted that 'eternal' life,—life in God,—was never withheld from any one who would give up the evil will which his own sin, or a tempter more powerful than his own will, had corrupted; that eternal death was never God's decree, but the doing only of evil powers resisting God.

How far this teaching is, in an ecclesiastical sense,

heretical, the present writer is hardly theologian enough to know, especially in relation to the very fluid and variable standards of the English Church. A great deal in very orthodox writers comes very near to it. Dr. Newman, for instance, in his beautiful story of the martyr "Callista," represents eternal death from very much the same point of view, as not inflicted by any decree of God, but simply the natural result of an immersion in self so habitual and complete that the vision of God, if it could be granted, would be more exquisite pain than even the loss of it. Only he does not recoil as Maurice did from the thought that God's will to save every man could ever be finally defeated by the powers of evil. If Maurice were an heresiarch, he was so from his inability to piece together the spiritual truths he had so powerfully grasped, by a tissue of intellectual system in which he could not feel any spiritual force; from his inability to let intellectual tradition dominate his direct spiritual apprehensions. It was a ground of heresy, if heresy it was, which he shared with Fénelon,—the teacher of the past whose spirit was most like his, though in fire and force of personal conviction he was greatly Maurice's inferior.

XXXVI

DR. GEORGE MACDONALD ON HELL

1884

DR. GEORGE MACDONALD, in the interesting preface which he has appended to the *Letters from Hell*,[1] just translated into English from the German version of a Danish book,—originally published eighteen years ago,—expresses at least one conviction of great importance. It is the conviction that we make our own misery, after death,—our own future, as well as occasionally our own present, hell, "*in unmaking ourselves.*" Dr. MacDonald amplifies this terse and remarkable phrase, by explaining his meaning to be "that men, in defacing the image of God in themselves, construct for themselves a world of horror and dismay; that of *the outer darkness*, our own deeds and characters are the informing or inwardly creating cause; that if a man will not have God, he never can be rid of his weary and hateful self."

It would be hard to find a finer expression than that which I have quoted as Dr. MacDonald's condensation of the process of moral disintegration, the "unmaking of ourselves." But is it always

[1] Published by Messrs. Bentley and Son.

applicable to those who are really living in "the outer darkness"? No doubt it suggests a perfectly true account of all that can involve moral guilt, and of all that therefore entails moral despair. It is, however, only right to remember that that *unmaking* of man which is guilt in those who are the causes of it, is often really effected by ancestors, and not by the existing beings in whom its effect is now chiefly seen. One of the gravest of the difficulties in the ordinary teaching about the future state is the failure to distinguish between the condition of those who have been unmade by themselves, and those who have been unmade by the guilt of their forefathers. Our Lord, indeed, tells us that the distinction ought to be insisted on, that from those to whom little has been given little will be required, that it is only those who have known their Master's will, and failed to do it, who will be beaten with many stripes, while those who have more or less unwittingly failed in doing it, will be beaten only with few. Still, that teaching has not been taken up as it ought to have been, for it involves the further teaching that the process of remaking in man what has been "unmade" by the sins of his forefathers, and not by his own, will be much less painful and terrible than the process,—if ever it can be performed,—of remaking the image of God which it has been a man's own doing to deface. This very book, which Dr. George MacDonald asks us to admire,—and which certainly deserves a certain amount of admiration for its occasional imaginative vigour and lurid intensity,—appears to draw no substantial difference at all between those who are expiating the sins of others, whose consequences they inherited, and those who are really expiating their own. Surely, if that "unmaking" of the divine image in which man was created, is the doing not so much of the offspring, as of parents and parents' parents,—if the atmosphere into which any being is born is one of moral evil, and the character inherited by that being is one almost specially adapted, as it were, for the assimilation of that moral evil,—then, though the apparent spiritual condition may be the same, the penalty ought not to be, and cannot be, the same, while God is just. Those who unmade the image of God in themselves must be held responsible for having transmitted to others a nature in which that image was hardly recognisable. And no account of that evil condition into which the unclothed spirit falls, when it finds itself alien from God, and trying in vain to be satisfied from itself, can be a reasonable one, unless it discriminates in the broadest way, not only between different degrees of incapacity for seeing and loving God, but also between the different causes of that incapacity, some of them being absolutely involuntary, others wholly voluntary, and others, again, a compound of voluntary and involuntary elements.

Dr. MacDonald's main principle evidently is that the state of misery into which men fall when the interests of earth are taken away, is not of God's decreeing, but wholly of their own making, or rather unmaking; that God wills us all to live in Him, and creates our nature so that its only perfect satisfaction is in Him, as the Psalmist implied when he said, "All my fresh springs shall be in thee"; but that we unmake ourselves whenever we detach ourselves from these spiritual aims, and try to put other and smaller ends above the only aims for which it is possible to live always and with an ever-increasing volume of life. But is that assumption of the full responsibility of every mind, living in the outer darkness, for its own misery when it loses its hold of earth, true? Is not the disintegrating process in which Dr. MacDonald truly regards guilt as consisting, begun for us all more or less in the evil tendencies we inherit, and more than begun,—well-nigh completed,—for some of those who are born into a world from which God seems almost to have disappeared? Surely that is a kind of incapacity for true life which ought to involve far less misery to the individual who suffers from it, than an incapacity which he had himself freely made for himself; and yet it leaves him for the time in "the outer darkness" all the same. This is why I cannot absolutely endorse Dr. MacDonald's view that the state in which man lives without God is always one of self-inflicted misery. It arises, more or less, surely, from the guilt of others, and not always from man's own. And where it arises from the guilt of others, and not chiefly from the guilt of those who suffer from it, it must, I believe, be a very different kind of misery,—one much more easily removed, one much more permeable by divine grace,—than the incapacity which is strictly self-made. It is one of the dangers, as I think, of the new school of theology — which explains all misery as a natural state, and not as the consequence of divine judgment—that it does not distinguish between a naturally-inherited and a personally-incurred blindness to things spiritual. The naturally-inherited blindness must, if we are to believe fully in God's justice, find another probation in the future state, a probation which it has never had in this. Of the personally-incurred blindness, I could not say the same. I should judge of it even less hopefully than Dr. MacDonald. I might admit virtually Dr. MacDonald's premiss that "it would be nothing less than injustice to punish infinitely what was finitely committed"; but I should deny that this assumption is involved in every theory of eternal suffering. No doubt, to justify unceasing suffering, you must assume unceasing guilt; you must hold that there is no divine barrier ever placed between the sinner and repentance; that if he does not turn away from his own evil heart with loathing, it is his own act; that he is always "unmaking" himself, to use Dr. MacDonald's expression, if he continues to cling to his own evil; and that so, and so only, he earns,— if he does earn, —unceasing suffering. But then, is not such a conception perfectly justified by the experience of life? If any one ever voluntarily sinks further and further into evil, knowing what he is about, where is the evidence that he will ever turn back? What happens for months may happen for years; what happens for years, may happen for centuries. It is essential, to the conception of the divine goodness and mercy, no doubt, to believe that God never leaves any one without some witness of Himself, to believe that He will be to all eternity willing to receive the penitent. But where is the evidence that that which goes on in many hearts, in spite of that witness, for a lifetime, may not go on in some of them for ever?

The book to which Dr. MacDonald gives such praise, is a book of extremely unequal power, and parts of it are really vulgar and contemptible,—I allude especially to the passage as to the consultations of Satan with his granddam concerning the best means of destroying man's soul. Its strength consists in the vivacity with which it represents the nakedness and emptiness of the soul,—the emptiness of all desire, the nakedness of the miserable self,—in the condition to which death reduces the sinful heart. Its weakness consists in the absolute dead-level to which it appears to reduce all who are not saved by their faith in and love for Christ. Now, as we know perfectly well that the absence of that faith and love at the moment of death may be due to very different causes, and that some of these causes need not be moral causes at all, the reality of the writer's thought is greatly injured by his very conventional view of this subject. Of course, there are many theologians who, with the author of this book, would not shrink from saying that souls often suffer eternally, and without hope of any alleviation, who have never done anything in this world for which they felt the sting of conscience. I can only say that if that be so, eternal suffering is unjustly awarded to those who have never had a chance of true salvation. Dr. MacDonald, of course, would be as eager to repudiate such a notion as I am; but even his teaching seems to make the suffering of the spiritual state too much of a *natural* consequence of alienation from God, instead of depending, as I maintain on our Lord's principle that it must depend, on the *causes* of that alienation. Alienation from God must, no doubt, always involve either suffering, or the blankness of heart which is worse than suffering. But it does not, and cannot involve, in the case of those who have not themselves brought about that alienation, a suffering of the same kind as it involves when it comes as the consequence of voluntary sin. I hold that no theory of the final character of future sufferings can be just at all which does not give in the next life a genuine probation to all who have not had it here, and which does not hold open, even for those who have had and have rejected it here, the power of repenting at any time, if at any time those who have so often refused to repent are willing to turn their back upon themselves, and the evil into which they have been slowly hardening. Hell may be, and no doubt is, a *state*, and not a place; but it is a state which must differ infinitely in hopefulness or hopelessness, for every one who is conscious of it, according to the character of the moral antecedents which ushered in that state.

XXXVII

BISHOP MAGEE ON THE ETHICS OF FORGIVENESS

1884

"Do you not see," says the Bishop of Peterborough, in the course of an Oxford University sermon on the Ethics of Forgiveness, which he has just republished,—and with important extensions if I am not mistaken,—in the remarkable volume called *The Gospel and the Age*,—"Do you not see that all this magniloquent and windy talk about a merciful and compassionate God, so facile and easy in His forgiveness, is a mere conception of modern Theism?—that it is, after all, the poorest and lowest idea we can form of God? that it does not rise above the low thought of the savage, which pictures Him merely as an angry and offended man? Rise but one degree above that, rise up in your thought to the idea of Him as the judge of all the earth: rise one degree higher to the idea of Him as the author and controller of the moral universe, and all this talk about easy, good-natured forgiveness vanishes in your nobler but more awful conceptions of God, as the cloud-wreath vanishes at the rising of the sun?" Now, I can imagine that passage having been written with a drift with which I should heartily agree, and I believed at the time the sermon was first published by a Missionary Society which hoped, by the help of it, to remove some of the difficulties which stand in the way of the reception of the Christian doctrine of the atonement, that the drift of the Bishop was one with which, in the main, I did agree. But that hope is greatly diminished by the form in which the sermon is now republished, and I fear that the Bishop's sermon will do more to throw new difficulties in the way of the understanding of the Christian doctrine of the sacrifice of Christ, than to remove any. What the Bishop seems to be aiming at is not to show how great, how infinite almost, is the difficulty of moving man to a true abhorrence of sin, and of reconciling him to God by infusing into him the divine abhorrence of sin, but how impossible it is, *even after that difficulty is surmounted*, to conceive God as forgiving sin, except by the help of something which the Bishop calls a "moral miracle" to enable Him to do it. Now, far as my conception of God —far as the Christian conception of God—is from that of a Being who is "easy and good-natured" in His forgiveness of sin, not even that view seems to me less like the Christian view than one which would tell us that a "moral miracle" is required to enable God to forgive even those sins which are truly and earnestly repented. And though the Bishop of Peterborough does not always appear to distinguish between the saving of the sinner from the "consequences of sin" and the divine forgiveness of sin itself—two totally different matters, as it appears to me—yet I regret to think that the main drift of his sermon is that, even assuming true repentance on the part of man, it takes some special suspension of the ordinary moral laws of the universe in which we live, to enable God to forgive the sin thus heartily repented of. At least, if this be not the preacher's drift, I do not know what can be the meaning of this passage, the earlier part of which is, as I believe, new in the sermon as Dr. Magee now republishes it. "Is it alleged, however," he asks, "that God forgives, not of mere compassion, but on condition of penitence, and that he who truly repents has thereby satisfied His requirements, and may, therefore, claim to be forgiven; while he who remains impenitent does so of his own act and choice, and therefore deserves his fate?" I should have supposed that nothing could be plainer than the apostolic affirmative to that question, which, however, the Bishop, as we shall soon see, answers in the negative. "If we say that we have no sin," says St. John, "we deceive ourselves, and the truth is not in us. If we confess our sins, he is *faithful and righteous to forgive us our sins, and to cleanse us from all unrighteousness.*" But the Bishop does not appear to agree with St. John that the matter is so simple as that. It takes something more than fidelity and righteousness, he evidently thinks, in God, to justify the forgiveness of the penitent. "Surely the answer to this is obvious," he continues. "The refusal of the impenitent to repent is either a sin or a defect; either he will not or he cannot repent. If it is a sin, why not forgive it like any other sin? If it is only an imperfection, why punish it at all? Is it not clear, moreover, that if God forgives only the penitent He is less compassionate than He bids us to be, when He tells us to forgive all our debtors whether penitent or impenitent? And if, on the other hand, penitence is a necessary antecedent condition of forgiveness, arising out of the nature and constitution of things, then equally so, for aught we can tell, may atonement and mediation be such conditions too. Then there is this further difficulty. God is the author of that very constitution of things, of those inexorable and unalterable laws, under which, as we have seen,"— let me say parenthetically that if I rightly understand the sermon, we have seen nothing of the kind, —" forgiveness is scarcely conceivable. Are we to suppose then, that He will deflect those laws at our bidding?" No, we are to suppose nothing of the kind. But all that the Bishop has shown is not in the least that under the moral laws of the universe "forgiveness" is scarcely conceivable, but a very different thing indeed, that under the moral laws of the universe, it is hardly, or not at all, conceivable, that the *consequences* of sin in disturbing and undermining society should cease with repentance; that it is next to impossible either that we can regard ourselves as free from responsibility for the evil that we have done, even when we have repented it, however heartily; or that others should regard us as having finally and fully expiated that evil. But this is surely a totally different thing from saying that *forgiveness* is hardly conceivable. If there be any meaning in Christ's Gospel at all, true penitence is as sure of true forgiveness, as sin is sure of punishment. The Bishop's attempt to represent the breaking of the divine law, and impenitence for the breaking of the divine law, as distinct sins, the latter of which is as much entitled to forgiveness as the former, is surely a very forced march in logic. How is it possible that if true penitence be the necessary condition of God's forgiveness, impenitence should be as much entitled to forgiveness as any other sin? Can an impenitent man be penitent for his impenitence? If so, he is not impenitent. If, on the contrary, he *is* impenitent for his impenitence, he has no claim for forgiveness. God forgives only him who resolutely separates himself from the evil he has committed, and abhors himself for it; but once assume the will to do that, and as I understand Christ's teaching, not only God, but all good beings rejoice, and feel no longer alienated in heart from him who has thus put the evil away from him. As for its requiring a "moral miracle" to forgive such a one, it would seem to me to require a moral miracle, and the most astounding of all moral miracles, for any good Being *not* to forgive him; but by forgiveness I only mean the removal of all alienation of spirit, and by no means the restoration of the penitent to the same position in the moral world in which he stood before he did what he knew to be evil.

What I dread in the attempt to make of the atonement a miracle primarily essential to the granting of God's forgiveness even to the truly penitent, is this, that it appears to present God as divinely averse to that which Christ assures us to belong to the very essence and constitution of His nature. It seems to me the very denial, not only of Christ's revelation, but of all that the prophets had taught, to represent the obstacle to forgiveness as being in the reluctance of God to restore the penitent to His own love and favour. Doubtless the mystery of the doctrine of sacrifice is magnified even in the prophets, and grew constantly before the minds of all the great Hebrew teachers till it culminated in the life and death of Christ. But that mystery consists in the infinite sacrifice needed to bring hatred of sin home to the hearts of men, not in the infinite magnitude of the obstacle presented by the Divine mind to the forgiveness of evil, in cases where it had once been so brought home to the heart, and hated as it deserved to be. Surely the mystery in the doctrine of sacrifice, great as it is, is a mystery because it measures the difficulty which an infinite Being has in bringing a finite being to his senses, and not because it measures the difficulty which an infinite Being has in finding a sufficient excuse for doing that which love and righteousness alike prompt Him to do. I agree with the Bishop of Peterborough in thoroughly rejecting the shallow doctrine of a "good-natured God"; but I do not agree with him in thinking,—as he leads us to believe that he does think,—that the mystery of evil lies in the difficulty of according true divine forgiveness to the penitent; for I hold that the only mystery in this matter is the mystery of evil itself,—the strange difficulty of producing in not merely finite, but even very weak creatures, that penitence which alone perfect righteousness can possibly forgive.

XXXVIII

MR. GLADSTONE ON THE ATONEMENT

1894

It seems to me a great pity that Mr. Gladstone's interesting and thoughtful article on the meaning of vicarious redemption should have been connected with the criticism of such a book as Mrs. Besant's *Autobiography*, which really only shows how a thoroughly undisciplined mind can go off at a tangent from one superficial mode of error to another, more because the thinker has exhausted one false mode of apprehending the glimpses permitted us of the infinite purposes of our life, than because she has gained any truer or more steady vision of it. It is like choosing the most unmeaning of all the accidents of human caprice as the text for a discussion of the most profound of all the purposes of divine goodness, to associate Mrs. Besant's sudden and unbridled freaks of religious or irreligious conviction with the mysterious but at the same time inspiring theme of divine sacrifice. Except by way of illustrating the contrast between the arbitrariness of human excuses for rejecting truth and the slow and steady development of divine teaching, there is no natural connection at all between Mrs. Besant's revolt against the doctrine of Christ's vicarious suffering and Mr. Gladstone's reason for holding fast to it.

I think, then, that it would be best to dismiss Mrs. Besant at once as a writer who must evidently be allowed to exhaust herself in a series of spasmodic feats of intellectual acrobatism before she has any chance of gaining a position of calm and peaceful trust. But Mr. Gladstone's paper is worth a great deal more than its accidental starting-point. To my judgment, he takes a very sound and luminous course when he starts from the assumption that pain, "though it is not lawfully to be inflicted except for wrong done, is not in itself essentially evil. It has been freely borne again and again by good men for the sake of bad men; and they have borne it sometimes with benefit to the bad men, but always with benefit to themselves." The only question is whether there is anything in the divine character and omnipotence which renders it impossible to acquiesce, in relation to the voluntary acceptance of pain by a divine mind, in a view which we have no difficulty at all in taking, of the willing human endurance of it for the sake of others. When one man consents to suffer acutely in order that he may lighten the burden of another who has brought his misery upon himself, we are not scandalised, but subdued into genuine reverence by the spectacle. Is there anything in the mystery of infinite power and purpose which renders it impossible to reconcile with the righteousness of God, what we so eagerly associate with righteousness in man? I think that Mr. Gladstone omits to notice one of the most conspicuous links in the true interpretation of a divine atonement, when he passes over this question, which I should answer simply in the sublime words of St. James,—" Every good and every perfect gift is from above, and cometh down from the Father of lights with whom is no variableness, neither shadow of turning." That surely is the master-principle of divine revelation. What is good and perfect in man, has its origin and starting-point in God, who is the prompter of all good. This does not imply, of course, that what is good but painful in human action is not only good but also painful to the divine prompter, for, as Mr. Gladstone truly says, God prompts us to do what is to us painful because we are imperfect, because our human nature is made up of more or less incompatible instincts and desires, and what must therefore wound and gall some of our cravings, while it gratifies and exalts others. "If we are told," says Mr. Gladstone, that "God in His perfection could receive no good from pain," as men who take upon themselves the burden of others' sufferings certainly do, the answer is that, "by the Incarnation, Christ took upon Him a nature not strictly perfect but perfectible, for He grew in wisdom and stature and in favour with God and man"; and that, therefore, the divine prompting to take up and bear the infirmities of human nature, and to endure the stripes by which we are healed, though it came down from "the Father of lights with whom there is no variableness, neither shadow of turning," did not imply anguish in Him who prompted the renunciation, but only in that human nature which at that prompting the Son of God assumed. Once grant that "every good and every perfect gift cometh from above," and we must grant that the willingness to assume the burden of others' sins came from above; and that, however mysterious it may be, the wish and the power to suffer the most terrible of the agonies of human sympathy, is a gift from above, even though it proceeds from a nature which, on its divine side, is as incapable of anguish as on its human side it is infinite in its capacity for a kind of passion of which ordinary human beings are utterly unable to measure the grandeur and the scope. This capacity for infinite passion in a divine humanity seems to me the very central light of revelation. Without it I should be tempted to say that the capacity for vicarious suffering in man would in some sense put man above God, did we not learn from revelation that the very root of that capacity in man is of divine origin, and that it rises to its highest flood in the mystery of that divinely human nature which by its organic union with our own gives us all the little power we have for sharing and lightening the burdens of others. If Christ had been man alone, we might have been moved to the deepest reverence by His example, but we could not have recognised, what we now recognise, that it is by virtue of our spiritual union with Him, and by that alone, that we derive the impulse to suffer for others on which we might otherwise pride ourselves. The mysterious union of a divine life led within all the cruel pressure of human limitations seems to me the only explanation of the joy in bearing "the heavy and the weary weight of all this unintelligible world," on which our greatest spiritual poet descants as transmuting sorrow into—

> "Sorrow that is not sorrow, but delight;
> And miserable love that is not pain
> To hear of, for the glory that redounds
> Therefrom to human kind and what we are."

Mr. Gladstone puts what is called the "forensic" analogy for the "scheme" of atonement, with great delicacy and discrimination, showing where it fails, and how far it may be regarded as well founded; but I think with him that the directions in which it fails are far more conspicuous than those in which it holds good. "Pardon," as I understand it, is not so much a magnanimous concession of God's pity to human repentance, as a necessary and immediate consequence of all true penitence, though Mr. Gladstone is certainly right in saying that pardon to the truly penitent in no way involves the remission of all the shame and suffering which are the necessary consequences of sin; for the extinction of that shame and suffering would really imply not the reality, but the unreality of the penitence. To my mind, indeed, the "forensic" analogy for the Atonement, with which Mr. Gladstone deals so subtly and delicately, has been from the first a great theological mistake, which has done far more to cloud the true meaning and grandeur of the vicarious sacrifice of Christ, than to illustrate or explain it. I am grateful to Mr. Gladstone for using his great influence to clear away this cloud of false analogy, and to restore the grandeur of the great truth that without a regenerating impulse from the divine mind, man would never have been able to appreciate the true glory of vicarious suffering; in other words, that the divine justification and the beginning at least of sanctification in man, are not the consequences but the conditions of a pardon which is sometimes gravely represented as preceding and causing, instead of following and involving, penitence. The slowly crystallised doctrine of Atonement not only affords us a measure of the infinite evil of sin, but also evidence of the growing anticipation visible in the prophetic writers of the only event which could have brought us any healing for the magnitude of the evil it had disclosed.

XXXIX

PRINCIPAL TULLOCH ON SPIRITUAL EVOLUTION

1876

Principal Tulloch delivered on Sunday, March 19, in Edinburgh, the first of a series of lectures on the Christian doctrine of Sin, and dwelt in his opening address chiefly on the bearing which the recognition of the fact of sin should have on the modern theory of evolution. He pointed out that there is nothing in Christian teaching in the least inconsistent with the theory of development of which Mr. Darwin, for instance, is the chief exponent. What is inconsistent with it is the notion, he said, that everything can be accounted for as a mere growth out of antecedent states, and that all divine agency is excluded; that Nature is not merely a sphere of action, but the acting power itself, beyond which there is nothing. That the doctrine of evolution, by natural selection or in any other way, may describe the true method in which life rises from the lower to the higher levels, Principal Tulloch not only did not deny, but held it to be in every sense consistent with the evolution of conscious life, as we know it ourselves, on those higher levels. It is no longer supposed, as he very justly remarked, that theology is merely the classified arrangement of Scriptural teachings properly interpreted, it is held by all the better thinkers to be the vital growth of the moral and spiritual experience of man as enlightened by Scripture, and its business is to trace the various links in the organised structure of Christian history and thought. Now, if this be true, so far is a doctrine of gradual evolution of the forms of life from being inconsistent with Christian teaching, it is but the anticipation in lower stages of creation of the highest application of that teaching. Only, just as in interpreting the gradual development of Christian doctrine and Christian thought, we never think of assuming that the later stage is nothing but the earlier stage in transformation, but rather assume that the later stage is a fuller unfolding of that divine mind which was less perfectly seen in the earlier stage, so with regard to physical evolution, the assumption of the Christian faith is that it is the divine power which is seen in evolution throughout all the stages of the gradual growth of life, only more fully manifested in the more complex organisms of the higher creation than in the simpler organisms of the lower. Christian faith has not only nothing to say against evolution, but recognises evolution as one of the most important phases in the method of revelation itself. But such faith is wholly inconsistent with the radical idea dominating materialistic conceptions of evolution,—namely, that the process of growth really explains the cause as well as the history of life on the earth,—and also with the radical idea dominating the view of Matthew Arnold and the modern Dutch school of divines,—that there is nothing but an abstract ideal which is higher than man, that religion is only "morality touched with emotion," and God an expression for "a stream of tendency, not ourselves, which makes for righteousness," in other words, not the foundation of our life, but its visionary goal. Now with both these conceptions, as Dr. Tulloch showed, the Christian teaching as to sin,—a teaching which, like all other similar lessons of the Church, had its history of gradual growth, and was no more fully developed at first than the doctrine of divine grace,—is entirely inconsistent. If sin represents a fact at all in human experience, it is a fact which cannot be explained on the principle of finding in every new phase of existence nothing but the transformed shape of some antecedent state of existence. If sin were to the previous condition of circumstances and character what the blossom is to the bud, or the fruit to the blossom, then though it might be a morbid growth, a parasitic growth, a growth tending to disfigure and ruin the character out of which it grows, it would no more call for remorse, or penitence, or judgment, than the gall-apple on the oak, or water on the brain. Yet the attempt to eliminate the sense of sin from human consciousness is just as ineffectual as the attempt to eliminate the sense of cause and effect, or the sense of hope and fear. The "historical method," as it is called, which recognises everything as having some real right to an appropriate commemoration in the life of man which is found alike in all ages, and developed as the life of the race is developed, demands that the sense of sin should be recognised as a constituent part of human history, no less than the feeling for art, or the thirst for knowledge, or the life of imagination. Indeed, it is far more pervading than any of these. While they are developed by only a portion of the community, the moral feeling of deep self-reproach and remorse for voluntary evil is shared by all, not least by the most ignorant who do not participate at all in the life of culture or of abstract thought.

In the early history of every people, it is indeed remarkable how uniformly the nation feels that all its guilt or goodness is shared by all, that the penalty of impiety will light upon all alike, even when it seems to be due only to the acts of a few. As the Jews recognised that Egypt suffered for the tyranny of its king, and themselves expected that, in the long wanderings of the wilderness, all would incur the penalty of acts committed only by a few,—as the Athenians regarded their whole city as liable to a curse for the acts of desecration committed by a few thoughtless youths,—so the early literature of all nations is full of the Nemesis which descends on one member of a family for the sins of his ancestors, a conception of which the earliest dogmatic trace is probably found in the story of the Fall and the wide extermination which followed it in the Flood. It will be said that this fact only proves that, originally at least, sin is no more distinguished from the antecedent conditions from which it is "evolved," than other human characteristics or qualities; that the peculiar remorse attending it, whatever it may be due to, is not due to any keen sense of personal responsibility. But it might be as well said that because in a dim light we cannot distinguish from each other the shadows of contiguous objects, we have no impression of the true meaning of a shadow. The line of discrimination between the range of the suffering, and the exact range of personal or tribal responsibility for the suffering, is necessarily a delicate line to draw. Society is so constituted, especially in its earlier stages, that it sins and suffers collectively,—that it is often impossible to distinguish who is and who is not responsible for a calamity which overshadows all alike. Early tribes were units, rather than collections of units. What they did was done perhaps by the chief, but then the chief carried the whole tribe with him, and what he did, they consented to. In such cases, the sense of sin was necessarily almost as collective as the suffering which came of it. No one was in the same way separately responsible as in more individualised societies, but no one was in the same way distinctly innocent of the guilt. It is only in later stages of society that it is possible to distinguish effectually between the range of the guilt and the range of the suffering caused by that guilt, which last necessarily spreads far beyond the limits of the guilt itself. When a whole city trembles because one or two of that city have done something impious, as Athens trembled at the mutilation of the Hermes, it is probable that all feel, though not perhaps responsible for the impiety, yet accountable for the moral recklessness and selfish audacity which caused the impiety. Athenian awelessness seemed almost the contradiction of Athenian superstition, but the Athenian mob felt in some dim way, I presume, that the cruel awelessness of the young scapegraces, and the cruel superstition which cried out for vengeance on them, were somehow a growth of the same stock. And to us, looking back at the history of Judæa and Athens, the real identity between the impiety of individual offenders, and the cruel vindictiveness which asked for vengeance on them as a mode of absolving the people from the consequences of such offences, seems plain enough. But as the history of a race develops, the time inevitably comes when finer distinctions are rendered necessary between sin and suffering, and when the notion of expiation is connected rather with the voluntary disinterestedness of more than human love, than with the compulsory suffering of arbitrarily chosen victims. The notion of sin is individualised, the range of the collective suffering which comes from it is better defined, and the conception of the intense and yet willing suffering which is its only adequate cure, comes out in its full grandeur in the doctrine of atoning love.

Thus, as Principal Tulloch truly urges, the history of the sense of sin is the truest example of the sort of 'evolution' which should be our standard in interpreting the sense to be attached to lower kinds of evolution. In the first instance, the ideas of guilt, responsibility, punishment, expiation are all more or less confused in a vague notion of common evil, common penalty, and common hope of some sort of penance and purification. Then gradually the guilt is discriminated from the penalty, and the penalty from the expiation. It is seen that the doers of evil cannot suffer alone, but that they suffer differently, and in a much more permanent way, than those who only share the evil consequences and not the evil of the cause; and again, it is felt that those who only share involuntarily the evil consequences are in no way helping to remove the evil cause, while the divine love which accepts voluntarily, and for the sake of the guilty, that pain, of the origin of which it was quite innocent, is restoring the moral order which the guilty broke. Now, can 'evolution' of this sort be in any sense the mere growth of more organised out of less organised structures? Does not the whole story imply the conception of a divine horror of sin, and a more and more complete discrimination of its origin, its consequences, and its remedy, every step in which renders the divine groundwork of creation more evident? Surely Principal Tulloch is right in saying that the Theistic and Christian conception of evolution excludes the idea of the growth of the higher forms of life out of the lower, and requires that of the gradual revelation of divine purposes which in the earlier stages of human life are only roughly and dimly discerned.

XL

MR. J. S. MILL'S RELIGIOUS CONFESSION

1874

I HAVE just received more posthumous confessions of John Stuart Mill's. I do not pretend to have studied or even completely read as yet the *Essays on Nature, the Utility of Religion, and Theism*, which Messrs. Longman have just published. But the fragments of these Essays which unaccountably leaked out in the Northern papers, with the fuller expositions of the book itself, are, at all events, sufficient to give a very clear general impression of his point of view. And it is obvious that the moral and intellectual authority for which, in future, his name will be quoted in theological controversy, will be one of a very complex, hesitating, and ambiguous character. No one could have anticipated, at the time when Mr. Mill published his *Logic* and his *Essays on some Unsettled Questions of Political Economy*, that when his career came to an end, he would have influenced his age chiefly as a kind of potent intellectual yeast or ferment, instead of as a great inculcator of definite truths. He began life chiefly as the antagonist of the *a priori* school of philosophy and as an advocate of the empirical school which found the germs of all our knowledge in particular sense-impressions and the law of association; partly also as one of the most severe disciples of the great teachers of 'the dismal science,' —Malthus and Ricardo. But we of the present generation shall now look upon these elements of his teaching as mere infinitesimal constituents in the powerful stimulus which he gave to the various conflicting tendencies of the seething and distracted thought of our times. The general effect of his writings will not be any definite teaching at all, but a sort of impregnation of the waters of a cold and empirical school of thought with foreign sources of agitation and ebullition rendering them apparently ardent and exciting. His experience-philosophy was soon saturated with at least the deepest admiration for the methods, if not for the results of Coleridge's speculations; his political economy was modified by the warmest sympathy with the peasant and the labouring class, and the profoundest desire to mingle moral with economical motives in the distribution of wealth and industry. In politics his abstract democratic principles soon exhibited a strong deflection in the direction of Conservative scorn for the vaunted omnipotence of Radical machinery; and then afterwards, during his short political career, displayed a strong reaction towards "heroic measures" and popular sympathies. And in the region of ethics and religion his name is likely to be remembered chiefly for the heterogeneous character of the intellectual germs which floated about his mind like the light seed-vessels of plants of the most mutually incompatible habits of growth and nutrition. It will be said of him that while he was a strict Utilitarian, finding the sanctions of all the ethical principles he admitted in their tendency to promote the happiness of the race, he yet thought it not only right, but obligatory on a high-minded man to defy even an *omnipotent* being who should threaten men with eternal sufferings for refusing to surrender their finite notions of virtue to his own arbitrary will and law; that he regarded the *direct* pursuit of happiness—*i.e.* of the only final end of life—as fatal to the happiness pursued; and that he felt far more reverence for the enthusiastic emotions which arise incidentally during the pursuit of benevolent objects, than even for those benevolent objects themselves. And now that the posthumous *Essays on Nature, Religion, and Theism* have appeared, it must be added, that while he doubted everything, from the existence of God and the divine mission of Christ to the immortality of the soul, he distinctly rejected nothing, except the divine omnipotence, nay, that he preached the duty of saturating the imagination with possibilities of religious truth which he did not rate high, rather than stint the elastic force of hope by a rigid adherence to a rational standard of intellectual expectation. In short, Mr. Mill professed his wish that human nature should feed itself, consciously and deliberately, on very dubious, not to say slender hopes,—without, however, disguising from itself the slight character of those hopes,—by way of reinforcing its otherwise too small resources of aspiration; that it should store up for itself new impulses through the habitual contemplation of spiritual contingencies the prospect of ever realising which would hardly exceed the chance of a prize in a very hazardous lottery, and this solely on the ground that all the anticipations in which men may indulge themselves with real confidence, are inadequate to the work of providing sufficiently inspiring and elevating themes. The following are his words:—

"To me it seems that human life, small and confined as it is, and as, considered merely in the present, it is likely to remain, even when the progress of material and moral improvement may have freed it from the greater part of its present calamities, stands greatly in need of any wider range and greater height of aspiration for itself and its destination which the exercise of imagination can yield to it, without running counter to the evidence of fact; and that it is a part of wisdom to make the most of any, even small, probabilities on this subject which furnish imagination with any footing to support itself upon. And I am satisfied that the cultivation of such a tendency in the imagination, provided it goes on *pari passu* with the cultivation of severe reason, has no necessary tendency to pervert the judgment; but that it is possible to form a perfectly sober estimate of the evidences on both sides of a question, and yet to let the imagination dwell by preference on those possibilities which are at once the most comforting and the most improving, without in the least degree overrating the solidity of the grounds for expecting that these rather than any other will be the possibilities actually realised" (pp. 245-6).

Thus, Mr. Mill was an empiricist who attached more importance to the secondary than to the primary forms of pleasurable satisfaction; a Utilitarian who was more of a believer in the sacredness of disinterested emotion than transcendentalists themselves; an economist who carried sentiment with a high hand into the very heart of questions affecting the accumulation and distribution of wealth; a necessarian who was the most passionate advocate of liberty; a democrat who eagerly defended the rights of culture and the full representation of independent thought; nay, he was a sceptic who held the character of Christ all but divine, and who wished men to cling to the belief in even a slender hope of divine guidance and personal immortality for the sake of the new moral resources such a hope must give;—and in practical matters, he was the enthusiastic advocate of a change which would tend to deprive women of the highest influence they have, while gaining for them a power for which they seem to most of us little suited. Of course, the mind which threw so much ardour into such paradoxical positions must appear to future ages as one of the most incalculable of the intellectual influences of his day,—one who fostered enthusiasms rooted in doubt, and revolutionary changes founded on visionary hopes,—one who acted like a ferment on almost all schools of intellectual tendency, developing rapidly all the floating germs in their authors' minds, and yet which robbed even that which it stimulated most, of anything like the firmness and stability of a steady conviction.

And no doubt the total influence which John Stuart Mill will exercise on the development of English thought will be rather this,—that he will have rendered it difficult for sceptics to shut themselves up in a shell of repellent theory,—that he will have taught them to sound all the doubtfulness of doubt, to enter into all the paradoxes of an empirical philosophy, to appreciate the religious enthusiasm consistent with a utilitarian belief,—than that he will have made any fundamental truth or any fundamental denial clearer than it was before. He will have given an ideal tone to political economy, and grafted a Conservative vein into democratic theory. He will have persuaded not a few of the disciples of Bentham that they ought to delight in emotions which it is impossible on Bentham's principles to justify, and to flush with joy at the prospect of changes the advantageous results of which are as yet visible only to the most sanguine eye. He will have convinced many Materialists that, though there can be no omnipotent God of perfect holiness, there may be a very powerful, invisible Being who is helping us to struggle against impossible conditions, not much more or not much less mighty than himself. And he will have induced certain Rationalists who smile at revelation, to believe that it becomes a sceptic to reserve the possibility at least that Christ actually was exactly what in the first three Gospels He declares Himself to be,—*i.e.* not, in Mr. Mill's belief, God at all, but a divine messenger of God's, sent into the world to declare the will and unveil the nature of the Being who sent Him. No doubt the effect of all this, not only on Mr. Mill's philosophical allies, but on their opponents of all schools, must be to increase very much the sense of ultimate uncertainty;—on his allies, because it shows them how much a negative thinker could sympathise with tendencies which his philosophy went to undermine; on his opponents, because bewildering them with the vision of sympathies where they looked for prejudices, and yet sympathies which only permitted their subject to throw them the crumb of comfort involved in a 'perhaps.'

But even that is not the most curious feature of his total moral effect as a thinker. The most curious seems to me to be that, while mediating to some extent between opposite tendencies, and increasing the sense of ultimate uncertainty about the foundations of things, Mr. Mill was the very apostle of noble emotions, panegyrising the disinterested feelings generated like phosphoric flames by the decay of the earthly objects of desire, and making a sort of religion of personal enthusiasm, without much relation either to the calculable advantages of the course he advocated, or to the hopefulness of the campaign. This gives something of a hectic effect to the character of his teaching. The enthusiasm looks more like the enthusiasm of fever than the enthusiasm of health, when one considers how it derives its origin from selfish sources which fail to justify its existence, and how it flames upwards towards objects, the very existence of which is expressly stated to be involved in a haze of doubt. One cannot but admire and even reverence the nobility of the mind which felt so keenly the sacredness of the glow of disinterested enthusiasm, alien as it was to his philosophy of things, as passionately to welcome it, and eagerly to dwell on the ambiguous and shadowy hopes on which it was most likely to gain strength. It is impossible to feel anything but profound admiration for the delicate love of truth which makes Mr. Mill array so carefully all the half-tangible grounds of the hope to which he clings, and yet sadly confess how small individually they seem. Still how strange it is to contrast what Mr. Mill has written concerning the genius and character of our Lord, with his own view of the slender probability of Christ's own beliefs!—

"And whatever else may be taken away from us by rational criticism, Christ is still left,—a unique figure, not more unlike all his precursors than all his followers, even those who had the direct benefit of his personal teaching. It is of no use to say that Christ, as exhibited in the Gospels, is not historical, and that we know not how much of what is admirable has been superadded by the tradition of his followers. The tradition of followers suffices to insert any number of marvels, and may have inserted all the miracles which he is reputed to have wrought. But who among his disciples or among their proselytes was capable of inventing the sayings ascribed to Jesus, or of imagining the life and character revealed in the Gospels? Certainly not the fishermen of Galilee; as certainly not St. Paul, whose character and idiosyncrasies were of a totally different sort; still less the early Christian writers, in whom nothing is more evident than that the good which was in them was all derived, as they always professed that it was derived, from the higher source. . . . But about the life and sayings of Jesus there is a stamp of personal originality, combined with profundity of insight, which, if we abandon the idle expectation of finding scientific precision where something very different was aimed at, must place the Prophet of Nazareth, even in the estimation of those who have no belief in his inspiration, in the very first rank of the men of sublime genius of whom our species can boast. When this pre-eminent genius is combined with the qualities of probably the greatest moral reformer and martyr to that mission who ever existed upon earth, religion cannot be said to have made a bad choice in pitching on this man as the ideal representative and guide of humanity; nor even now would it be easy, even for an unbeliever, to find a better translation of the rule of virtue from the abstract into the concrete than to endeavour so to live that Christ would approve our life. When to this we add that, to the conception of the rational sceptic, it remains a possibility that Christ actually was what he supposed himself to be,—not God, for he never made the smallest pretension to that character, and would probably have thought such a pretension as blasphemous as it seemed to the men who condemned him, but a man charged with a special, express, and unique commission from God to lead mankind to truth and virtue, we may well conclude that the influences of religion on the character which will remain after rational criticism has done its utmost against the evidences of religion are well worth preserving, and that what they lack in direct strength as compared with those of a firmer belief, is more than compensated by the greater truth and rectitude of the morality they sanction."

Now what is the very stamp of the genius or originality on which Mr. Mill so justly insists in this estimate of Jesus? Is it not precisely that certainty of insight into divine things which Mr. Mill decides to be wholly unjustified and unjustifiable by his review not merely of Christ's own career, but of all that happened previous to and all that followed that career? Not to refer to the Gospel of John, of which Mr. Mill's estimate is so strangely contemptuous, was he not thinking as he spoke of the profundity and originality of Christ's genius of the calm confidence of " Blessed are the pure in heart, for they shall see God," "Every plant which my heavenly Father hath not planted shall be rooted up," "Be ye therefore perfect, even as your Father which is in heaven is perfect," "Who is my mother, and who are my brethren? Whosoever shall do the will of my Father which is in heaven, the same is my brother, and sister, and mother." Now, where is the 'genius' in such sayings, if they represented not insight into the truth, but the overmastering might of a potent delusion,—if the true state of mind on these subjects should be that which Mr. Mill delineates in these remarkable essays, the anxious hoarding-up of a number of doubtful indications of the supernatural influence of a Being of limited power,—" evidence insufficient for proof, but amounting only to one of the lower degrees of probability" for the existence of any God at all? If this be so, surely the certainty and simplicity of Christ's insight would be a mark, not of genius, but of hallucination,— unless, indeed, the sceptic takes the view hinted at by Mr. Mill, that Christ may have really been what He assumed Himself to be, *i.e.* may have had evidence which we cannot recover of the divine life in which He lived. Only from any confident belief of this kind Mr. Mill is wholly shut out, for if he held it confidently, he must hold with precisely equal confidence the existence of the supernatural being whom Christ revealed. Yet if he thought it a mere possibility that Christ spoke of what He knew, when using the language of knowledge instead of the language of surmise,—surely he ought to think of the 'genius' of Jesus, as he calls it, only as of a very small possibility of the same order. On Mr. Mill's view, Christ was either a great genius, or had a wonderful aptitude for grand hallucinations, the last being to him much the more likely of the two, otherwise Mr. Mill's own slender 'hope' would take the form of a firm belief. Anyhow, nothing is stranger than the contrast between the language of the admirer, and the language of him whom he so profoundly admires, on divine subjects. The former is the language of hesitating feeble hope, hope of a low order, but which nevertheless warrants the attitude of enthusiasm and the glow of a poetic aspiration. The latter is the language of an absolute vision, of calm certainty, which warrants no such feverish emotion, but only undoubting trust and happy devotion. Will not the potent ferment which Mr. Mill has cast into the boiling cauldron of modern thought, end in making it seem far more reasonable to accept the quiet language of implicit faith, than the impassioned language of an idealising dream at once excited and despondent?

XLI

MR. JOHN MORLEY ON RELIGIOUS CONFORMITY

1874

THE new chapter of Mr. John Morley's Essay on *Compromise*, to be found in the July number of the *Fortnightly*, is as wholesome in doctrine as it is able and thoughtful in expression. Of course it is written from a point of view intellectually and religiously almost the opposite of my own, but I am not ashamed to feel far more sympathy with the nobler aspects of unbelief, than with the ignobler and shiftier aspects of so-called faith. A diplomatic Churchman, who has borrowed hardly anything from the Christian spirit except St. Paul's boast that he had been all things to all men, is a phenomenon which seems to me far more threatening to the Christian faith of our own day than the sturdy and, as far at least as this essay goes, the charitable 'I believe not' of such men as Mr. John Morley. To those who apply our Lord's universal test, 'By their fruits ye shall know them,' a religion which has not made a man religious must, in the form it has taken in his mind at least, be inferior to the want of religion, or if you please, even irreligion, of the man who shows as high a morale and as earnest a sense of duty as Mr. John Morley. What the explanation may be of the appearance of so keen a sense of obligation and so frank a tenderness for what Mr. Morley, not, we think, in intellectual pride, but apparently in downright conviction, calls Christianity, —" that sovereign legend of Pity,"—in combination with so sharp a denial of what seems to me the transparent personal background of the moral law, is no doubt puzzle enough, a puzzle which I am not at the present moment attempting to resolve. But this, at all events, is true; it is quite easy to confess God and Christ in a spirit much more pernicious and fatal to the growth of faith in God and Christ, than that in which others deny them. False visions may be much worse than no visions. The babble of imaginary voices may be much more perverting to the mind than the aching of an intense silence. Mr. Morley's present essay is a grave and earnest protest against the conventional conformity of men to creeds they sincerely and thoroughly disbelieve, and for my own part, I not only heartily agree with Mr. Morley, but think that true Christianity has much more to lose by the falsity which Mr. Morley attacks than has unbelief. A conformity which makes the inner life of the most intimate affections a hollow and conventional affair, is a conformity which is destructive of religion, not conservative of it. Directly we begin to act a part, we leave the region in which faith is possible, and what is worse, we infect all those for whose sake we act the part we do, indeed all who are concerned with us in the histrionic affair, with something of our own utter unreality. Therefore I have nothing to say to the substance of Mr. Morley's essay except to echo its teaching, with all my heart, from the opposite point of view. I should indeed refuse to acquiesce in Mr. Morley's exceptions to his doctrine of the duty of social frankness on the subject of any firmly-rooted and fixed denial. Mr. Morley seems to think that because children have not had anything to do with the selection of their own parents, they may owe it to their affection for those parents not to confess their rejection of the faith in which they have been brought up, though a similar reticence cannot be justifiable in wives, with whom men's relation is a voluntary one. "If parents are not wise," he says, "if they cannot endure to hear of any religious opinions except their own, if it would give them sincere and deep pain to hear a son or daughter avow disbelief in the inspiration of the Bible, and so forth, then it seems that the younger person is warranted in refraining from saying that he or she does not accept such and such doctrines. This, of course, only where the son or daughter feels a tender and genuine attachment to the parent. Where the parent has not earned this attachment, has been selfish, indifferent, or cruel, the title to the special kind of forbearance of which we are speaking can hardly have any existence. In an ordinary way, however, a parent has a claim on us which no other person in the world can have, and a man's self-respect ought scarcely to be injured, if he finds himself shrinking from playing the apostle to his own father and mother." It shows how oddly other differences of opinion are connected with differences of moral theory, that I should just have inverted Mr. Morley's qualification. He seems to think that to the parents you love you may fairly shrink from giving pain. I should have thought that from the parents you love you should shrink from withholding your true confidence on a subject that goes very near to their hearts, and that your obligation to let them know your true heart on such a subject, whether it give pain or not, is far more imperative than your obligation to spare them pain. No doubt this difference of view is one of the results of a difference of moral creed. To the Utilitarian, —and Mr. Morley is, I believe, a Utilitarian in Mr. Mill's sense,—the giving of pain must always assume what seems to me to be a thoroughly factitious importance in the moral conduct of human life.

But while I concur with Mr. Morley's doctrine without concurring in the exceptions by which he here qualifies it, I do not at all accept one leading view of his essay, by which apparently he hopes to minimise the social shocks and jars likely to result from the candour in relation to fundamental denials recommended by that essay. That view is that the Positivism (which means, of course, Negativism) of Mr. Morley's creed is to be the heir of Christianity, in the same sense in which Christianity was the heir of Judaism. "Whatever form," says Mr. Morley, "may be ultimately imposed on our vague religious aspirations by some prophet to come, uniting sublime depth of feeling and lofty purity of life with strong intellectual grasp and the gift of a noble eloquence, we may, at least, be sure of this, that it will stand as closely related to Christianity, as Christianity stood to the old Judaic dispensation. It is commonly understood that the rejectors of the popular religion stand in face of it, as the Christians stood in face of the pagan belief and rites in the Empire. The analogy is inexact. The modern denier, if he is anything better than that, or entertains hopes of a creed to come, is nearer to the position of the Christianising Jew. Science, when she has accomplished all her triumphs in her own order, will have to go back, when the time comes, to generate a new creed, by which man can live; will have to find material in the purified and sublimated ideas of which the confessions and rites of the Christian Churches have been the grosser expression. Just as what was once the new dispensation was preached *a Judæis ad Judæos apud Judæos,* so must the new, that is to be, find a Christian teacher and Christian hearers. It can hardly be other than an expansion, a development, a readaptation of all the moral and spiritual truth that lay hidden under the worn-out forms. It must be such a harmonising of truth with an intellectual conception as shall fit it to be an active guide to conduct. In a world '*where men sit and hear each other groan . . . where but to think is to be full of sorrow,*' it is hard to imagine a time when we shall be indifferent to that sovereign legend of Pity. We have to incorporate it in some wider Gospel of Justice and Progress." Mr. Morley writes with feeling, and with not more of benignant condescension to the moral and intellectual weakness of Christians than is perhaps inevitable from his point of view, but he will not be easily able to persuade any one who enters in the least into the drift and meaning of the Gospel, to see anything but an amiable, yet groundless dream in his hope that the new religion of humanity without God, can succeed in establishing any sort of historical heirship to the gospel of the divine humanity. A new religion which should stand in the same relation to historical Christianity as that in which historical Christianity stood to Judaism, can hardly be even imagined, just because historical Christianity claims to find its perfect and ideal life in Christ, while Judaism confessedly looked forward into the future, and was but anticipating that completion and fulfilment of which Christ's gospel declared itself the harbinger. But even if that point be waived, how is any religion to bear the same relation to Christianity which Christianity bore to Judaism, if it begins with denying the common root of both, the fact of a divine revelation to man? nay, more, if it denies, as Mr. Morley expressly affirms that it must, even the *possibility* of such a revelation. The essential life and form of Judaism was belief in the call of God to men, and the personal rule of God over men. That belief, so far from being diluted or softened down by Christ in the direction of "a religion of humanity," was made by Him indefinitely more explicit and absolute. The belief that man was nothing apart from God, that his whole good and his whole happiness lay in union with God, was of the very substance of the Jewish faith, but by Christ it was vivified with a totally new principle of emotion such as it never had before. That which dropped off from Judaism was forms and ceremonies, which were originally intended, but which had latterly quite failed, to express the sense of the perpetual penitence, obedience, and self-sacrifice due from man to God. But everything that expressed the depth of the personal relation, the passion of loving humility, of unquenchable trust, of exulting hope towards God, was not only retained and developed in Christianity, but exalted and glorified by the light of the new revelation. To talk of "developing" such a faith as that into a faith whose great boast it is that its root is in man, and in man alone, which begins by terming revelation a legend, and God a power at once unknown and unknowable, which brings as its special indictment against the Christian faith that "it tends to divert and misdirect the most energetic faculties of human nature," and which, if it could, would concentrate on man all the life of affection now wasted, as it holds, on God,—is to talk of developing a tree into a lichen, or the language of Shakespeare into the starved speech of a tribe of Esquimaux. Judaism had its knowledge and fear of God, where Christianity has its love of God; Judaism had its fore shadowings of a man who should be "as a hiding-place from the wind and a covert from the tempest, as rivers of water in a dry place, and the shadow of a great rock in a weary land," where Christianity has its Christ and Redeemer; Judaism had its hope that there should be a satisfying awakening after the likeness of God, that when "the flesh and the heart failed, God should be the strength of the heart and its portion for ever," where Christianity has its sure and certain hope of "the life that is hid with Christ in God;"—but how all these developments are to be further developed into the purely "agnostic" state of mind towards the Cause of the Universe, into active disbelief in all mediating love, and into the gospel of an altruistic immortality to consist in the tiny driblet of consequences contributed by each human life to the future of the race,—so long as the race may happen to last,—it would puzzle even the conjuring of the Hegelian logic to suggest. It is said of Mr. J. S. Mill, that when assured by some physicist that the sun must burn itself out, and that long before that happens the earth must pass into the sterile condition of our moon, and become perfectly lifeless, he turned pale at the mere thought, for in that prediction sentence was passed on the "religion of humanity" and the gospel of earthly

"Progress" which Mr. John Morley preaches. And surely Mr. Mill was right, from his point of view. A religion which depends on the eternity of astronomical conditions now existing, is not a religion at all, and most certainly is not a "development" of any form of faith in an eternal God and an immortal life for man. Development at least demands the preservation of the seminal idea, and even the most negative of the students of comparative theology would admit that the seminal idea of Judaism and Christianity is the idea of a divine descent into humanity, of light and love, from above, seeking out humility and faith beneath. Give up that idea, and it is about as wise to talk of the prophet of the new religion developing its teachings out of the heart of his own Christianity, as it would be to talk of Copernicus and Newton 'developing' the Ptolemaic astronomy, or Bishop Butler 'developing' the ethics of Hobbes. I suppose that what Mr. Morley means is, that there ought to be some vestige of the sublime disinterestedness of the Christian ethics in the new 'religion of humanity.' But if so, it will be apparently disinterestedness of the Utilitarian sort, ignoring with holy horror any mystery of origin,—disinterestedness which feeds itself on a totally different class of reflections, and which aims at a widely different class of ends, from those of the faiths which it aspires to supersede. If Mr. Morley and his friends could succeed, they would not diminish the jar or shock of their new ideas even in the very least degree, by their kindly consideration for "the sovereign legend of Pity" which they propose to dissipate. It is something, no doubt, to be able to say of each other, as Mr. Morley admits that he can of believers, that mutual moral respect is easy, even while fundamental belief is so profoundly different. But beyond that it seems to me childish to attempt to go. To try to develop a humanitarian religion out of one grounded in God, is to attempt an intellectual juggle, not a philosophical reconciliation. After all, the jars and shocks which Mr. Morley wishes to minimise may be wholesome things. We may get far more truth out of them than out of the tentative adjustment of radically incompatible convictions. Indeed I had hardly expected such mere wistfulness of sentiment, such impracticable though kindly endeavour at the impossible conciliation of mutually destructive creeds, as this new chapter shows, from so robust a thinker as Mr. John Morley.

XLII

MR. ARNOLD'S LAY SERMON

1884

Mr. Arnold's lay sermon to "the sacrificed classes" at Whitechapel contrasts doubly with the pulpit sermons which we too often hear. It is real where these sermons are unreal, and frankly unreal where these sermons are real. It does honestly warn the people to whom it was addressed, of the special danger to which "the sacrificed classes" are exposed, whenever they in their turn get the upperhand, the danger of simply turning the tables on the great possessing and aspiring classes. "If the sacrificed classes," he said, "under the influence of hatred, cupidity, desire of change, destroy, in order to possess and enjoy in their turn, their work, too, will be idolatrous, and the old work will continue to stand for the present, or at any rate their new work will not take its place." It must be work done in a new spirit, not in the spirit of hatred or cupidity, or eagerness to enjoy and appropriate the privileges of others, which can alone stand the test of time and judgment. So far, Mr. Arnold was much more real than too many of our clerical preachers. He warned his hearers against a temptation which he knew would be stirring constantly in their hearts, and not against abstract temptations which he had no reason to think would have any special significance to any of his audience.

On the other hand, if he were more real in what was addressed to his particular audience than pulpit-preachers often are, he resorted once more, with his usual hardened indifference to the meaning of words and the principles of true literature, to that practice of debasing the coinage of religious language, and using great sayings in a new and washed-out sense of his own, of which pulpit-preachers are seldom guilty. This practice of Mr. Arnold's is the only great set-off against the brilliant services he has rendered to English literature, but it is one which I should not find it easy to condemn too strongly. Every one knows how, in various books of his, Mr. Arnold has tried to "verify" the teaching of the Bible, while depriving the name of God of all personal meaning; to verify the Gospel of Christ, while denying that Christ had any message to us from a world beyond our own; and even,—wildest enterprise of all,—so to rationalise the strictly theological language of St. John as to rob it of all its theological significance. Well, I do not charge this offence on Mr. Arnold as in any sense whatever an attempt to play fast-and-loose with words; for he has again and again confessed to all the world, with the explicitness and vigour which are natural to him, the precise drift of his enterprise. But I do charge it on Mr. Arnold as in the highest possible sense a great literary misdemeanour, that he has lent his high authority to the attempt to give to a great literature a pallid, faded, and artificial complexion, though, with his view of it, his duty obviously was to declare boldly that that literature teaches what is, in his opinion, false and superstitious, and deserves our admiration only as representing a singularly grand, though obsolete, stage in man's development. Mr. Arnold is as frank and honest as the day. But frank and honest as he is, his authority is not the less lent to a non-natural rendering of Scripture infinitely more intolerable than that non-natural interpretation of the Thirty-nine Articles which once brought down the wrath of the world of Protestants on the author of "Tract 90." In this Whitechapel lecture Mr. Arnold tells his hearers that in the "preternatural and miraculous aspect" which the popular Christianity assumes Christianity is not solid or verifiable, but that there is another aspect of Christianity which is solid and verifiable, which aspect of it makes no appeal to a preternatural [*i.e.* supernatural] world at all. Then he goes on, after eulogising Mr. Watts's pictures,— of one of which a great mosaic has been set up in Whitechapel as a memorial of Mr. Barnett's noble work there,—to remark that good as it is to bring home to "the less refined classes" the significance of Art and Beauty, it is none the less true that "whosoever drinketh of this water shall thirst again," and to suggest, of course, by implication, that there is a living water springing up to everlasting life, of which he who drinks shall never thirst. Then he proceeds thus:—

"No doubt the social sympathies, the feeling for Beauty, the pleasure of Art, if left merely by themselves, if untouched by what is the deepest thing in human life religion—are apt to become ineffectual and superficial. The art which Mr. Barnett has done his best to make known to the people here, the art of men like Mr. Watts, the art manifested in works such as that which has just now been unveiled upon the walls of St. Jude's Church, has a deep and powerful connection with religion. You have seen the mosaic, and have read, perhaps, the scroll which is attached to it. There is the figure of Time, a strong young man, full of hope, energy, daring, and adventure, moving on to take possession of life; and opposite to him there is that beautiful figure of Death, representing the breakings-off, the cuttings short, the baffling disappointments, the heart-piercing separations from which the fullest life and the most fiery energy cannot exempt us. Look at that strong and bold young man, that mournful figure must go hand in hand with him for ever. And those two figures, let us admit if you like, belong to Art. But who is that third figure whose scale weighs deserts, and who carries a sword of fire? We are told again by the text printed on the scroll, 'The Eternal [the scroll, however, has 'the Lord'] is a God of Judgment; blessed are all they that wait for him.' It is the figure of Judgment, and that figure, I say, belongs to religion. The text which explains the figure is taken from one of the Hebrew Prophets; but an even more striking text is furnished us from that saying of the Founder of Christianity when he was about to leave the world, and to leave behind him his Disciples, who, so long as he lived, had him always to cling to, and to do all their thinking for them. He told them that when he was gone they should find a new source of thought and feeling opening itself within them, and that this new source of thought and feeling should be a comforter to them, and that it should convince, he said, the world of many things. Amongst other things, he said, it should convince the world that Judgment comes, and that the Prince of this world is judged. That is a text which we shall do well to lay to heart, considering it with and alongside that text from the Prophet. More and more it is becoming manifest that the Prince of this world is really judged, that that Prince who is the perpetual ideal of selfishly possessing and enjoying, and of the worlds fashioned under the inspiration of this ideal, is judged. One world and another have gone to pieces because they were fashioned under the inspiration of this ideal, and that is a consoling and edifying thought."

Now, when we know, as Mr. Arnold wishes us all to know, that to him "the Eternal" means nothing more than that "stream of tendency, not ourselves, which makes for righteousness," that "Judgment" means nothing but the ultimate defeat which may await those who set themselves against this stream of tendency, if the stream of tendency be really as potent and as lasting as the Jews believed God to be, I do not think that the consoling character of this text will be keenly felt by impartial minds. Further, we should remember that according to Mr. Arnold, when Christ told His disciples that the Comforter should "reprove the world of sin, and of righteousness, and of judgment; of sin because they believe not on me, of righteousness because I go to the Father, and ye see me no more; of judgment because the prince of this world is judged," we should understand this as importing, to those at least who agree with Mr. Arnold, only that, for some unknown reason, a new wave of feeling would follow Christ's death, which would give mankind a new sense of their unworthiness, a new vision of Christ's holiness, and a new confidence in the power of that "stream of tendency, not ourselves, which makes for righteousness," in which Christ's own personality would then be merged; and further, that this powerful stream of tendency would probably sweep away all institutions not tending to righteousness but opposing an obstacle to that tendency.

Well, all I can say is that, in watering-down in this way the language of the Bible, Mr. Arnold, if he is doing nothing else, is doing what lies in his power to extinguish the distinctive significance of a great literature. The whole power of that literature depends from beginning to end on the faith in a Divine Being who holds the universe in His hand, whose will nothing can resist, who inspires the good, who punishes the evil, who judges kingdoms as He judges the hearts of men, and whose mind manifested in Christ promised to Christ's disciples that which His power alone availed to fulfil. To substitute for a faith such as this, a belief—to my mind the wildest in the world, and the least " verifiable " —that "a stream of tendency" effects all that the prophets ascribed to God, or, at least, so much of it as ever will be effected at all, and that Christ, by virtue merely of His complete identification with this stream of tendency, is accomplishing posthumously, without help from either Father, Son, or Spirit, all that He could have expected to accomplish through the personal agency of God, is to extract the kernel from the shell, and to ask us to accept the empty husk for the living grain. I am not reproaching Mr. Arnold for his scepticism. I am reproaching him as a literary man for trying to give currency in a debased form to language of which the whole power depends on its being used honestly in the original sense. "The Eternal" means one thing when it means the everlasting and supreme thought and will and life; it is an expression utterly blank and dead when it means nothing but a select " stream of tendency " which is assumed, for no particular reason, to be constant, permanent, and victorious. "Living water" means one thing when it means the living stream of God's influence; it has no salvation in it at all when it means only that which is the purest of the many tendencies in human life. The shadow of judgment means one thing when it is cast by the will of the supreme righteousness; it has no solemnity in it when it expresses only the sanguine anticipation of human virtue. There is no reason on earth why Mr. Arnold should not water-down the teaching of the Bible to his own view of its residual meaning; but then, in the name of sincere literature, let him find his own language for it, and not dress up this feeble and superficial hopefulness of the nineteenth century in words which are undoubtedly stamped with an ardour and a peace for which his teaching can give us no sort of justification. "Solidity and verification," indeed! Never was there a doctrine with less bottom in it and less pretence of verification than his; but be that as it may, he must know, as well as I know, that his doctrine is as different from the doctrine of the Bible as the shadow is different from the substance. Has Mr. Arnold lately read Dr. Newman's great Oxford sermon on "Unreal Words"? If not, I wish he would refer to it again and remember the warning addressed to those who "use great words and imitate the sentences of others," and who "fancy that those whom they imitate had as little meaning as themselves," or "perhaps contrive to think that they themselves have a meaning adequate to their words." It is to me impossible to believe that Mr. Arnold should have indulged such an illusion. He knows too well the difference between the great faith which spoke in prophet and apostle, and the feeble faith which absorbs a drop or two of grateful moisture from a "stream of tendency" on the banks of which it weakly lingers. Mr. Arnold is really putting Literature,—of which he is so great a master,—to shame, when he travesties the language of the prophets, and the evangelists, and of our Lord Himself, by using it to express the dwarfed convictions and withered hopes of modern rationalists who love to repeat the great words of the Bible, after they have given up the strong meaning of them as fanatical superstitions. Mr. Arnold's readings of Scripture are the spiritual *assignats* of English faith.

XLIII

MATTHEW ARNOLD'S NEW CHRISTIAN CATECHISM

1885

Mr. Arnold's comment on Christmas in the April *Contemporary* is a very patronising one. He is very thankful for what he terms the Christmas legend. He thinks the belief in the miraculous birth a striking testimony to the universal feeling for the purity of Christ, and he rejoices that it embodies that feeling in a poetical form better calculated to impress the world than any pedantic inculcation of purity by those who have learnt the worthlessness of the legend, could pretend to be. Consequently, Mr. Arnold does not attempt to re-state the Christian teaching with regard to purity with any affectation of being able to enforce it the better for not associating it with supernatural sanctions. He even admits that the giving-up of all these supernatural sanctions,—which he chooses, not very candidly as I think, to speak of collectively as "miracles,"—is a matter of danger. "Undoubtedly the reliance on miracles is not lost without some danger; but the thing to consider is that it *must* be lost, and that the danger must be met, and, as it can be, counteracted. If men say, as some men are likely enough to say, that they altogether give-up Christian miracles, and cannot do otherwise, but that then they give-up Christian morals too, the answer is, that they do this at their own risk and peril; that they need not do it, that they are wrong in doing it, and will have to rue their error. But for my part, I prefer at present to say this simply and barely, and not to give any rhetorical development to it." And here surely Mr. Arnold is very wise, for as we want to know what will be left of Christianity, after all that is not mere human quality has departed, "a rhetorical development" would rather confuse than help to enlighten us. And I suppose that we get as near as possible to the heart of what Mr. Arnold discerns in Christianity, when all that is legendary and "unverifiable" has been ignored in it, in the following terse catechism,—certainly much nearer than we could get by the help of any kind of "rhetorical development":—"Therefore, when we are asked: What really is Christmas, and what does it celebrate? we answer, the birthday of Jesus. What is the miracle of the Incarnation? A homage to the virtue of pureness, and to the manifestation of this virtue in Jesus. What is Lent, and the miracle of the temptation? A homage to the virtue of self-control and to the manifestation of this virtue in Jesus. What does Easter celebrate? Jesus victorious over death by dying. By dying how? Dying to re-live. To re-live in Paradise, in another world? No, in this. What, then, is the kingdom of God? The ideal society of the future. Then, what is immortality? To live in the Eternal Order, which never dies. What is salvation by Jesus Christ? The attainment of this immortality. Through what means?

Through means of the method and the secret and the temper of Jesus."

Now, to get to the bottom of the drift of the answers here suggested to Mr. Arnold's catechumens, I should like to put to the distinguished author of the Catechism a few more questions intended to bring out its meaning. In what did the blessing of pureness, as enforced by Jesus, consist? Mr. Arnold himself tells us, "Blessed are the pure in heart, for they shall see God." What do you mean by God? Mr. Arnold has told us that, so far as the word "God" conveys a verifiable reality at all, it means, "A stream of tendency, not ourselves, which makes for righteousness." Did, then, Jesus hold that the blessedness of purity consisted in discerning "a stream of tendency, not ourselves, which makes for righteousness"? May not the impure see that just as well, and see that it makes for their misery? Again, what was the secret of resisting temptation "as manifested in Jesus"? We are told by those who learned the story of the temptation from Christ that it consisted in realising fully that "Man shall not live by bread alone, but by every word that proceedeth out of the mouth of God." Now, if you substitute here for "God," "a stream of tendency, not ourselves, that makes for righteousness," would you attach any meaning at all to the words of our Lord? Would it mean anything to say, "Man shall not live by bread alone, but by every word which proceedeth out of the stream of tendency that makes for righteousness"? Again, when Mr. Arnold says that Easter celebrates Jesus victorious over death by dying, and by dying to re-live, what is the account which Jesus Himself gives of this re-living; is it Mr. Arnold's—that He is to re-live "in the Eternal Order which never dies"? No; it is that He is to re-live in His Father, even as His disciples are to re-live in Him. "Yet a little while, and the world seeth me no more; but ye see me: because I live, ye shall live also. At that day ye shall know that I am in my Father, and ye in me, and I in you." Does not Mr. Arnold see that to substitute for "my Father" "a stream of tendency, not ourselves, which makes for righteousness," makes the purest nonsense of these promises, and yet that in these promises centres the celebration of Easter, and the essence of that "victory over death," which the death of Jesus was to bring? What Mr. Arnold truly calls "the secret of Jesus," the secret of dying in order to re-live, is a secret the whole significance of which is contained in the life in God. This life in God was assigned, not only as the special blessing of purity, and as the special source of strength in temptation, but as the infinite spring of joy which eye has not seen nor ear heard, and which it has not entered into the heart of man to conceive. Mr. Arnold's catechism has but this one defect, — it leaves out God. And if God be only a stream of tendency, Jesus Christ, instead of being One whose birth we ought to celebrate with imperishable joy, would be One who had misled mankind into believing in the wildest and most blinding of human illusions.

Mr. Arnold will now understand why I reproached him with lumping together all that is supernatural in Judaism and Christianity under the general head of "miracles." For my own part, I am no less sure that miracles occur, than Mr. Arnold is sure that they do not occur. But it is not on the occurrence or non-occurrence of miracles that the *essential* truth of Christianity hinges; it is on the reality or unreality of our Lord's personal life in God. And when I speak of God, I need hardly say that I do not use that great word in Mr. Arnold's sense of an "eternal order,"—which without God may be eternal or not, and may be order or not, for without Him it might be either temporary order, or temporary disorder, or eternal order, or eternal disorder, and no human being could tell us which. I mean by God, what Jesus Christ meant, not "a stream of tendency, not ourselves, which makes for righteousness," for without God such a stream of tendency, if it existed, might be very much weaker than the stream of tendency, not ourselves, which makes for unrighteousness, but God in the only sense in which Christ ever uses the term, namely, a being who both gives and asks the purest love of which the heart can form any conception, and who is wholly "unverifiable" by us unless He verifies Himself in us. Without such a being, Christ's beatitudes have no ground and no meaning; without such a being, Lent and Easter are but the mirage of the desert; without such a being, there is no re-living for dying saviours, except in that very idle and empty form,—the posthumous life; and even of that re-living a very large part would be mischievous, since it would consist in leading others to wander about after the same will-of-the-wisps which the exaltation of these dying saviours' hearts had led them to follow.

What I press is this:—Mr. Arnold's criticism of the Bible goes a great deal further than the exorcism of the miraculous from its pages,—it goes to the exorcism of the supernatural, the exorcism of

God. Now, if the Bible is not a revelation of the character of God, it is nothing in the world but a book the whole source of whose inspiration is illusion. And if it be, as I hold, the true revelation of the character of God, then the supernatural is *real;* and the questions as to the truth or falsehood of individual miracles is as nothing compared with the great fact that a source of spiritual power exists beyond what we call Nature, and independent of what we call natural laws, and that that power has revealed itself to us. Mr. Arnold's fond desire to keep the Bible without God, seems to me even wilder than the Nihilists' desire to protect liberty by destroying Governments,—for it is at least just conceivable that all men should consent to respect each other's liberty when government had disappeared; but if God be not a being to obey and love, the Bible becomes a bewildering chaos of false dreams and fancies and of distracting promises, on which no real and sober life can be built-up. Grant the supernatural, however, and Mr. Arnold well knows that he grants so much, that whether we accept all the rest or not is comparatively a detail. It is the supernatural with which he must dispense, if he wants to get back to scientific naturalism of any sort or kind. It is the belief that the soul can commune with God, can make itself heard by Him, can hear His word and obey it, can feel His love and return it, which is so out of keeping with the physical science of the day, and so subversive of scientific maxims and exhortations. If Mr. Arnold, in deference to the modern science, gets rid of that, he gets rid of the very stock of which miracle is the fruit. If he retains it, he retains that stock, and must not be surprised to hear men saying that what are usually called miracles,—results which really are due to the power of spirit over physical nature,—have happened in all ages, happen now, and will happen hereafter, though not of course with the frequency and the power with which they have happened in the wake of a few divinely-gifted natures. The truth is that Mr. Arnold wants to retain the right to strike-out both right and left,—to pity the credulity which revolts the science of the day, and to depreciate the science which revolts the credulity. He is very adroit in dealing blows at both; but none the less he does not prevail over either, for the simple reason that he cannot make his own choice between them. It is childish to give-in his adhesion to the spiritual world, and yet to empty that world of all which men have worshipped in it. It is childish to give-in his adhesion to the scientific world, and yet invest it with an atmosphere that physical science utterly repudiates. Christ revealed God; and without God, His teaching would be baseless. Physical science reveals only law; and if there be anything beyond law, its teaching is inadequate. Mr. Arnold will accept neither the gospel of Christ nor the gospel of Science, without excluding just that which is characteristic of it as a gospel; and so he falls between the two stools. His catechism of Christianity without God will be accepted whenever agnostics begin to take to gnosis, and Christians begin to ignore the one thread on which every lesson of Christ's teaching is strung,—not sooner. At present, Mr. Arnold fights "as one beating the air."

XLIV

AGNOSTIC DREAMERS

1884

Nothing is more surprising than the extravagances of Agnostics. After taking all the pains in the world to destroy the idols, as they think them, of Christian worship, after carefully demonstrating that a living God in the Christian's sense of the term is a contradiction in terms, and that the life everlasting cannot rationally be attributed to beings deprived of their bodily existence in any sense but that of posthumous activity, they immediately proceed to substitute for these idols mere dolls of their own fashioning and dressing,—dolls which they make no secret of having deliberately fashioned and dressed up for the occasion, and which, nevertheless, they dandle enthusiastically in their arms, and hold up to a sort of make-believe adoration, as the true and rational substitute for the old religions. Here, for instance, is Mr. Frederic Harrison, the President of the English Committee of the Positivist Society, delivering a long address on the last night of the old year, on "the Choir invisible" of the departed, by the pious contemplation of whose posthumous energy he seeks to kindle the gratitude of the living to something more of "depth, and breadth, and glow" than is usually accorded to them under the influence of "the old sentiment and practice,"— in other words, I suppose, to deeper gratitude than is usually accorded them by those who believe in "the communion of Saints." As no one could suppose that the mere dropping of a belief in the continued spiritual life of these benefactors of the human race would of itself add "depth, and breadth, and glow" to the gratitude with which we recall their services, I naturally turn with some curiosity to the eloquence of Mr. Harrison, in the hope of discovering from what source he expects to draw these new stores of deeper, broader, and more glowing gratitude. And even he does not affirm that those who believe in the complete cessation of personal existence with death, feel *additional* gratitude to former benefactors for having ceased to be. But as that is apparently the whole of the intellectual and moral difference between the ground of the Positivists' attitude towards the dead, and of our own, I am puzzled as to the source of Mr. Harrison's hopes. In point of fact it soon appears that Mr. Harrison trusts for his fresh stores of enthusiasm about the dead to rhetorical extravagances of language, and nothing else. He declares that Positivists see the dead "as still living around them, and as active as they ever were in their life,"— the activity, remember, being in his belief purely posthumous, and therefore passive,— not activity of their own at all. Nay, afterwards, Mr. Harrison goes further still. "We live by one another, we live again in one another; and often, indeed, much more after death than before it"; so that death not only need not, in his opinion, diminish the amount of influence exerted over others, it may often positively increase it. Mr. Harrison would, I suppose, explain himself as meaning that where any one's characteristic influence on his generation has been great, it grows and is multiplied with the growing number of persons to whom it is transmitted,—Shakespeare's poetry, for example, influencing the imaginations and feelings of thousands of persons in this generation, for every person so influenced in his own lifetime. That is not only true, but a perfectly irrelevant truism. Indeed, it is equally true of course, to say that the posthumous influence of rays of light and heat radiated by the sun in the ages of the past is at work now in the organism of a larger number of living people than ever in the past; but we do not pretend, on that account, that if the sun were extinguished to-morrow, it would be exerting greater influence over our earth than ever before; on the contrary, we regard the sun's past light and heat as blended indissolubly with the organisations into which it then entered, and through which it has been transmitted to our day. What should we think of a man who gratefully recognised the energy of the sun of the past, and the stars of the past, and the burned coal and wood of the past, and kindled himself into a "deeper and broader and more glowing" gratitude for their past services than anybody could feel who was actually warmed or lighted by them now? Would not some one at once say,— 'If life is to be spent in acts of homage towards all the antecedent conditions of our present life, we shall have no life left for ourselves to live'? And yet how do individuals who once lived and have absolutely ceased to live any personal life—who enter into the life of the present only through their influence on the people of the past, or through those contrivances by which the people of the present perpetuate the literature of the past,—differ from those rays of the sun which first generated and then burnt up the fuel of our ancestors, and which exist for us only through the transformations of energy by which the generations are prepared? Where Christians commemorate and are grateful to those who have done great things for them, it is because they feel gratitude not to the dead, but to the living,—to those who are living with God, even if they are not living with us, and who will once again be living with us when we pass from the visible scene. But to be grateful to the used-up intellectual and moral elements of the ancient world as they are transformed in our modern world, to the manufactured equivalents of the past as they are now found in combination with the present, is about as easy as to be grateful to the ancient forests which make our modern coal-beds. The difference between the Positivists' attitude towards the great dead and the Christians' is this,—that while the former think of them as the used-up materials of present-day life, the latter not only recognise what they owe them in the past, but think of them as still living an intenser life than before, and as looking back on their good and evil deeds in the past with that humble gratitude or that bitter self-reproach which good and evil excite in ourselves. It is clear that there is no *fresh* store of gratitude to be got out of the belief that the objects of that gratitude have ceased to live a personal life, and have become only part of the moral amalgam of history. The attempt to lash such artificial emotion into existence is an intrinsically absurd one; and so the Positivists really feel it, for by way of enhancing the artificial gratitude which they desire us to feel towards the dead, they tell us—for what reason, I know not, for they never offer any—that the worthless and the evil have no posthumous life, their worthlessness and evil dying away, in "the tide of progress and good." A more extraordinary doctrine was never propounded by so-called philosophers. If worthlessness exist where worth might have existed, does it not neutralise so much worth? Does not worthlessness reproduce itself, as well as worth? Are not the children of the bad apt to be bad too? Are not the companions of the bad corrupted? Is not the posthumous influence of falsehood, and hypocrisy, and lust as certain in its extent as the posthumous influence of truth, and candour, and purity? I do not hesitate to say that the Positivists, in their very scant materials for a religion, and their deep conviction that mankind needs one, dress up excuses for emotion at least as artificial as the dressed-up dolls which are supposed to stimulate piety in foreign churches. The ruined storehouses of the intellectual and moral materials embodied in the modern world can no more be permanently regarded with gratitude after they are really ruined, than the old shaft of a worked-out mine can be regarded with gratitude after all the ore it contained has passed into our manufactures. If, to use the favourite sociological metaphor, the teaching of Socrates has been assimilated by the tissues of our modern society, and Socrates be only the name which denotes the first spring of that teaching, why should Socrates be regarded with more gratitude than that with which we regard the sources of the Rhine, or the fossil ancestor of the modern horse?

But even Mr. Frederic Harrison excites in me less wonder than Mr. Herbert Spencer, who, in the new number of the *Nineteenth Century*, after carefully explaining to us how the belief in God began out of superstitions about ghosts, and how even the purified conception of God, as it is held by the highest minds to-day, involves contradictions in terms, goes on to explain to us that, nevertheless, the religion of the Agnostic is a much nobler thing than the religion of the Christian, and must become even nobler and nobler, as Agnosticism comes to be built on a higher and higher level of positive science. We must admit, says Mr. Spencer, an unknowable energy, which manifests itself alike in consciousness and in the external world; but we must also admit that human "explanation," when applied to that ultimate reality, "is a word without a meaning," and this even while we are compelled to think that there must be an explanation. Well, all I can say is that, if this be so, religion is a dream. Not at all, says Mr. Spencer; on the contrary, religion will always grow in its object-matter, and "the sphere of the religious sentiment" will always increase. We ask why, and we are told that this must be because scientific wonder is deeper than ignorant wonder; because the geologist is capable of realising better how long it took to denude the rocks than any mere rustic, or any traveller in search of the picturesque; because the astronomer who knows how big the spots on the sun are, can wonder at the energy of solar heat to better purpose than the Psalmist who talked of the heavens as declaring the glory of God and the firmament as showing His handiwork; finally, because the thinker who knows the necessarily finite character of intelligence, as he himself demonstrates it, must be much more deeply convinced of the absolute insolubility of the great enigma, than the credulous Christian who supposes that behind that great enigma is an infinite Being, capable of revealing Himself, if He will. Well, suppose all that to be so, how does that show that religion under such conditions has a future? Religion, to mean anything, must mean worship, must mean an influence "transfiguring"—to use Mr. Spencer's pet phrase—the will, and not merely puzzling the intellect. What is it to me, to be able to realise how many thousands of years the rocks were in getting themselves denuded; how many earths would go into one solar spot; how utterly insoluble the great enigma is? Even if I could realise these things better than any geologist alive, better than the most original of the astronomers, better than Mr. Spencer himself, I should be no nearer a religion. If "the Infinite and Eternal Energy" is simply beyond the reach of either vision or thought, and I can hope for no more living aid from it than from the unknown quantity of an insoluble equation, the "sentiment" which it must excite in me cannot but be the most barren and empty in the world. It comes very much, so far as I can see, to the old Oriental notion of "Om,"—as absolute being and also absolute nothingness. If God is righteous in any sense in which I may be righteous, however humbly, then religion means something, and worship a great deal. If God is love in any sense in which I can love, however feebly, then religion means something, and worship a great deal. But as for the emotion which I should feel towards the inexplicable, when I try in vain to find for it an explanation, it must be an emotion of a purely paralysing kind, if it is to have any characteristic influence at all. So far as religion is worth a farthing, it is founded on a real vision of what is far above us, and, nevertheless, more or less within our reach, and on an intense yearning to reach after it. But as for the emotion springing out of the vision of a mighty mist, and the conviction that a mighty mist it must always remain, it is a pure confusion of language to call it religious emotion at all. It is at best a state of dreary amazement at the infinitude and eternity of a blank,—without influence on the will or the affections, on the individual or society, on the present or on the future. Positivists and Agnostics at least are bound not to be dreamers, yet few dreamers seem to me to dream dreams so wild as the Positivists and Agnostics of the present day.

XLV

GOD, AND IDEAS OF GOD

1880

Dr. Carpenter, in a letter published three weeks ago, on the 24th of July, maintained with much vigour that "every believer's God is neither more nor less than his own idea of God," and that growth in religious life is nothing in the world but such growth in man's own conception of moral good as enables him gradually to "project upon infinity" a higher and higher conception of himself. In two or three remarkable letters which have since been published, especially in that of Mr. Moggridge, published on the 31st of July, this opinion was challenged, and so limited and modified as to be reconciled with a belief with which, in the strong form in which Dr. Carpenter stated it, it appeared to me to be quite inconsistent—though, of course, in Dr. Carpenter's opinion, it was perfectly consistent with it, and is proved to be so by the letter published on August the 14th—I mean, the belief in the reality and independence of the divine agency. For, of course, if God be for us nothing more than our own idea of God, there is nothing acting freely upon us from outside our own finite understanding which tends to widen and elevate that idea,—a conception fatal to true Theism. I was from the first very sure that this was not what Dr. Carpenter meant. And he now clearly admits, as freely indeed as the correspondent of last week, that if a child's father were not something very much above the child's idea of its own father, the child would be very badly off for a father indeed. And so, too, the difference between an infinite Being whom man only faintly takes in, and man's faint idea of Him as "projected on infinity," is the whole difference between God and Ludwig Feuerbach's gigantic shadow of man. The one is an inexhaustible life, which besets us behind and before, and is constantly pressing in on our own, so as to compel us to open our hearts wider and wider; the other is a notion of our own making, which will only grow as we grow and if we grow, and which, in any case, cannot do for us anything beyond what in reality we do for ourselves. It is all the difference between a living being who is constantly helping us to apprehend, what unassisted we could not apprehend, and a philosophic view, which may indeed widen from time to time, but only as we get time and leisure and capacity to reconsider and extend it. Dr. Carpenter, of course, will say that he never for a moment intended to deny that it is God Himself whose agency modifies and expands our human "ideas" of Him, nor that our ideas should always be kept open and elastic, so as to be recast at once under every new experience which God may provide for us. And I am quite aware, as no one doubts Dr. Carpenter's earnest Theism, that the issue between us, momentous as it is, is at bottom rather one as to the best form of expressing what we mean, than as to the thing itself. But then, sometimes a great deal of truth of belief is involved in choosing the best mode of expressing our belief. What at one time led physical science more astray than the mistaken antithesis between heat and cold, heaviness and lightness, as though either of these opposites expressed something of a kind essentially antagonistic to the other?—yet this was at bottom an inexact mode of expressing actual observation. And so, too, what has led our religious life more astray than the notion that God is for each of us only what we have recognised Him to be, and that the stress of our religion, therefore, should be thrown upon clearing up our own finite notions of God rather than on practically following His mysterious inward guidance, a guidance of the true rationale of which even the most lofty intellects can give themselves so inadequate an account? The great difference, I take it, between the mode of looking at things which starts from "the idea of God" formed by each man as if it were the equivalent of God Himself, and that, on the other hand, which recognises that the divine agency is infinitely wider and more various in its influences and its pressure upon us than anything of which our finite intelligence can give an account, is this: that the former tends to a purely self-conscious religion, which never takes a step until the mind has given itself a clear account of the principles which justify that step; while the latter tends to a faith that often goes in advance of what it can see, because it believes in a guidance higher than the human intellect can at present grasp, drawing us towards what the human intellect will creep slowly after, and perhaps, for ages more, rather throw doubts upon than verify.

Of course, it will be said, as it always has been

said, that this conception of God as acting upon us
by a great many more influences than we can apprehend
or analyse, tends directly to fanaticism, pietism,
and all kinds of dangerous mysticism. As Dr.
Carpenter has well pointed out, there is hardly any
religious mischief going, which has not been justified
by insane intuitions of divine commands; and, of
course, it is no news to anybody that those who allow
themselves to be guided by influences which they
cannot clearly define and explain, are, so far as that
goes, and if they know nothing more of these influences
than that they cannot explain them, more
likely to be guided in the wrong direction than in
the right. But then no one who believes in divine
revelation at all, thinks that, because we are unable
clearly to discriminate what it is which assures us of
the divine hand, there is nothing which can so assure
us. The child cannot discriminate in the least what
it is which teaches him to rely on his father, but,
none the less, he is quite right in so relying; and
if he did not so rely, it would be all the worse for
him. What I maintain is, that every great religious
advance has been due to following some guidance
which went far beyond what the people so guided
could at the time clearly comprehend or rationally
justify, and yet which, acting upon the teaching of
their whole inward nature, they felt to be a guidance
better than their own, and worthy to be trusted, as
proceeding from a higher source. Take the Jewish
legislation, for instance, which so carefully provided
against idolatry in the midst of idolatrous instincts
of the most potent kind,—which so carefully provided
strict limitations on the accumulative instincts of the
Jews in relation to property, accumulative instincts
which have always been stronger amongst the Jews

than amongst other nations,—which so early and so solemnly forbade covetousness, as a sin of the first order, and that among a people peculiarly exposed to covetousness. Now was not the Jewish legislation in all these cases quite beyond the rational justification, in any clear intellectual sense, of the people who were called upon to obey it? And yet was there not enough in the heart and mind of the people to make it inexplicably certain to them—though by no means explicably clear—that they ought to obey these laws? It was the same with the later prophets, when they protested so powerfully against holding by the letter of the sacrificial law, and demanded instead the divine spirit of self-sacrifice,—the sacrifice of the will, instead of the mere sacrifice of expensive external dues and of conventional earthly observances. Was not the teaching of Isaiah far in advance of the mind of the people whose obedience Isaiah demanded? But though far in advance of their mind, was there not enough in their hearts and minds to justify that demand, even though they could not explain how it was justified? And so, too, with the teaching of Christ. Do not His Apostles tell us expressly that they misunderstood His language, that they often did not even follow what He was driving at in His teaching, that they put the most earthly interpretations on His promises, and protested passionately against His purposes? Yet they followed Him, and though in a sense blindly, yet in a much better sense not blindly at all, because though they knew not what they did, there was something in them, and that the highest thing in them, which assured them that what they did was good. Well, what I say is that the power to trust to this spirit of God which leads men in *advance* of their "ideas of

God," is of the very essence of religious development; that if men had not felt that they must obey a voice which prompted them to break through the limits imposed by their "ideas of God," we should never have had religious advance at all. Every religious reformation has broken through the best and most approved notions of the day about religion, and has broken through these without its own characteristic ideas having first mastered the intellects and enlarged the understandings of those who made up the bulk of the reforming party. Religious advance has always consisted in moving onward to a divine beckoning, and that before the rational justification of that movement had presented itself to the people. Patriarch, prophet, apostle,—not one of them, if we can trust history at all, could be said to have acted in conformity with his "idea of God"; every one of them was startled by what he was prompted to do, as by a novelty which involved falsehood to his most sacred traditions and conceptions of God; and though he knew he ought to do it, he did it, shrinking and wondering, and at a loss to justify to his own intellect what he was about. This is just the difference between trusting in God, and trusting in your own "idea of God": the man who trusts in the former is ready to move out beyond the field of his own ideas, at the impulse of the living Power who is greater than those ideas, and who is always trying to show us the insufficiency of them; while the man who trusts only in the latter, is kept a prisoner in the vicious circle of his own inadequate notions. God can enlarge our ideas of Him, can show us how imperfect they are, by gently leading us beyond them, as when He taught St. Peter, while priding himself in his horror of what was "common and unclean," that what God had cleansed he was not to regard as common; but an "idea of God" can never enlarge itself, and has in itself no principle of life and movement.

If it be said that this view leads directly to a superstitious and fanatical trust in imaginary "calls" and "voices," I utterly deny it. Such fanaticism or superstition always consists in the false emphasis laid on some fanciful coincidence, such as an illusion of the senses, or the wording of a text of Scripture that the eye alights on in a moment of indecision, or a dream, or vision, or anything that is specially impressive to some susceptible part of our lower nature. What I maintain is that all such dispositions to attach vast importance to a minute aspect of mere circumstance is unhealthy, morbid, insane. But, on the other hand, it is clearly false to suppose that we can safely trust our whole nature to the guidance of our clearest "ideas." There is much more in man than he has ever understood, and those have never been the greatest men who have acted solely on the light of their "ideas," instead of trusting in a guidance which led them upwards, even in despite of the fixed protest of some of their ideas. Only you must feel, by the evidence of your whole nature, that it is *upwards* you are being borne, and not sideways or downwards by a mere caprice of unhealthy instinct. And of what constitutes such evidence there is, of course, no abstract test whatever. It is just the difference between true wisdom and poor self-confidence, that the one recognises what is highest,—recognises true revelation,—even when it draws us away from our preconceived notions; while the other adheres obstinately to its own fixed ideas,—and will not give them up even for a nobler life. The difference between trusting in God and trusting in an "idea of God," is the difference between waiting for guidance from above, and preparing carefully for your own ascent from beneath.

XLVI

THE LIMITS OF FREE-WILL

1892

THE case of the "Conscious Automaton," if he can be said to have a case, does not certainly consist in the conspicuously false analysis which he makes of the phenomena of volition, but in the tendency of the free-willist to exaggerate greatly the sphere within which there can be said to be moral freedom. It is perfectly true that nothing can be conceived that is more important and more significant than the part which free volition plays in the drama of human life. It represents the woof where the constituents of our life over which we have no control represent the warp. It impresses more or less of deliberate purpose on the whole wealth of human faculty, and stamps with its seal even the passive sufferings of which our existence is partly made up. The voluntary efforts by which we mould what would otherwise be the drift of our characters, whether in doing or in enduring, to our higher purposes, are all unintelligible without free-will. And yet it is true that probably of all the minutes of an average life, barely one in a day dates a fresh volition, though, of course, very many date the direct consequences of former volitions which have long been incorporated in our habits and assimilated into the very tissue of our active or passive moods. It is effort, and effort only, which betrays free-will. A mind that is the sport of its various desires, and that yields itself without a struggle to the resultant of its contending desires, is no more conscious of effort than a straw which dances on the eddies of a whirlpool, and is borne hither and thither as those eddies may determine, is conscious of effort. We may all of us satisfy ourselves of this by carefully watching ourselves during the conflict of various desires and emotions, when we deliberately give ourselves up to the spontaneous operation of those complex feelings. We are conscious of the vehemence of some, of the steady persistence of others, of the submergence and disappointment of those which are overwhelmed, of the victory and gratification of those which carry the day. But we are not conscious of *effort*, unless we ourselves bring out of our own will and purpose some new force which allies itself with one or more of our desires, and which forcibly suppresses, or at least subdues and mortifies, those which rage against our deliberate purpose. Effort is self-created force from within,—from within the very innermost source of personality. It often gives the victory to the desire which is intrinsically the weakest, and defeats the passion which is intrinsically the richest in spontaneous vigour. But efforts of this heroic kind are rarely, perhaps, as numerous as the years of a human life; and even genuine but much less costly efforts are numbered rather by days than hours or minutes. Of those vital conditions over which we neither have, nor even so much as imagine that we have, any control, we can enumerate a host without even a moment's hesitation. No man supposes that he is responsible for his own physical constitution, for his own keenness or defectiveness of sight or hearing, for his height or his descent, or for his hereditary tastes and prepossessions. Nobody supposes that he can be independent of the climatic influences in which he was born, or the scenery and human associations which have moulded his habits and expectations. No man supposes that by the exercise of his own free-will he could have supplied all the defects of a bad education, and cancelled all the evil influences of vicious companionship. No man supposes that he could have made his original faculties and instincts different from what they were, or that he could have warded off all the attacks of disease, or materially altered the character of his earliest affections. All these influences are of the very warp of our nature, and are conditions as determinate as the solar light and heat and the atmospheric and magnetic currents by which our bodies are affected, and our perceptions and sensations developed. Free volition starts and sustains many a new exercise of energy, alters essentially many a habit of thought, and many a sphere of practical activity; but it can only work on a mighty web of determinate conditions so numerous and so complex, that it is safe to attribute the actual complexion of any man's mind and character to a thousand potent influences over which he has no control, for every one which he either has actually moulded or might have moulded by his own free-will.

And I may note especially that the most conspicuous parts of character, those on which the charm or repulsiveness of character depends, are very seldom completely, or even in any large degree, under the control of the will. The sweetest and most affectionate persons are usually sweet and affectionate by nature rather than by virtue of any self-education or self-control. No man who was naturally secretive and self-occupied ever became characteristically frank and ingenuous by any amount of effort that he could apply in the period of this brief existence, though, of course, many a one of this type has become far less secretive and self-occupied, far more nearly of the type at which he aims, than he was in his childhood and youth. No man who was by nature timid, and even cowardly, ever succeeded in making himself distinctly bold and remarkable for courage within the period of this life, though such a one may and often does succeed in stifling his timidities, and forcing his naturally cowardly impulses into the background,—into the suppressed and conquered region of his life. Still, it remains true that most of those who particularly attract and fascinate their fellow-men, attract and fascinate them not by any qualities which the exercise of free-will has given them, but by the beauty of inborn and inherited dispositions, and that most of those who repel us by their hardness and dryness and self-consciousness and vanity and pride, repel us by virtue of dispositions which they could no more extirpate than they could extirpate the faults of their physical constitution or raise the temperature of their blood.

How, then, it may be asked, is the part which free-will plays in the life of man so all-important, if it can only modify, and that not always with very much visible effect, the original constitution which nature and circumstance and inheritance combined to confer? It is all-important, because it is the one helm by which we guide our course, by which we impose the *tendencies* which change our characters for the better or the worse, by which we arrest degeneration and stimulate aspiration, by which we determine whether the higher or lower impulses of our nature shall have their way, whether we shall serve the desires and aims which most exalt us, or the desires and aims which most debase us,—in a single word, by which we become responsible beings. It is quite true that in the case of so short a life as that which men pass on earth, they cannot revolutionise entirely the very grain of their character. If that grain is coarse, they may render it somewhat finer; if it is fine, they may make it finer still; but they can only work on the conditions into which they are born, and can neither eradicate all that they find faulty, nor, as a rule, even transfigure the surrounding influences and circumstances which tend to aggravate those faults. Still, everything is saved if responsibility for the limited changes of which life admits is saved, and that is precisely what the gift of free-will really saves. We are not responsible for the conditions, favourable or unfavourable, with which we start in life; but we are responsible for the full use and development of the favourable conditions, and the attenuation and repression of the unfavourable. The petty mind cannot suddenly spring into grandeur and magnanimity; but the petty mind may become fair and open to the knowledge of its own stiffness and limitations. The ambitious mind cannot suddenly abolish the temptations which spring from its own restlessness and audacity, but it may force itself to see the manifold snares and sins to which these audacities lead, and so bank up its eagerness and its insatiable cravings, as to control and turn to a nobler use the imprisoned force of which it can dispose. The strict limitations of free-will are visible on every side. Free-will is no magician to transform by a wave of the wand sullen passions into exalted affections, or plodding industry into flashing genius,—a hut into a palace, or a rusty knife into a Damascene scimitar. But it is free-will, and free-will alone, that can transmute mere graceful dispositions into high and steadfast character; that can imbue the finer feelings with the depth and constancy of deliberate purpose; that, in short, can saturate the automatic spiritual vitality of childhood and youth with the full personality of those fixed intentions and motives which lift instinct and impulse into the loftier region of divine life.

XLVII

THE LIMITS OF DIVINE POWER

1897

A CORRESPONDENT to the *Spectator* suggests that the enigma of the terrible catastrophes which so often eclipse the faith or startle the consciences of men, like the earthquake of Lisbon in the last century, or that of Krakatoa in this, or such disasters as the great fire in the church at Santiago, when so many hundreds of women perished, or the gruesome tragedy in the Roman Catholic bazaar the other day in Paris, may practically have no solution beyond this, —that the Creator, in forming man out of the dust of the earth, may have set limits to His own power, and accepted for Himself a set of conditions which render it necessary for Him to choose between alternatives *either* one of which involves what seem to us enormous evils and even horrors, so that whichever alternative He actually selects must appear an act which a loving and omnipotent being would have rejected as absolutely inconsistent with His character as Revelation presents it to us. I cannot say that this seems to me at all an applicable explanation of such tragedies as I have named, though I fully admit, and even maintain, that such an idea as that of unqualified omnipotence is inconceivable as involving the most absolute contradictions. Thinkers who suppose that God can overrule the laws of thought, and create a being for whom even moral or mathematical contradictions are perfectly reconcilable, for whom two and two make either four or five, as God pleases, or *both* four and five, if He so rules it; for whom evil is good and good evil, if God chooses; thinkers who suppose that God, if He will, can both bring into existence a human being, and yet *not* bring him into existence, seem to me to confound all the distinctions without which life would not be life at all. Indeed, they both assert and deny in the very same breath assumptions which any sort of communion between God and man absolutely involves. Omnipotence does not and cannot mean that it is in the power even of the Creator of the Universe to mean and not to mean the very same thing at the very same time. If it were so, Omnipotence and the absolute extinction of all power would be perfectly compatible. How could a Revelation be possible at all if the very contents of Revelation were born of a mere breath of caprice which the very next act of the revealer might dissipate? God would not be God if there were any "variableness or shadow of turning" in Him, much more if at His own choice He could, as it were, annihilate Himself for us by showing us that He can unteach us all that He has taught, just because it is His arbitrary pleasure so to do. A God who could be holy or unholy at His own pleasure would in no sense whatever be God, but would be more than incomprehensible, inapprehensible, a mystery of self-contradiction. Any being who could profess to unveil to us his own nature, and then unveil to us that it had never been unveiled, would be the very opposite of divine,—a bewilderment, not the author of light. So far I entirely go with the correspondent to the *Spectator* that the divine nature does not cease to be necessarily definite only because it is infinite. When our Lord tells us that to God "all things are possible," He certainly does not mean that it is possible for Him to make Himself impossible, to be at once good and evil, light and darkness. The sense in which Christ declared that to God all things are possible, was the sense in which it is easy for God to do what is in full accordance with His own nature but far beyond the possibilities of man's; not the sense in which it is possible for Him both to be Himself and not to be Himself: in other words, so absolutely omnipotent as to have no definite nature of His own to communicate or reveal.

But I cannot go with the *Spectator*'s correspondent when he appears to suggest that God may have submitted Himself to limits which really place the attribute which has been specially called His Providence in relation to man's life, utterly beyond His own reach. If in any sense God *could* not have prevented such a disaster as the Santiago or the Paris tragedy, even if He would, then such teaching as our Lord's, that "not a sparrow falleth to the ground without him," and that the hairs of our heads are all numbered, is, if not erroneous, at least thoroughly misleading; for its obvious drift and its actual effect have been, and still are, to inspire the most absolute trust in God's personal love and care. And if in choosing to subject us to material laws He has put it beyond His power either to guide our wanderings in the world, or to inspire us with the courage and presence of mind requisite to prevent such tragedies as the frightful horrors to which I have referred, surely all our Lord's teaching as to the both mighty and minute Providence of God is a teaching the natural and actual effect of which cannot be justified. Practically speaking, all that is essential to justify these lessons is the existence of real communion between God and man, so that the divine voice which instigates and controls our actions is to be recognised as a real influence of the first magnitude in the ordering of our life. If that is a real influence, then the great doctrine of Providence is true, and is at the very foundation of all human religion. If it is a mere illusion, the assumption of almost all the greater religions of the world is a false assumption, and we can no longer venture to believe that in God "we live and move and have our being." In that case we are shut out from intercourse with Him by the very laws of the material bodies that He has given us. Now, as it appears to me, it is of the very essence of the teaching of Revelation, and not only of the highest ultimate Revelation, but of that earlier Revelation which is contained in the songs of the Psalmists and the declarations of the Prophets, that whatever may be the riddle of the material universe, it is one which can be far better solved by the divine half-lights which penetrate its obscurities than by the scientific keys with which human study and observation furnish us. "The Lord is my shepherd, I shall not want," "His name shall be called wonderful, counsellor, the mighty God, the everlasting father, the Prince of Peace, and the government shall be upon his shoulder," are teachings in which the mind that attends to the inner voice, settles down, even after all that study can do to classify and search out the secondary causes at work in our universe has been done, and done successfully. It is the teaching of the conscience and of the spiritual insight, which shines through all the obscurities of the outward framework by which we are enveloped. Nothing can be more certain than that the whole course of the development of the Jewish conception of God fully recognised the difficulty of reconciling the physical order of creation with the spiritual testimony of the conscience with reference to God's immanent intercourse with the soul of man, and yet insisted that the two could and must be reconciled. The very subject of the Book of Job was that, and that alone. And many of the Psalms and large passages in the greater Prophets concern themselves with the same problem. "Oh that thou wouldst rend the heavens, that thou wouldst come down, that the mountains might flow down at thy presence," says the later Isaiah, as though he were overwhelmed by the opaque though feebly translucent veil with which the physical universe often seems to hide the presence of God and to weaken the testimony of the conscience and spirit of man to the divine authority. But none the less that testimony is constantly repeated with greater and greater emphasis, till at last we are told plainly that the divine light "shineth in darkness and the darkness comprehendeth it not,"—the darkness being of our own making, not of God's. I heartily believe that there is no omnipotence which can at once reveal the divine nature and yet ignore the very characteristics which make it divine. An omnipotence that can at

will establish the great foundations of all mental
and moral order, and yet at will dissolve them only
to demonstrate its own arbitrary power, would be
an omnipotence that exploded the essential meaning
of divine power. But none the less, divine power
without divine providence, divine power which
found itself so fatally manacled by the physical
conditions of the universe that it could not inspire
in men the deep sense of divine love and grace,
would be rather divine weakness than divine power.
And it seems to me remarkable that it is the very
catastrophes which most amaze and paralyse mere
lookers-on, that also elicit specimens of that highest
kind of piety and heroism best fitted to awaken our
wonder and awe. Such examples as those set by
the Duchesse d'Alençon at one end of the social
scale, and the poor plumber who rescued so many
victims from the burning Paris bazaar at the other
end of the social scale, and who nearly lost his
reason in the effort, are the best possible proofs
that it is not those who are really full of piety and
enthusiasm who lose their religion in the moment
of supreme peril. The very terrors which paralyse
the faith of mere onlookers, stimulate the trust
which has been fostered in the hearts of true
piety.

XLVIII

HUMAN SYMPATHIES AND RELIGIOUS CAPACITY

1892

IN discussing last week the distinct character of religious capacity, I assumed that there is a close analogy between the effect of human sympathy in quickening the insight of those who possess it into human character, and the effect of divine sympathy, —of what I may with reverence term sympathy with God, — in quickening the insight into the spiritual meaning of the divine ordinances and the various paradoxes of human life. Indeed, the only theologian, properly so called, among the twelve who received the commission to preserve and publish the teaching of Christ, gives the best possible authority for the assumption that there is a very close analogy between the effect of human and divine sympathy. "He that loveth not his brother whom he hath seen, how can he love God whom he hath not seen?" And yet there is a good deal in human life which seems to tell just the other way. I believe that there is no more fertile source of religious scepticism than what I may truly call a tender and passionate love for man. How many cases have we not had of late years of a philanthropy like Robert Owen's, which was all the more generous from his complete rejection of any sort of individual life or spiritual judgment beyond the grave? That attitude of mind is really systematised in the teaching of the Positivists. The more they reject as an altogether baseless assumption the faith in God, the more lavishly they pour out on Humanity the rapture of feeling which they no longer render to the Creator. It might almost be said of many of our modern philanthropists, that it is the very depth and earnestness of their love for the brother whom they have seen which renders them indignant at the suggestion that there is any being in whose image they are created who has the power to save man from the manifold sufferings to which he is subjected, and who yet in multitudes of instances refuses to wield that power. How can any one, they ask, who truly loves the brother whom he hath seen, manage to love the God whom he hath not seen, but who, if He really has the omnipotence ascribed to Him, permits,—nay, brings about by His own agency,—all these horrors of earthquake, and volcano, and flood, and avalanche, and innumerable tragic destinies of other kinds, which it almost breaks human hearts to contemplate, and yet which it does not apparently even grieve the divine heart to bring about? If love of one's brother be the first condition for true love of God, how is it that God does so much, which if it were deliberately done by men, would be most simply described as being a manifestation, not of love but of hate, not of mercy but of cruelty? Surely it is by no means difficult to understand why sympathy with men so often eclipses and extinguishes sympathy with God. Yet St. John tells us that without the former the latter is simply impossible. And yet without the latter the former seems to be not only possible enough, but not unfrequently unusually vivid and impetuous. What was Shelley's atheism but a passionate protest against the inexorable severity of the divine government? What even was such ordinary and commonplace atheism as the late Mr. Bradlaugh's but a more materialistic and less refined protest of the same kind. There is surely a sense in which sympathy with men, far from leading directly to sympathy with God, renders this sympathy difficult, and in some cases all but impossible.

Such a sense there certainly is, and yet it is none the less true that a sympathy with God which is not *founded* on sympathy with men is a spurious and irreligious, not a genuinely religious, emotion. It is, of course, in the human character of the Divine Son that we must look for the true kind of sympathy with God, and what do we find there? The tenderest human sympathy, the sympathy which vibrated to every pang of human nature, which felt the hardness of the fate of those eighteen upon whom the tower of Siloam fell and slew them, just as we feel the hardship of the fate of those who perish in the scalding water of an exploded boiler, or the scores who are swept to destruction by a bursting glacier. Indeed, this sympathy was so strong, that it led Him to forbid His disciples to regard such a fate as a divine judgment on exceptional sin. Yet far from shrinking at these mysterious and unearned sufferings, He predicted the steady multiplication of such mysterious calamities amongst His own people unless they should repent of the hardness of heart which rendered them inaccessible to His appeals. There was nothing which He condemned more severely than the readiness to see the vengeance of God in the sufferings of His countrymen,—for example, in the exceptional privations of the man born blind, and in the sudden death of those whose blood Pilate mingled with the sacrifices. His heart thrilled with their pangs, just as His heart thrilled with delight at the self-sacrifice of the poor widow who cast two mites into the treasury, or with the grief of the widow who was following her only son to the grave. But these sufferings, though they moved His tenderest compassion, did not appal Him. He felt no disposition to arraign the goodness of God because these mysterious pangs fell upon His people. On the contrary, He foresaw their increase, their gathering into tempests and hurricanes of darker and deadlier omen, if the effect of them should not be to soften the hearts of His people towards God. His sympathy with God was a mightier form of His sympathy with man. He entered deeply into the sufferings of the blind and the halt and the palsied and the insane, and was ever ready to heal them; but He entered more deeply still into the love of Him who inflicted these sufferings with the purpose of bringing human nature back into the attitude in which it could receive most humbly and simply the impress of the divine mind. It never even appears to have occurred to His human nature that what, if purposely inflicted by man, would have implied the deepest malignity in man, implied, when inflicted by God, anything but the purpose to turn the hearts of the disobedient to the wisdom of the just. For He knew that though he who inflicts suffering, seeing nothing beyond the suffering which he inflicts, is evil-minded, there is a prophetic knowledge in the government of the world which transforms, and indeed transubstantiates, its most fearful calamities into possibilities and even promises of a totally new kind of blessing, a blessing which reverses the apparent significance of pain, and stimulates the latent core of goodness, even where happiness only acted on it like an opiate, or stifled it in the vivid ripples of distracting sensation. "Blessed are ye when men shall revile you, and persecute you, and do all manner of evil against you, falsely, for my sake," was not the saying of One whose foresight was limited to the immediate pangs which He knew that His followers would be compelled to endure. His sympathy with the good in man was too keen to render it possible that He should overlook that greater good lurking in the heart of the mighty calamities of the world, which makes of overwhelming and even overawing anguish a transfiguring power competent to elicit the highest elements of the human character. He who could see through the temptation and even the temporary fall of Peter, the growth of something higher and sterner and steadier in St. Peter's character, could see, of course, through the shock of national or even of terrestrial catastrophes the gleam of brighter and more constant and nobler qualities in man. In Christ, at all events, it was not for want of the more transient and, so to say, superficial sympathies, that the human tragedy so completely failed to blind Him to the light beyond. He showed by almost every one of His mighty works how tenderly He entered into the immediate pang when He beheld it, and how ready He was to assuage it. All the more, however, He felt, as it is impossible for mere man to feel, the beneficence latent in the most heart-rending calamities, the secret meaning in the most prolonged and enigmatic sufferings. His sympathy with man was so deep, that it contained the prophecy of what man should become under the purifying and strengthening fire of divine discipline. What Matthew Arnold called " the secret of Jesus," was simply the knowledge that willing acquiescence in any weakness of divine origin is in itself a source of strength, that willing acquiescence in suffering of divine origin is in itself a source of blessing. This was not a secret which any human being not created entirely in the divine image, and not fully conscious of having been so created, could have guessed. For no philosophical attempt was ever more disastrous than Matthew Arnold's to divorce that " secret " from the permanent and immanent divine inspiration which could alone have breathed it into any human ear, and to make it the mere lesson of human " experience." A lesson of human experience, no doubt it is, but a lesson which is inextricably bound up with that other lesson, that the weak things of the world, and the things which are not, are so moulded by the power of the creative spirit as to bring to naught the things which are, and that without the vivifying touch of that creative spirit, they remain just as inert and dead as are human genius, pride, and presumption in their splendid failures, their magnificent imbecilities.

XLIX

THE CHRISTIAN ETHICS OF FORBEARANCE

1894

In a very interesting little book on Christian Ethics, by Professor Knight, of St. Andrews, which Mr. Murray has just published, I find an admirable description of the virtues and the sins on which Christ's teaching lays most stress, and especially, of course, on that contrast between Pantheism and that assertion of the interpenetration of the human with the divine,—of the coexistence in real humanity of a vivid human life with the divine nature which enfolds it,—which is, of all the characteristics of Christ's teaching, the most characteristic. "Hebraic theism," says Professor Knight, "pure and simple, looking upon the Divine and the human as two natures standing apart, with a wide chasm between them—natures between whom a contract could be made, or a covenant adjusted—did not fully recognise the counter truth of the unity of the two. Pantheism threw emphasis on that truth, but it accomplished the union of the two natures—the finite and the Infinite—by silencing one of them, or extinguishing it. If the finite disappears and is lost to view, there can be no reconciliation of the one with the other." But, while Professor Knight recognises fully the great contrast between the Pantheism which practically extinguishes human limitations, and that sympathy of God with man which maintains, enforces, and refines without extinguishing them, I do not think that he lays enough stress on one of the most impressive of the aspects of Christ's teaching and practice, namely, that which I may perhaps call the duty not merely of recognising the infinite tenderness of God for man, and His divine sympathy with our limitations, but in some feeble and germinal fashion of entering into sympathy with God's large forbearance with human wilfulness, and recognising frankly that there is that in the large tolerance of the divine nature which in some sense claims our sympathy even while it far transcends our powers of complete comprehension. What can be more remarkable than the element in the Sermon on the Mount which has given it its paradoxical character,—the command, for instance, not to resist evil, but if any man will sue thee at the law and take away thy coat, "let him have thy cloak also," —if any one would compel another to go a mile, to go with him twain,—if any man should smite thee on one cheek, to turn to him the other also? This thread of teaching, which runs through the whole discourse, and which insists that man should emulate God in allowing His sun to shine and His rain to fall alike on the evil and the good, on the just and the unjust, is surely not so much a series of literal practical injunctions, as a series of efforts to inculcate sympathy with the amazing tolerance and forbearance of divine providence, which so often, when it meets with the grossest ingratitude, turns as it were the other cheek to that ingratitude, which so often resists not evil, but allows us to fill up to the brim the measure of our wilfulness that we may the better enter into its true spirit, and which, in short, yields purposely to our waywardness only that it may conquer it. It seems to me that half the paradox of the Sermon on the Mount is due to our interpreting as literal precepts of human conduct what are really intended to give us an insight into, and put us in sympathy with, the largeness of divine purpose. Of course, in the vast majority of ordinary human cases, the practice of letting an unjust man see that the more greedy and unjust he is, the more he will gain, would not benefit but harm him. That is just the difference between the human order and the divine, that if you let explicit reward follow explicit transgression, human society becomes a chaos, and human life impossible; indeed, the moral law, the Ten Commandments, are all opposed to any such bestowing of rewards on the evil and of penalties on the good; and Christ came not to abolish the law, but to fulfil it. But what is impossible in human society is often not only possible, but beneficent, when embodied in the half-hidden principles of the divine order. Christ is always teaching this. The tares are not to be rooted up, lest the wheat that grows with them should also be rooted up. The wheat and tares are to grow together till the harvest. Evil is to be suffered long in order that it may be the more effectually destroyed. God's providence is far more long-suffering than human society can afford to be, simply because its motives, being hidden in mystery, take their time in ripening, and do not therefore directly encourage, but only permit, the evil heart to indulge its evil passions till they overflow in conspicuous and open sin. But none the less it is true that God's providence yields freely to human wilfulness, giving it free scope in order that it may recognise its own character, and that Christ in His Sermon on the Mount claims to point this out to His disciples as a characteristic of the divine government which demands their sympathy, and, so far as is consistent with the established order of human society, their own practical concurrence.

But what this sympathy and concurrence with the largeness of the divine purpose practically means, no one can understand by merely studying Christ's precepts without also studying His life. Nothing in that life seems to me half so remarkable as the detached way in which our Lord looked at His own human destiny and sufferings as if they were in some sense external to Himself and had to be regarded, not as if they concerned in any way the divine judgment on His own human life, but solely what would bring out more fully the wider purposes of the divine mind. It does not so much as occur to Him that there was hardship to Himself in being tried, and scourged, and condemned, and crucified. What His mind seems always full of is the danger that His disciples would be betrayed into false views of God's providence by this apparent collapse of the divine justice. He is always seeking to prepare them for the true interpretation of the great paradox of the triumph of the world over God, and to prepare the Jewish people in general for the catastrophe which was at hand in their history, and which they could not construe rightly unless they understood that the suffering of the Son was essential to the carrying out of the purpose of the Father. "Daughters of Jerusalem, weep not for me, but weep for yourselves and for your children."

"Jerusalem, Jerusalem, that killest the prophets and stonest them that are sent unto thee, how often would I have gathered thy children together, as a hen gathers her chickens under her wings, and ye would not. Behold, your house is left unto you desolate." Nothing seems further from His mind than any consternation at the shame and disaster of His own destiny. It is with the largeness of the divine purpose that He sympathises, and seeks to lead His disciples to sympathise. How, otherwise, as He is always asking, could the Scriptures, the oracles of that divine purpose, be fulfilled?

And it is just the same even in the case of the stumblings and falls and betrayals into which His disciples are led by their weakness and cowardice. In their case, too, He knows when it is a mistake to resist evil, when He must let them learn the depth of their own evil before that evil can be purged away. "All ye shall be offended because of me this night"; and yet He does not plead with them not to be offended. "I tell thee, Peter, before the cock crows twice, thou shalt deny me thrice"; but He addresses no passionate reproach even to His most trusted apostle, no entreaty not to fall under the power of darkness, but calmly enjoins upon him, so soon as he has recovered himself, to strengthen his brethren. He turns to Judas, and says: "What thou doest, do quickly." There is no trace in Him of any effort to avert the agony as it approaches. He is simply possessed with the divine view of the catastrophe. To Pilate He says: "You could have no power at all against me unless it were given you from above." He regards Himself with perfect equanimity as simply fulfilling the divine purpose in His sufferings, and does not address a word to

His judges or the Roman Governor which might tend to bias their judgment in His favour. "As the sheep before her shearers is dumb, so opened he not his mouth." It is His sympathy with God's largeness of purpose, not with the shrinkings and tremblings of His mortal nature, which determines His whole action during the very crisis of His fate. Professor Knight sketches briefly and vigorously the characteristics of the human ethics which made Christ's teaching the very flower and completion of all the earlier ethical teaching which had ever moulded human conduct; but he seems to me to pass by too much that strange and perfectly unearthly sympathy with God, which transformed His life into a living embodiment of the Sermon on the Mount, with its calm surrender to evil, which He yielded to only that He might the better overcome it, and only yielded to when He saw, with a divine prescience, that it must overflow before it could be subdued. There is a deep vein of prescience in Christ's ethics, which gives them their peculiar tone of divine equanimity, and reduces the sense of storm and conflict in them to a minimum. No purely human mind could have delivered the Sermon on the Mount. It is the teaching of one who foresees, by virtue of His sympathy with God, as much as He discerns of the temper of the immediate present. That interference of our wishes with our judgment which disturbs our human vision never troubled the clear depths of that divine equanimity.

L.

THE MODERN POETRY OF DOUBT

1870

SOME fine anonymous stanzas in the February number of *Macmillan's Magazine*, written on occasion of the meeting of the Œcumenical Council on the Feast of the Epiphany, give us a fresh illustration of one of the most curiously marked and constantly recurring features of the unbroken succession of English poets between Shelley's day and our own,—the always bitter and sometimes almost tragic cry of desolation with which one after the other, as they gaze eagerly into the spiritual world, they nerve themselves to confess what they have not found and cannot find there. It is true that the Laureate, with that comprehension of grasp, that deliberate rejection of single strands of feeling, which always distinguishes him, has rarely allowed himself to echo the mere wail of agonising doubt without shedding some glimpse of faith, some ray of light from Him whom he "deems the Lord of all," upon the darkness, but even Mr. Tennyson's gleams of light have rarely quite equalled his "shadow-streaks of rain." There is no lyric in all his volumes quite equal to that which tells us how

> ". . . the stately ships go on
> To their haven under the hill;
> But O for the touch of a vanish'd hand,
> And the sound of a voice that is still!"

If the greatest of our living poets is unequalled in touching the dreariest landscape with some beam of living hope, he is even greater in creating the passionate need and craving for it, the almost unspeakable fear that we may be left alone with that Nature utterly careless of the "single life," and almost equally careless of "the type,"—of Nature "red in tooth and claw" ravening on the lives she sacrifices in millions, in that process of selection which science has so triumphantly established, but which only a poet can picture to us in all its terror. Yet no one can fairly deem the Poet Laureate one who takes any pleasure in depicting such moods of desolation as Shelley abounds in. He has saved the higher poetry of our generation from despair, and it is remarkable enough that every other poet of note has so far felt either *his* influence, or some influence which he and they have felt in common, as to mingle with even the most profound expressions of unsatisfied longing, a tacit assumption that it is something of the nature of faith—as surely it is—which confers the power to pour out doubt so truthfully and yet so sadly to the silent skies. There was nothing of this in Shelley's song as he shuddered on the edge of the void he thought he saw. The English language does not contain lines of despair at once so calm and so poignant, as those with which he closed the unequal but marvellous poem of "Alastor," and painted the immeasurable emptiness, the piercing vacancy, which so often robs the whole

universe of its meaning when one mortal life dies
out :—

> "It is a woe 'too deep for tears' when all
> Is reft at once, when some surpassing Spirit
> Whose light adorned the world around it, leaves
> Those who remain behind not sobs or groans,
> The passionate tumult of a clinging hope,
> But pale despair and cold tranquillity,
> Nature's vast frame, the web of human things,
> Birth and the grave, that are not as they were."

Nor was it, of course, only in a passage here and there that this vivid sense of unutterable desolation of spirit, boldly faced and confessed to himself, found expression in Shelley. It was a thread of pain running through his whole poetry, though now and then, as in "Adonais," it was replaced for a moment by flashes of almost triumphant hope. Passionate but hopeless desire wailed like the wind in an Æolian harp in more than half his lyrics. When will any chord be struck of a despair deeper than this?—

> "When the lamp is shattered
>   The light in the dust lies dead;
> When the cloud is scattered
>   The rainbow's glory is shed;
> When the lute is broken,
>   Sweet notes are remembered not;
> When the lips have spoken,
>   Loved accents are soon forgot.
>
> "As music and splendour
>   Survive not the lamp and the lute,
> The heart's echoes render
>   No song when the spirit is mute:—

> No song but sad dirges
>   Like the wind in a ruined cell,
> Or the mournful surges
>   That ring the dead seaman's knell."

No doubt, the two modern poets who have most nearly taken up the same intellectual ground as Shelley in gazing into the spiritual world, Mr. Clough and Mr. Arnold, have, as has been already intimated, interwoven with his tone of utter desolation a thread of manly and solemn conviction that "there is more faith in honest doubt," as Tennyson himself says, than in all the creeds. The student of their poetry is not unnerved by their boldest confessions as he is by Shelley's desolate cry. Even when Mr. Clough paces about the "great sinful streets of Naples," murmuring to himself,—in order to relieve the wonder and the heat with which his heart burns within him as he gazes on all that fermenting mass of evil,—

> "Christ is not risen. No,
>   He lies and moulders low;
> Christ is not risen,"

—there is an under-current of faith in the power which enables him to confess his doubt. Nay, even as he goes over the familiar old ground of those 'evidences' which he had imprinted on his heart in his intense desire to believe in the Gospel, and link by link declares them all untrustworthy, there is a burning remnant of hope, very different from Shelley's thrilling desolation, in the ascetic minuteness of the vigilance with which he cuts away his own hope from under him:—

"What if the women ere the dawn was grey,
  Saw one or more great angels, as they say
  (Angels or Him Himself)? Yet neither there nor then,
  Nor afterwards, nor elsewhere, nor at all,
  Hath He appeared to Peter and the ten,
  Nor save in thunderous terrors to blind Saul ;
  Save in an after Gospel and late Creed,
  He is not risen indeed,—
  Christ is not risen."

Nor are we surprised to find this wonderfully fine piece of spiritual asceticism, in which a great mind filled with a passionate love for Christ flings away one after another the grounds of hope which he thought he could not honestly retain, followed by one—of far less poetical intensity, indeed,—but of evident sincerity, in which the poet asserts his confidence that,—

"Though He be dead, He is not dead,
  Nor gone though fled,
  Not lost, though vanished ;
  Though He return not, though
  He lies and moulders low ;
  In the true creed,
  He is yet risen indeed,
  Christ is yet risen."

For of Mr. Clough it is plain that though the doubt and difficulty and denial were immense, though the intellect of the poet sternly denied his heart many a once cherished and still longed-for faith, yet beneath the doubt and difficulty and denial there was a residuum of victorious trust which alone,—if we may so express it,—gave him heart to doubt. And so again in some true sense it is with Mr. Arnold.

His poetry indeed is not so full of bitter and almost heart-rending resolve to surrender every grain of belief its author cannot justify. And as the confession is the confession of a milder pain, so the reassertion of the faith behind the doubt is less triumphant. But there is nothing in our modern poetry more touching in its quiet sadness than this:—

> "While we believed, on earth He went
>   And open stood His grave;
>   Men called from chamber, church, and tent,
>   And Christ was by to save.
>
> "Now He is dead. Far hence He lies
>   In the lorn Syrian town,
>   And on His grave with shining eyes
>   The Syrian stars look down.
>
> "In vain men still, with hoping new,
>   Regard His death-place dumb,
>   And say the stone is not yet to,
>   And wait for words to come.
>
> "Ah, from that silent sacred land
>   Of sun and arid stone,
>   And crumbling wall, and sultry sand
>   Comes now one word alone!
>
> "From David's lips this word did roll,
>   'Tis true and living yet;
>   'No man can save his brother's soul
>   Nor pay his brother's debt.'
>
> "Alone, self-poised, henceforward man
>   Must labour; must resign
>   His all too human creeds, and scan
>   Simply the way divine."

Yet here, too,—and it is a fair specimen of a whole thread of feeling penetrating everywhere Mr. Arnold's poetry,—this confession of a great doubt is mellowed by the confession of a fainter yet deeper trust.

And it is just the same with the fine poem just published in *Macmillan*, which gives out evanescent flavours of many other poets,—of Clough, of Arnold, even of Morris. The author describes first, in a far from Roman Catholic spirit, and with something of the Chaucerian pity of the last-named poet, the procession of the Bishops :—

> "Thereby the conclave of the Bishops went,
> With grave brows, cherishing a dim intent,
> As men who travelled on their eve of death
> From everywhere that man inhabiteth,
> Not knowing wherefore, for the former things
> Fade from old eyes of bishops and of kings."

And then after a very picturesque passage on the various elements of the conclave, and a digression in eulogy of St. Francis and his Franciscans, he draws a picture of two figures seen by his, though not by every eye, in the great Council Hall. One of them is but a faint vision, a vision, as the prophet says, " neither clear nor dark :"—

> "To my purged eyes before the altar lay
> A figure dreamlike in the noon of day ;
> Nor changed the still face, nor the look thereon,
> At ending of the endless antiphon,
> Nor for the summoned saints and holy hymn
> Grew to my sight less delicate and dim :—
> How faint, how fair that immaterial wraith !
> But looking long I saw that she was Faith."

But the other figure is neither delicate nor dim. It is the figure of some Oriental seer, who for a hundred years had sought passionately for truth and rejected dreams:—

> "His brows black yet and white unfallen hair
> Set in strange frame the face of his despair,
> And I despised not, nor can God despise,
> The silent splendid anger of his eyes.
> A hundred years of search for flying Truth
> Had left them glowing with no gleam of youth,
> A hundred years of vast and vain desire
> Had lit and filled them with consuming fire."

And it is this eager and angry seer who first stamps his mark on the assembly, addressing them in lines of which we extract the greater part:—

> "Better for us to have been, as men may be,
> Sages and silent by the Eastern sea,
> Than thus in new delusion to have brought
> Myrrh of our prayer, frankincense of our thought,
> For One whom knowing not we held so dear,
> For One who sware it, but who is not here.
> Better for you, this shrine when ye began,
> An earthquake should have hidden it from man,
> Than thus through centuries of pomp and pain
> To have founded and have finished it in vain,—
> To have vainly arched the labyrinthine shade,
> And vainly vaulted it, and vainly made
> For saints and kings an everlasting home
> High in the dizzying glories of the dome.
> For not one minute over hall or Host
> Flutters the peerless presence of the Ghost,
> Nor falls at all, for art or man's device,
> On mumbled charm and mumming sacrifice,—
> But either cares not, or forspent with care
> Has flown into the infinite of air.

> "Apollo left you when the Christ was born,
> Jehovah when the Temple's veil was torn,
> And now, even now, this last time and again,
> The presence of a God has gone from men.
> Live in your dreams, if you must live, but I
> Will find the light, and in the light will die."

But while his speech still paralyses the Council, Faith rises in the likeness of the Virgin Mary, and is rapt away,—her "translation" to heaven,—the poet's equivalent for the assumption of the body of the Virgin, which it is supposed that the Council will decree,—being thus described in some fine lines, containing more than an echo of Mr. Clough's:—

> "And yet, translated from the Pontiff's side,
> She did not die, O say not that she died!
> She died not, died not, O the faint and fair!
> She could not die, but melted into air!"

And with that hope that Faith had only become invisible, had not died,—a hope weaker than Mr. Clough's, less definite than Mr. Arnold's, but yet containing no echo of Shelley's poignant wail, the poet leaves us to content ourselves as we may.

Is there not something striking about this consensus of the higher poets of our day in this frank and sad confession of Doubt with an undertone of faith,—an undertone that varies with the individual strength of the poet,—rising in Mr. Tennyson to the assertion that "the strong Son of God, immortal Love," will unquestionably prevail even over all those doubts which he sings in so unflinching and yet sad a strain,—falling in the poet of these new and beautiful stanzas, as he records the disappearance of Faith from mortal sight, to the trembling entreaty, "O say not that she died!" It seems to me to show one of two things,—either that we are on the eve of a long and uncertain era of spiritual suspense,—scepticism qualified by a yearning hope,—or that the way is preparing for a day of clearer and more solid trust than the world has yet known. And for which issue of the two it is that "the generations are prepared," every man will decide according as he perceives, or fails to perceive, that when the great controversy between faith and suspense has been pleaded to its last plea, a supernatural Power steps in which fastens upon every really candid and open heart a final compulsion of faith, enabling the soul to beat up against the strongest head-winds of sceptical theory, and "flee unto the mountain" where from all these troublings there is rest.

LI

BROWNING'S THEOLOGY

1891

Mrs. Sutherland Orr has not the art of perspicuous exposition. Her new contribution to the discussion concerning Browning's religious attitude makes vagueness vaguer and mysticism more mystical. Probably Mrs. Sutherland Orr is right in contending that Browning,—in this respect resembling other poets, even Wordsworth, for example,—was very jealous of its being supposed that he accepted literally the cut-and-dried formulas of any Christian Church. Great idealists see farther into the significance of the spiritual faith they adopt than the ordinary catechists, and very naturally shrink from binding themselves by dogmatic phrases which may very inadequately represent the insight of an elevated imagination. In "Saul," in "Christmas Eve and Easter Day," in *The Ring and the Book*, and fifty other poems, Browning has endeavoured to depict the very heart of his own faith, and of course he prefers his own mode of indicating that faith to that of the narrow-minded Evangelical preacher, or the technical scholastic theologian, or the cold rationalistic critic. No doubt he told Mr. Buchanan that in his (Mr. Buchanan's) sense of the term, he did not profess to be a Christian; but, as Mrs. Sutherland Orr puts it, we want to know exactly what meaning Mr. Buchanan had put upon the term, before we can attach any great importance to this asserted denial. It is as plain as vivid imaginative expressions can make it, that if Browning was not in some very deep and true sense a Christian,—a believer even in the divinity of Christ,—his language is elaborately adapted rather to conceal and misrepresent his mind, than to express it. Nor do I know at all what Mrs. Sutherland Orr means by distinguishing between belief in Christ and belief in Revelation, and even asserting the former belief strongly on Mr. Browning's behalf, while denying the latter. Belief in the divinity of Christ is absolutely inconceivable without the belief in Revelation. Such a belief implies not only the hearty acceptance of Christ's humanity as our ideal, but of Christ's humanity as setting forth and embodying the mind of God. What does Revelation mean except the unveiling of God, the lifting of the veil from the otherwise inscrutable nature of the Creator? Yet Mrs. Sutherland Orr, in her new *Contemporary* article, while she declares Browning to have been a hearty Christian in the sense of holding, and holding with more and more confidence as life advanced, the divine love to have been manifested in Christ's cross and passion, declares that "the one consistent fact of Mr. Browning's heterodoxy was its exclusion of any belief in Revelation." I do not hesitate to say that whatever a "consistent fact" in the abstract may mean, such a fact as this is not at all consistent with the definite Christianity she has conceded to him. If Mr. Browning believed (as he did) in Christ as manifesting God's love to man, he believed in Him as revealing God. If he did not hold that Christ revealed God, he did not believe in His divinity at all,—the one reality in which he evidently did believe. Mrs. Sutherland Orr asserts, indeed, that the possibility of Browning's belief in the Christian Revelation is practically "excluded" by the fact that he insists on the uncertainties of faith, and that he speaks as follows in one place of the relation of Christ to our belief:—"The evidence of divine Power is everywhere about us; not so the evidence of divine Love. That love could only reveal itself to the human heart by some supreme act of *human* tenderness and devotion; the fact or fancy of Christ's cross or passion could alone supply such a revelation." Here, as Mrs. Sutherland Orr triumphantly points out, we find Mr. Browning declaring that even if the story of Christ's cross and passion be a fancy, it still seizes on the human heart, and accounts for the hold taken upon human faith. And again, Mrs. Sutherland Orr points out that in *The Ring and the Book*, Mr. Browning makes his meditative Pope deplore the dogmatic certainties in which men rest too idly; and further, that he represents the evangelist John as predicting that an age of doubt,—of receding certainty,—will quicken men's spiritual life, which has been too much petrified by mechanical clinging to ossified creeds. Besides, says Mrs. Sutherland Orr, Browning's whole attitude towards the belief in immortality is an attitude not of confident assurance, but of lively hope. And lively hope implies at least some uncertainty of the thing hoped for. Well, if Mrs. Sutherland Orr will extend that reasoning, she will be able to prove that the Apostles did not believe in any revealed Immortality. "We are saved by hope," says St. Paul; "if in this life only we have hope in Christ, we are of all men most miserable." "Be ready always," says St. Peter, "to give an answer to every man that asketh you a reason of the hope that is in you." St. John, speaking of the prospect of seeing God as He is, says: "Every man that hath this hope in him, purifieth himself even as He is pure." Hence it seems to me ridiculous to argue that because Mr. Browning spoke of immortality as a hope, and, I may truly say, as a more and more confident hope as life drew on, he could not have believed in Christ's revelation in a sense closely similar to that in which the Apostles themselves believed in it. If his hope was not strictly apostolic in degree, it was apostolic in kind. As for the phrase, "The fact or fancy of Christ's cross or passion could alone supply such a revelation," I think the context shows that Browning regarded the need of man as so deep that even the fancy, if it had been a mere fancy, would have proved itself a revelation of the divine love which had inspired such a fancy. There is what may seem a still stronger passage quoted by Mrs. Sutherland Orr:—"I know all that may be said against it [the Christian scheme of salvation] on the ground of history, of reason, of even moral sense. I grant even that it may be a fiction. But I am none the less convinced that the life and death of Christ, as Christians apprehend them, supplies something which their humanity requires, and that it is true for them." That means surely that Mr. Browning conceives the possibility that Christians may have misunderstood completely the theology implied in the life and death of Christ, but that whether they have misunderstood it or not, —and he only puts the possibility that they may have misunderstood it,—the very misunderstanding involves a glimpse of the deep, tender, and inexhaustible love of God. Such a conception is doubtless what is called heterodox. It is not the conception of the Christian Church. But it is a conception leading men to the Christian faith (just as a sign-post leads a man to the place to which it points), since it points to a great revelation,— "revelation" is Mr. Browning's own word,—of the love of God such as the Christian faith was intended to announce. Even on the chance that the scheme of Revelation was a fiction, Browning certainly held that it was a fiction based upon a great subjective truth; and even had he thought it a fiction, he would have agreed more with those who held it to be a fact, than he would have agreed with those who simply ignored it as an idle fable. And, as a matter of fact, these hypothetical admissions were only hypothetical. No one who reads Browning's greater poems can doubt for a moment that the whole drift and tendency of his mind and life went in the opposite direction, towards a deeper and deeper value for the Christian Revelation, and not towards a more decided distrust of it.

I do not doubt in the least that Browning was not what could be called an orthodox disciple of any Christian Church. To my mind, he often verges on Pantheism in his optimistic treatment of all forms of evil as in some sense necessary and of divine causation. No doubt his mind held to what is called universalism, and to optimism generally. He never laid any hold of the notion that there was a tradition and a Church which might be a safer guide to Christian truth than the individual instincts of each separate soul. He was an individualist to the core, and believed much more in the guidance of the affections to which his heart inclined, than in the guidance of the reason. Still, the one deepest belief of his life was that Christ revealed the divine mind and the divine purpose in a sense so profound, that the doctrine of the Incarnation was to him a real word of God. He was not an Athanasian. Perhaps even he did not hold theologically the whole of the Nicene Creed. But he held to the Incarnation in a sense much more eager and much more progressive and much more constant, than he held to any of the doubts or hesitations which the opponents of that doctrine had suggested to him. Browning had no faith in any ecclesiastical guidance, sectarian or otherwise. Though brought up a Dissenter, all that he retained of Dissent was his intense individualism, his inability to submit himself to any mediate guide to God. But certainly I may say this of him, that his hypothetical doubts had far less part in him than his growing and passionate belief. Mrs. Sutherland Orr has not made things much plainer by her disquisitions on the obscure passages in *Ferishtah's Fancies* and *La Saisiaz*, or any other of Browning's crude transcendentalisms of later years. These half-baked compositions, which mark rather his later impatience of the difficulty of expressing thought in adequate speech, than his earlier power to mould for himself a rough but most effective and impressive form of speech, will never count much for the exposition either of his faith or his genius. But they at least show that he became more and more convinced that Christ is the great revelation of God, as he grew older, incoherent as many of his attempts to affirm this were. To the world in general, "Saul," "Christmas Eve and Easter Day," the story of the Arabian physician concerning the resurrection of Lazarus, and *The Ring and the Book*, will remain Browning's high-water mark as a religious poet, though not perhaps his high-water mark as a Christian believer. He was a heterodox Christian, no doubt, with certain pantheistic leanings, but he was a Christian of the utmost intensity. He believed, from his heart, that Christ revealed God, and was personally the divine Son of God, in a sense a great deal deeper and a great deal more vivid and personal than most orthodox Christians.

LII

THE HUMILITY OF SCIENCE

1889

MR. AUBREY DE VERE had not, in all probability, read the discussion on "Astronomy and Theology" which appeared in the columns of the *Spectator* a few months ago, when he wrote the fine poem on Copernicus which appears in the September number of the *Contemporary Review;* but if he had read it, he could hardly have put more impressively than he has, the true criticism on such a view as Mr. Frederic Harrison's, that the moment you establish the heliocentric view of the solar system, you disprove that conception of Revelation which makes the Incarnation its central fact. Mr. de Vere supposes Copernicus,—who wrote, by-the-way, nearly a century before Galileo's brush with the Papacy, and who is said to have got a Pope's personal authority for his publication of his treatise on the heliocentric view of the planetary system,—on the eve of his death to be musing on the effect of the new doctrine on the religious belief of the age; to be anticipating that it may produce some consternation, and yet confident that it will in the end prove to be not only reconcilable with the theology of the Church, but even that it will give new significance to that theology,—or at least that it will give a new emphasis and a new illustration to the meaning of the word "humility" as it applies to the attitude of men of science towards that infinite world of knowledge on the margin of which, as Newton has since said, they are permitted, like children on the seashore, to pick up a few shells. What does humility in men of science really mean? Does it mean an inveterate belief that, to the mind of such a being as man, the unknown will always be immeasurably vaster than the known? Such an inveterate belief is consistent not only with intellectual pride, but with intellectual pride of the worst type,—the pride that consists half in rash but confident inferences derived from its own knowledge, and half in still rasher and more confident inferences derived from its own ignorance. The true humility proper to science means something very different. It means the docility of learners towards a teacher infinitely above them not only in the knowledge to be imparted, but in the wisdom which recognises the true relations between the different kinds of knowledge and the great danger of undermining the foundations of moral knowledge by showy physical knowledge. Humility really means keeping low, keeping on the ground, not walking on stilts, not delighting in a position of advantage over other men. And science is humble only when it uses its knowledge and its ignorance alike to help other men, and not to lord it over them. Mr. de Vere makes Copernicus say that to his mind the heliocentric view which makes so little of the earth is a revelation made rather to the soul than to the intellect of man, one that gives us a vivid lesson as to what we mean

when we call God Infinite. And yet, he adds, that
lesson might have misled if it had come before we
had gained a sufficiently deep conviction of the
spiritual essence of God's nature, and while we were
still in danger of thinking only of the grandeur of
His architecture :—

> "The Stars do this for men,
> They make Infinitude imaginable:
> God by our instincts felt as infinite,
> When known, becomes such to our total being,
> Mind, spirit, heart, and soul. The greater Theist
> Should make the greater Christian. Yet 'tis true
> Best gifts may come too soon.
>   No marvel this:
> The earth was shaped for myriad forms of greatness,
> As Freedom, Genius, Beauty, Science, Art,
> Some extant, some to be: such forms of greatness
> Are through God's will greatness conditional:
> Where Christ is greatest these are great; elsewhere
> Great only to betray. Sweetly and safely
> In order grave, the maker of the worlds
> Still modulates the rhythm of human progress;
> His angels, on whose song the seasons float,
> Keep measured cadence: all good things keep time
> Lest Good should strangle Better."

And the drift of his poem is that Good *would* have
strangled Better, if our knowledge of the scientific
scale and wonders of the universe had preceded
instead of succeeded the revelation of God's purity
and righteousness and love. But having once well
learned that these characteristics of His,—purity,
righteousness, and love,—are even more essentially
divine than physical infinitude, the lesson as to
what physical infinitude really includes, becomes
one of incalculable value, since it gives definiteness

to our mind when we repeat the words, "My thoughts are not your thoughts, neither are your ways my ways, saith the Lord; for as the heavens are higher than the earth, so are my ways higher than your ways, and my thoughts than your thoughts." In that passage it is almost asserted in so many words that the astronomical scale of the heavens, as compared with that of the earth, is a mere *hint* to us of the infinitude of God's moral and spiritual world as compared with our moral and spiritual world, and that, if we are to feel humbled when we reflect on the inconceivable grandeur of the celestial architecture, we are much more to feel humbled when we reflect on the inconceivable grandeur of God's purity, righteousness, and love. And this is how Mr. de Vere works out that thought as regards the objection that the earth, being so poor a fraction of the infinite universe, the Incarnation could not have taken place for the redemption of such a race as ours:—

"This Earth too small
For Love Divine! Is God not Infinite?
If so, His Love is infinite. Too small!
One famished babe meets pity oft from man
More than an army slain! Too small for Love!
Was Earth too small to be of God created?
Why then too small to be redeemed?

 The sense
Sees greatness only in the sensuous greatness:
Science in that sees little: Faith sees naught:
The small, the vast, are tricks of earthly vision:
To God, that Omnipresent All-in-Each,
Nothing is small, is far.

. . . . .

 They that know not of a God
How know they that the stars have habitants?

'Tis Faith and Hope that spread delighted hands
To such belief; no formal proof attests it.
Concede them peopled; can the sophist prove
Their habitants are fallen? That too admitted,
Who told him that redeeming foot divine
Ne'er trod those spheres? That fresh assumption granted
What then? Is not the Universe a whole?
Doth not the sunbeam herald from the sun
Gladden the violet's bosom? Moons uplift
The tides: remotest stars lead home the lost:
Judæa was one country, one alone:
Not less who died there died for all. The Cross
Brought help to vanished nations: Time opposed
No bar to Love: why then should Space oppose one?
We know not what Time is, nor what is Space;—
Why dream that bonds like theirs can bind the Un-
    bounded?
If Earth be small, likelier it seems that Love
Compassionate most and condescending most
To Sorrow's nadir depths, should choose that Earth
For Love's chief triumph, missioning thence her gift
Even to the utmost zenith!"

That seems to express adequately the true humility of science, which consists not merely in acknowledging the vastness of its ignorance,—for in that it often takes a genuine pride, as in the use of a weapon wherewith it can browbeat not only the unwise but even the wise credulities of man,—but in recognising that while science, such science as the inductive astronomy at least, stands on the common ground of slowly accumulated experience, and even mathematical science stands only on the commanding heights of necessary truth dictating within what limits our experience must be confined, there is a sort of truth which is higher than either, because it comes with a force of moral authority that proclaims its origin in a higher nature, and that, without forcing us to obey it, compels us to own that disobedience is full of the anguish of self-condemnation. The humility of science consists in this recognition of a higher *kind* of knowledge than any which pure science, whether inductive or deductive, can convey,—a kind of knowledge which is not knowledge of *things* at all, and not *mere* knowledge of men, but which announces itself as knowledge strong enough to bind man to some Being who is to human nature a lawgiver and an inspiration. Copernicus, in this fine poem, is made to recognise with awe,—nay, as matter of history, he did recognise, — the danger that the knowledge which he had painfully accumulated concerning the motions of the heavenly bodies, might be made the means of subverting the knowledge which he recognised as something far higher, because it regulated the living principles of heavenly minds,—minds to whose authority ours are in a voluntary though wholesome subjection, which we may, if we will, repudiate. He saw that the popular teaching in which the highest illumination vouchsafed by God to man is necessarily contained, was not teaching concerning the motions of the heavenly bodies at all, and was teaching which did not imply any special study of the motions of those bodies; so that what that teaching did bring home to us as to the power and purposes of God, might seem to be more or less invalidated by the special inferences which the work of astronomers had enabled him to gather concerning astronomical laws. And he felt that any such rash inference would involve the human race in far greater loss than his science could procure it gain. That was true scientific humility, the humility of a man who, though he had learned something new, and something new which was of magnificent proportions, yet recognised that it was nothing at all in comparison with the higher knowledge conveyed in terms suggesting false impressions as to the science of astronomy, though true impressions as well as impressions of the most infinite value as to the character of God. "He hath made the round world so fast that it cannot be moved," was not true if it meant that God did not move it, and was not constantly moving it through space at an almost inconceivable velocity; but it was true in its real meaning,—namely, that God had put it beyond the reach of any power but His own to interfere with its destiny, and to prevent the ripening of His purposes for those who dwelt on it. And that meaning is a meaning of infinitely higher value to the children of men than any knowledge which astronomers could give us, even though it enables sailors to sail the sea with comparative safety; for without moral law and reverence for the divine spirit in the heart, every ship might be a little hell of anarchy, and every crew beyond the power of astronomical knowledge to help or save. Without the benefit of the law which binds man to God, and therefore also to man, and sets his self-will bounds which it can only pass at the cost of becoming hateful to itself, students would not only be destitute of the tranquillity of mind requisite for the accumulation of scientific observation, but deficient in that confidence that they are under the sway of a great and righteous character, seeking to reveal itself, which is at the root of all hope of progress. What we call "faith" is, indeed, moral knowledge, though knowledge of a very different kind from that which the perception of the senses, when preserved by memory, stores up for us. It is knowledge of the better and the worse, knowledge that obedience to the teaching of the light we have, is better even than the increase of that light without obedience to its teaching. Inductive science is humble (or *humilis* is the true sense), when it consciously works on the ground of common experience, that is, on a level below that of mathematical science, for the latter compels us to recognise that it can lay down the law to experience; but even mathematical science, though it may claim to provide us with the very conditions of experience, is of the earth earthy compared with the moral revelation which preceded both the one and the other in the order of human development, and laid down the rule of man's duties almost before science, properly so called, had begun to train man's eyes and hands to discriminate duly between appearance and reality. This is what Copernicus had more or less dimly recognised, and what Mr. Aubrey de Vere at least makes him effectually proclaim.

LIII

TENNYSON'S THEOLOGY

1892

THE posthumous volume of Lord Tennyson's poetry [1] contains two, at least, of his most characteristic and vigorous poems,—"Akbar's Dream" and "The Church-warden and the Curate." The latter is one of the series of those poems in dialect in which he shows his great and humorous dramatic insight, though not what dramatists mean by dramatic power. I shall not refer to it further, for I wish to draw attention chiefly to the considerable series of poems in which Tennyson has treated definitely ethico-theological or strictly theological subjects from his own individual point of view as a reflective poet. "The Two Voices," "The Vision of Sin," "The Palace of Art," "St. Simeon Stylites," "In Memoriam," "Will," "The Higher Pantheism," "The Ancient Sage," "Vastness," and "Akbar's Dream," all of them deal principally with theological problems, to say nothing of the thread of theological idealism which runs through all the "Idylls of the King," and, indeed, many others of his poems. Let me try and sketch, so far as I may, the theology of

[1] Macmillan and Co.

Tennyson. In the first place, Tennyson is no pantheist. He does not dream, like Shelley, that the personality of man is a mere temporary manifestation of the *anima mundi*. In "The Higher Pantheism" he expressly distinguishes the spirit of man from the God whom he is born to worship, and treats the spiritual and moral limitations of man, whether voluntary or involuntary, as the real causes why we cannot adequately discern God :—

"Earth, these solid stars, this weight of body and limb,
Are they not sign and symbol of thy division from Him?
Dark is the world to thee: thyself art the reason why;
For is He not all but that which has power to feel 'I am I'?"

Tennyson's conviction of the direct relation of the soul to God, and of the chasm between the soul and God, is as deep as that of Cardinal Newman. In the next place, his profound belief in the freedom of the human will, and, consequently, of the reality of both virtue and sin, is conspicuous in almost every one of the poems to which I have referred. In the poem on "Will," he pictures the backslider as gazing back on some Sodom he would fain turn to :—

"But ill for him who, bettering not with time,
Corrupts the strength of heaven-descended Will,
And ever weaker grows thro' acted crime,
Or seeming-genial venial fault,
Recurring and suggesting still!
He seems as one whose footsteps halt,
Toiling in immeasurable sand,
And o'er a weary sultry land,
Far beneath a blazing vault,
Sown in a wrinkle of the monstrous hill,
The city sparkles like a grain of salt."

And in the still more impressive poem called "The Vision of Sin," though he will not admit that the cynical and hardened sinner who loathes the world in which, by his own default, he finds himself, is beyond all hope, still he treats the hope as dim, distant, and dubious in the highest degree.

Tennyson's Christian ethics are shown in nothing so much as his profound belief that humility is the only true and healthy attitude of the soul. This he expressed early in the fine poem called "The Palace of Art," and he expressed it last of all in the poems which chiefly distinguish his new book, "Akbar's Dream," and the pieces which conclude the volume. The sin of self-idolatry was, in Tennyson's mind, the deepest of all sins. The soul which builds itself a "Palace of Art," as a stronghold in which it can rejoice in its own grandeur, is brought to the most signal despair :—

> "Deep dread and loathing of her solitude
> Fell on her, from which mood was born
> Scorn of herself; again, from out that mood
> Laughter at her self-scorn."

And at length she had to shriek her misery, and to confess, "I am on fire within!" And the same deep abhorrence of all self-worship penetrates the "Idylls of the King."

Again, Tennyson is no despiser of that anthropomorphism, as its opponents call it, which maintains that the highest revelation of God which is possible to us must come through the incarnation of the divine spirit in a human life. No theologian ever held more earnestly than Tennyson that if we are to have a clear vision of God at all, we must have it under the conditions of our human life and action. He has expressed this conviction in many poems, and never more powerfully than in "Akbar's Dream." Religious "forms," Akbar says, are "a silken cord let down from Paradise, when fine Philosophies would fail, to draw the crowd from wallowing in the mire of earth," and then he goes on,—

> "And all the more, when these behold their Lord,
> Who shaped the forms, obey them, and himself
> Here on this bank in *some* way live the life
> Beyond the bridge, and serve that Infinite
> Within us, as without, that All-in-all,
> And over all, the never-changing One
> And ever-changing Many, in praise of Whom
> The Christian bell, the cry from off the mosque,
> And vaguer voices of Polytheism
> Make but one music, harmonising 'Pray.'"

But while Tennyson certainly held that what sceptics call Anthropomorphism is really the highest view of God that man can reach, and that anything which is not more or less anthropomorphic is not above, but below anthropomorphism, he shows no trace of any disposition to follow Christian teaching into its more dogmatic and elaborate distinctions. He affirms that in the "strong Son of God, immortal Love," we have our highest glimpse of God. He declares :—

> "Thou seemest human and divine,
>   The highest, holiest manhood, thou ;
>   Our wills are ours, we know not how ;
> Our wills are ours, to make them thine."

But then he immediately goes on:—

> "Our little systems have their day;
> They have their day and cease to be:
> They are but broken lights of Thee,
> And thou, O Lord, art more than they."

And that describes, I imagine, Lord Tennyson's attitude, not only towards the religious philosophies, but the dogmatic creeds of the Christian Church. It would hardly be possible for him to have spoken as he did of "The Shadow cloaked from head to foot, who keeps the keys of all the creeds," if he had felt that any Church gave him the full certainty he desired of the revealed will and nature of God. There was an agnostic element in Tennyson, as perhaps in all the greatest minds, though in him it may have been in excess, which kept reiterating: "We have but faith, we cannot know," and which, I should say, was never completely satisfied even of the adequacy of those dogmatic definitions which his Church recognised. Tennyson insists, from first to last, on the inadequacy of our vision of things divine. He finds no authoritative last word such as many Christians find in ecclesiastical authority. On the contrary, he dwells again and again on the dimness and faintness of the higher hope, and draws even no broad line of distinction between that which revelation appears to forbid our hoping for, and that which it encourages us to hope for:—

> "Behold, we know not anything;
> I can but trust that good shall fall
> At last—far off—at last, to all,
> And every winter change to spring.

> So runs my dream : but what am I?
> An infant crying in the night :
> An infant crying for the light :
> And with no language but a cry."

That tone of wistful faith, of tender, beseeching confidence, of humble but tenacious resolve not to be repelled by any accumulation of doubts and difficulties,—though without ignoring for a moment the sometimes, to him at least, overwhelming character of these doubts and difficulties,—is perfectly characteristic of Tennyson's religious poems. He certainly held that without faith life was not worth living, but he certainly held also that faith falls immensely short of certainty,—indeed, so short of it that faith itself must always utter itself with a sort of sob, with a thrill of pity for the tremulousness of its own daring. To him certainly faith was a venture, a venture which he held to be far better worth making than it would be to aim at anything more clearly within his grasp, though worth infinitely less than the less certain prize for which he strove :—

> " If death were seen
> At first as death, Love had not been,"

he wrote. And he argued,—not quite confidently,—from the audacity of love to the unreality of death, but only with that resolute determination to act on the one assumption which made life noble, with which a man goes into battle with his life in his hand. It is clear, I think, that though Tennyson clung to Christ with all the ardour of an ardent nature, he did not regard any Church as the authoritative interpreter of Christ's teaching and meaning, but rested chiefly on the profound attraction for the souls of men, which goes forth from the record of Christ's life on earth. And this was a great part of the secret of the popularity of his poetry. For the age has, like Tennyson, felt much more wistful faith than clear conviction. It "faintly trusts the larger hope." It refuses to act on the assumption that we are all ephemeral phantoms in an ephemeral world; but it cannot, except in rare instances, conquer all dread that that assumption may not be groundless and unreasonable. The generally faltering voice with which Tennyson expresses the ardour of his own hope, touches the heart of this doubting and questioning age, as no more confident expression of belief could have touched it. The lines of his theology were in harmony with the great central lines of Christian thought; but in coming down to detail it soon passed into a region where all was wistful, and dogma disappeared in a haze of radiant twilight.

LIV

THE LATE LORD TENNYSON ON THE FUTURE LIFE

1893

MRS. WELD, in the short but interesting paper which she entitles "Talks with Tennyson," in the March number of the *Contemporary Review*, tells us that, in his conversations with her,—she is his wife's niece,—he always loved best to talk "about spiritual matters," and that "no clergyman was ever a more earnest student of the Bible" than the late Poet-Laureate. "The Ancient Sage," she says, "sets forth his own views more fully than any of his other poems." This I doubt,—though it may set forth the views which he would have held had there been no Christian revelation, more accurately than any other poem. But as "The Ancient Sage" declares itself the picture of a sage's faith " a thousand summers ere the time of Christ," I cannot suppose that Tennyson, with the passion that he has expressed for Christ, the "Strong Son of God, Immortal Love," could image his own convictions in the dim anticipations of an ancient seer, as adequately as he images them in the "In Memoriam," or "The Idylls of the King," or "Crossing the Bar," where he writes frankly out of the very heart of Christian faith. Indeed, Mrs. Weld entirely admits this when she records Tennyson's confession of faith in Christ in the following remarkable words:—"I believe that beside our material body we possess an immaterial body, something like what the ancient Egyptians called the *Ka*. I do not care to make distinctions between the soul and the spirit, as men did in days of old, though perhaps the spirit is the best word to use of our higher nature, that nature which I believe in Christ to have been truly divine, the very presence of the Father, the one only God, dwelling in the perfect man. Though nothing is such a distress of soul to me as to have this divinity of Christ assailed, yet I feel we must never lose sight of the unity of the Godhead, the three persons of the Trinity being like three candles giving together one light. I love that hymn, 'Holy, holy, holy, Lord God Almighty,' and should like to write such a one. We shall have much to learn in a future world, and I think we shall all be children to begin with when we get to heaven, whatever our age when we die, and shall grow on there from childhood to the prime of life, at which we shall remain for ever. My idea of heaven is to be engaged in perpetual ministry to souls in this and other worlds."

What Mrs. Weld means by saying that Tennyson expressed his own faith better in "The Ancient Sage" than in any other of his poems, is rather that he explained his *philosophy* of faith better in it than even in "The Two Voices," or "The Idylls of the King." And the lines she quotes from "The Ancient Sage" do express, with admirable precision, the secret of the power which faith bestows:—

> "Cleave ever to the sunnier side of doubt
> And cling to Faith beyond the forms of Faith!
> She reels not in the storm of warring words,
> She brightens at the clash of 'Yes' and 'No,'
> She sees the Best that glimmers thro' the Worst,
> She feels the Sun is hid but for a night,
> She spies the summer thro' the winter bud,
> She tastes the fruit before the blossom falls,
> She hears the lark within the songless egg,
> She finds the fountain where they wailed 'Mirage'!"

Without forecasting the harvest, no man could deliberately sow his seed. No man whose heart had not passed fully into the effect, could painfully and laboriously bring about the cause. But still, the deliberate choice of "the sunnier side of doubt" is one thing, and the "distress of soul," with which Tennyson contemplated the assaults on the divinity of Christ, was quite another and a higher thing. And nothing could better prove it to be another and a higher thing, than the great explicitness with which Tennyson confessed to Mrs. Weld his belief that the heavenly state would consist in the "perpetual ministry to souls in this and other worlds," as compared with the extreme vagueness of that hope which "the ancient Sage" is made to express as to the possibility of another world:—

> "My son, the world is dark with griefs and graves,
> So dark that men cry out against the Heavens.
> Who knows but that the darkness is in man?
> The doors of Night may be the gates of Light;
> For wert thou born or blind or deaf, and then
> Suddenly heal'd, how would'st thou glory in all
> The splendours and the voices of the world!
> And we, the poor earth's dying race, and yet

> No phantoms, watching from a phantom shore
> Await the last and largest sense to make
> The phantom walls of this illusion fade,
> And show us that the world is wholly fair."

That is an anticipation worthy of a noble nature a thousand years before Christ, but it is not nearly so adequate an expression of faith for nearly two thousand years *after* Christ, as Tennyson felt that he could personally avow without exaggerating in the least the depth of his conviction.

There is certainly something singularly inane, and, I might also say, even un-English, in the ordinary idea which English believers in immortality so often seem to accept,—that it will consist in mere rest and praise, in repose and expressions of wonder at the goodness of God. The notion appears to be derived from the passage in Scripture in which it is briefly said that the good who die in the Lord may "rest from their labours, and their works do follow them," which certainly does not promise them any indolent repose in the satisfaction of already achieved and rewarded effort, but would rather seem to convey, on the contrary, a restoration of energy in the next life which will fall into the same grooves with the energy of this. The vision in the Apocalypse of exalted beings who are perpetually ascribing glory to God, has no doubt given rise to the feeblest of all conceptions of the character of that doxology. As human beings do not show their true reverence for men by indolent cries of admiration, but by throwing their whole hearts and energies into the attitude which they so much admire, so what Catholics call the "beatific vision," is certainly far less to be construed as passive and supine rapture, than as an exalted form of the same state of mind in which human beings show their human reverence. Who is it that best indicates his reverence for the great travellers, or the great biologists, or the great mathematicians, or the great astronomers, or the great philanthropists of the past? Surely, he who treads in their footsteps,—who explores Africa with the patience and fortitude of Mungo Park, or follows up the clue of evolution with the humble assiduity of Darwin, or extends the calculus of number with the masterly concentration of Newton, or explores the heavens with the patient search of Herschel, or alleviates human misery with the self-sacrifice of Howard or Elizabeth Fry. And it is almost childish to suppose that it can take less energy and less effort to enter into the glory of the Creator than it takes to enter into the glory of the creature,—to follow in the footsteps of the Infinite Wisdom and Righteousness than it takes to follow in the footsteps of finite curiosity and finite goodness. The sense in which men rest from their labours while their works follow them, is surely not the sense in which human beings fall asleep in glad fatigue with a feeling upon their hearts of having earned their rest, for that would imply a cessation rather than an expansion of life,— a long night of half-conscious or unconscious repose, instead of a great increase of divine power. It seems almost monstrous to regard the initiation into divine life as implying a cessation of all that we most closely associate with life here,—as the happy trance of languid ecstasy instead of the new glow of creative vigour. Clearly, the "beatific vision" must there, as here, be the vision which *makes* happy; and the vision which makes us happiest is never a vision of indolent contemplativeness, but a vision to which we lend all our powers and all our vitality. It is, in fact, a vision in which the will is as much alive as the intellect, the sympathies as the imagination; in which the whole nature springs into a new vividness of activity as well as insight. The ordinary anticipation of the blessedness of the future is of a kind of happy trance. But a trance is not the fulness of life, rather, on the contrary, a kind of half-death, half-life, in which the mind catches a glimpse of something beyond the verge of its ordinary horizon. Heaven, we may be sure, produces not a trance but a steady growth in the knowledge of God; and growth in the knowledge of Him whose very Sabbath of rest is glad work still, cannot be mere contemplation. "My father worketh hitherto and I work," said our Lord, when justifying on the Sabbath, the restoration of power to the paralytic. And the "beatific vision," however free it may be from the sense of *exhaustion*, which really means the inadequacy of our powers to the work they have to do, can certainly never be free from the sense of growing life and strength and of that divine energy which we call creative. No wonder Tennyson could not endure that conception of Heaven which made it a mere contrast to the very best life of earth, instead of a transfiguration of that very best life. If we cannot really do honour to men without catching something of their power,—and surely this is self-evident, for how are we to know what they were without appreciating the difficulties they have overcome and the triumphs they have achieved?—it is infinitely more true that we can only ascribe glory to God in any true sense, as we slowly and humbly learn to understand the infinitude of His life, and the infinitude of His gifts of life to others. Divine life, whatever else it is, is one immeasurable gift; and even to strive to enter into the secret of one immeasurable gift without at least measurable giving, is simply impossible. The "beatific vision" is a vision of giving; but a vision of giving can only grow into truth, as the life of giving grows into reality. It is not more certain, I take it, that we cannot spring at one bound into purity without purification, than that we cannot spring at one bound into beatitude without slowly learning that which is of the essence of beatitude,—the infinite munificence and passion of the divine generosity.

THE END

Printed by R. & R. CLARK, LIMITED, *Edinburgh*.

www.ingramcontent.com/pod-product-compliance
Lightning Source LLC
Chambersburg PA
CBHW030543300426
44111CB00009B/846